GLOBAL TRENDS 2030:

ALTERNATIVE WORLDS

a publication of the National Intelligence Council

MW00764209

GLOBAL TRENDS 2030:

ALTERNATIVE
WORLDS

a publication of the National Intelligence Council

DECEMBER 2012
NIC 2012-001

ISBN 978-1-929667-21-5
To view electronic version:
www.dni.gov/nic/globaltrends

Dear Reader:

Global Trends 2030: Alternative Worlds is the fifth installment in the National Intelligence Council's series aimed at providing a framework for thinking about the future. As with previous editions, we hope that this report will stimulate strategic thinking by identifying critical trends and potential discontinuities. We distinguish between megatrends, those factors that will likely occur under any scenario, and game-changers, critical variables whose trajectories are far less certain. Finally, as our appreciation of the diversity and complexity of various factors has grown, we have increased our attention to scenarios or alternative worlds we might face.

We are at a critical juncture in human history, which could lead to widely contrasting futures. It is our contention that the future is not set in stone, but is malleable, the result of an interplay among megatrends, game-changers and, above all, human agency. Our effort is to encourage decisionmakers—whether in government or outside—to think and plan for the long term so that negative futures do not occur and positive ones have a better chance of unfolding.

I would like to point out several innovations in ***Global Trends 2030.*** This volume starts with a look back at the four previous Global Trends reports. We were buoyed by the overall positive review in the study we commissioned, but cognizant too of the scope for needed changes, which we have tried to incorporate in this volume.

Our aim has been to make this effort as collaborative as possible, believing that a diversity of perspectives enriches the work. We have reached out to experts far beyond Washington, D.C. We have held numerous meetings, many in universities, in Indiana, Texas, California, New Mexico, Pennsylvania, Massachusetts, Colorado, Tennessee, New York, and New Jersey.

We also sponsored a public blog which featured blog posts and comments by experts on key themes discussed in ***Global Trends 2030.*** The blog had over 140 posts and over 200 comments. As of mid-October, it had 71,000 hits and had been viewed by readers in 167 different countries. To ensure that the blog posts can continue to be consulted, we are linking them to the web and e-book versions of the final published report.

We expanded our engagement overseas by holding meetings on the initial draft in close to 20 countries. Many times this was at the invitation of governments, businesses, universities, or think tanks. One beneficial outcome of the NIC's quadrennial efforts has been the growing interest elsewhere in global trends, including elaboration by others on their own works, which we encourage. Because of the widespread interest in how ***Global Trends 2030*** is seen elsewhere, we have detailed the reactions of our international experts to the initial draft in a special box following the introduction.

In this volume, we expanded our coverage of disruptive technologies, devoting a separate section to it in the work. To accomplish that, we engaged with research scientists at DoE laboratories at Sandia, Oak Ridge, and NASA in addition to entrepreneurs and consultants in Silicon Valley and Santa Fe. We have also devoted strong attention to economic factors and the nexus of technology and economic growth.

Finally, this volume contains a chapter on the potential trajectories for the US role in the international system. Previous editions were criticized—particularly by overseas readers—for not discussing at greater length the US impact on future international relations. We believe that the United States also stands at a critical juncture; we have devoted a chapter to delineating possible future directions and their impact on the broader evolution of the international system.

Scores of people contributed to the preparation of *Global Trends 2030,* and we have sought to acknowledge the key contributors from outside the NIC in a separate entry. Within the NIC, Counselor Mathew Burrows was our principal author in addition to orchestrating the entire process from beginning to end. He was assisted by Elizabeth Arens as senior editor; Luke Baldwin, who established the first-ever NIC blog; Erin Cromer, who oversaw logistical support; and Jacob Eastham and Anne Carlyle Lindsay, who created the design. Dr. Burrows worked closely with regional and functional National Intelligence Officers, who reviewed and contributed to the draft. Among NIC offices, the NIC's Strategic Futures Group under Director Cas Yost rates special mention for its participation across the board in Global Trends-related work. I would especially like to acknowledge the work of the late senior analyst Christopher Decker who provided critical help with the forecasts on global health and pandemics before his untimely death.

I encourage readers to review the complete set of *Global Trends 2030* documents, which can be found on the National Intelligence Council's website, www.dni.gov/nic/globaltrends, and to explore possible scenario simulations using the interactive material. We also have published the work in an e-book format so readers can download it for their use on a tablet. These formats are available for downloading from our website.

As with our previous Global Trends studies, we hope this report stimulates dialogue on the challenges that will confront the global community during the next 15-20 years—and positive and peaceful ways to meet them.

Sincerely,

Christopher Kojm,
Chairman, National Intelligence Council

TRACK RECORD OF GLOBAL TRENDS WORKS

Before launching work on the current volume, the NIC commissioned an academic study of the four previous Global Trends studies, beginning with the first edition in 1996-97. The reviewers examined the Global Trends papers to highlight any persistent blind spots and biases as well as distinctive strengths. A subsequent conference focused on addressing shortcomings and building on the studies' strong points for the forthcoming work. We sought to address the reviewers' concerns in designing the present project.

The key "looming" challenges that our reviewers cited for GT 2030 were to develop:

- **A greater focus on the role of US in the international system.** Past works assumed US centrality, leaving readers "vulnerable" to wonder about "critical dynamics" around the US role. One of the key looming issues for GT 2030 was "how other powers would respond to a decline or a decisive re-assertion of US power." The authors of the study thought that both outcomes were possible and needed to be addressed.

- **A clearer understanding of the central units in the international system.** Previous works detailed the gradual ascendance of nonstate actors, but we did not clarify how we saw the role of states versus nonstate actors. The reviewers suggested that we delve more into the dynamics of governance and explore the complicated relationships among a diverse set of actors.

- **A better grasp of time and speed.** Past Global Trends works "correctly foresaw the direction of the vectors: China up, Russia down. But China's power has consistently increased faster than expected . . . A comprehensive reading of the four reports leaves a strong impression that [we] tend toward underestimation of the rates of change . . ."

- **Greater discussion of crises and discontinuities.** The reviewers felt that the use of the word "trends" in the titles suggests more continuity than change. GT 2025, however, "with its strongly worded attention to the likelihood of significant shocks and discontinuities, flirts with a radical revision of this viewpoint." The authors recommended developing a framework for understanding the relationships among trends, discontinuities, and crises.

- **Greater attention to ideology.** The authors of the study admitted that "ideology is a frustratingly fuzzy concept . . . difficult to define . . . and equally difficult to measure." They agreed that grand "isms" like fascism and communism might not be on the horizon. However, "smaller politico-pycho-social shifts that often don't go under the umbrella of ideology but drive behavior" should be a focus.

- **More understanding of second- and third-order consequences.** Trying to identify looming disequilibria may be one approach. More wargaming or simulation exercises to understand possible dynamics among international actors at crucial tipping points was another suggestion.

We will let our readers judge how well we met the above challenges in this volume.

EXECUTIVE SUMMARY

This report is intended to stimulate thinking about the rapid and vast geopolitical changes characterizing the world today and possible global trajectories during the next 15-20 years. As with the NIC's previous Global Trends reports, we do not seek to predict the future—which would be an impossible feat—but instead provide a framework for thinking about possible futures and their implications.

" . . . the idea of the future being different from the present is so repugnant to our conventional modes of thought and behavior that we, most of us, offer a great resistance to acting on it in practice."

John Maynard Keynes, 1937

GLOBAL TRENDS 2030: AN OVERVIEW

MEGATRENDS

Individual Empowerment	Individual empowerment will accelerate owing to poverty reduction, growth of the global middle class, greater educational attainment, widespread use of new communications and manufacturing technologies, and health-care advances.
Diffusion of Power	There will not be any hegemonic power. Power will shift to networks and coalitions in a multipolar world.
Demographic Patterns	The demographic arc of instability will narrow. Economic growth might decline in "aging" countries. Sixty percent of the world's population will live in urbanized areas; migration will increase.
Food, Water, Energy Nexus	Demand for these resources will grow substantially owing to an increase in the global population. Tackling problems pertaining to one commodity will be linked to supply and demand for the others.

GAME-CHANGERS

Crisis-Prone Global Economy	Will global volatility and imbalances among players with different economic interests result in collapse? Or will greater multipolarity lead to increased resiliency in the global economic order?
Governance Gap	Will governments and institutions be able to adapt fast enough to harness change instead of being overwhelmed by it?
Potential for Increased Conflict	Will rapid changes and shifts in power lead to more intrastate and interstate conflicts?
Wider Scope of Regional Instability	Will regional instability, especially in the Middle East and South Asia, spill over and create global insecurity?
Impact of New Technologies	Will technological breakthroughs be developed in time to boost economic productivity and solve the problems caused by a growing world population, rapid urbanization, and climate change?
Role of the United States	Will the US be able to work with new partners to reinvent the international system?

POTENTIAL WORLDS

Stalled Engines	In the most plausible worst-case scenario, the risks of interstate conflict increase. The US draws inward and globalization stalls.
Fusion	In the most plausible best-case outcome, China and the US collaborate on a range of issues, leading to broader global cooperation.
Gini-Out-of-the-Bottle	Inequalities explode as some countries become big winners and others fail. Inequalities within countries increase social tensions. Without completely disengaging, the US is no longer the "global policeman."
Nonstate World	Driven by new technologies, nonstate actors take the lead in confronting global challenges.

The world of 2030 will be radically transformed from our world today. By 2030, no country—whether the US, China, or any other large country—will be a hegemonic power. The empowerment of individuals and diffusion of power among states and from states to informal networks will have a dramatic impact, largely reversing the historic rise of the West since 1750, restoring Asia's weight in the global economy, and ushering in a new era of "democratization" at the international and domestic level. In addition to individual empowerment and the diffusion of state power, we believe that two other **megatrends** will shape our world out to 2030: demographic patterns, especially rapid aging; and growing resource demands which, in the cases of food and water, might lead to scarcities. These trends, which are virtually certain, exist today, but during the next 15-20 years they will gain much greater momentum. Underpinning the megatrends are **tectonic shifts**—critical changes to key features of our global environment that will affect how the world "works" (see table on page v).

Extrapolations of the megatrends would alone point to a changed world by 2030—but the world could be transformed in radically different ways. We believe that six key **game-changers**—questions regarding the global economy, governance, conflict, regional instability, technology, and the role of the United States—will largely determine what kind of transformed world we will inhabit in 2030. Several potential **Black Swans**—discrete events—would cause large-scale disruption (see page xi). All but two of these—the possibility of a democratic China or a reformed Iran—would have negative repercussions.

Based upon what we know about the megatrends and the possible interactions between the megatrends and the game-changers, we have delineated four archetypal futures that represent distinct pathways for the world out to 2030. None of these **alternative worlds** is inevitable. In reality, the future probably will consist of elements from all the scenarios.

MEGATRENDS AND RELATED TECTONIC SHIFTS

MEGATREND 1: INDIVIDUAL EMPOWERMENT

Individual empowerment will accelerate substantially during the next 15-20 years owing to poverty reduction and a huge growth of the global middle class, greater educational attainment, and better health care. The growth of the global middle class constitutes a tectonic shift: for the first time, a majority of the world's population will not be impoverished, and the middle classes will be the most important social and economic sector in the vast majority of countries around the world. Individual empowerment is the most important megatrend because it is both a cause and effect of most other trends—including the expanding global economy, rapid growth of the developing countries, and widespread exploitation of new communications and manufacturing technologies. On the one hand, we see the potential for greater individual initiative as key to solving the mounting global challenges over the next 15-20 years. On the other hand, in a tectonic shift, individuals and small groups will have greater access to lethal and disruptive technologies (particularly precision-strike capabilities, cyber instruments, and bioterror weaponry), enabling them to perpetrate large-scale violence—a capability formerly the monopoly of states.

MEGATREND 2: DIFFUSION OF POWER

The diffusion of power among countries will have a dramatic impact by 2030. Asia will have surpassed North America and Europe combined in terms of global power, based upon GDP, population size, military spending, and technological investment. China alone will probably have the largest economy, surpassing that of the United States a few years before 2030. In a tectonic shift, the health of the global economy increasingly will be linked to how well the developing world does—more so than the traditional West. In addition to China, India, and Brazil, regional players such as Colombia, Indonesia, Nigeria, South Africa, and Turkey will become especially important to the global economy. Meanwhile, the economies of Europe, Japan, and Russia are likely to continue their slow relative declines.

The shift in national power may be overshadowed by an even more fundamental shift in the *nature* of power. Enabled by communications technologies, power will shift toward multifaceted and amorphous networks that will form to influence state and global actions. Those countries with some of the strongest fundamentals—GDP, population size, etc.—will not be able to punch their weight unless they also learn to operate in networks and coalitions in a multipolar world.

MEGATREND 3: DEMOGRAPHIC PATTERNS

We believe that in the world of 2030—a world in which a growing global population will have reached somewhere close to 8.3 billion people (up from 7.1 billion in 2012)—four demographic trends will fundamentally shape, although not necessarily determine, most countries' economic and political conditions and relations among countries. These trends are: aging—a tectonic shift for both for the West and increasingly most developing countries; a still-significant but shrinking number of youthful societies and states; migration, which will increasingly be a cross-border issue; and growing urbanization—another tectonic shift, which will spur economic growth but could put new strains on food and water

resources. Aging countries will face an uphill battle in maintaining their living standards. Demand for both skilled and unskilled labor will spur global migration. Owing to rapid urbanization in the developing world, the volume of urban construction for housing, office space, and transport services over the next 40 years could roughly equal the entire volume of such construction to date in world history.

MEGATREND 4: GROWING FOOD, WATER, AND ENERGY NEXUS

Demand for food, water, and energy will grow by approximately 35, 40, and 50 percent respectively owing to an increase in the global population and the consumption patterns of an expanding middle class. Climate change will worsen the outlook for the availability of these critical resources. Climate change analysis suggests that the severity of existing weather patterns will intensify, with wet areas getting wetter and dry and arid areas becoming more so. Much of the decline in precipitation will occur in the Middle East and northern Africa as well as western Central Asia, southern Europe, southern Africa, and the US Southwest.

We are not necessarily headed into a world of scarcities, but policymakers and their private sector partners will need to be proactive to avoid such a future. Many countries probably won't have the wherewithal to avoid food and water shortages without massive help from outside. Tackling problems pertaining to one commodity won't be possible without affecting supply and demand for the others. Agriculture is highly dependent on accessibility to adequate sources of water as well as on energy-rich fertilizers. Hydropower is a significant source of energy for some regions while new sources of energy—such as biofuels—threaten to exacerbate the potential for food shortages. There is as much scope for negative tradeoffs as there is the potential for positive synergies. Agricultural productivity in Africa, particularly, will require a sea change to avoid shortages. Unlike Asia and South America, which have achieved significant improvements in agricultural production per capita, Africa has only recently returned to 1970s' levels.

In a likely tectonic shift, the United States could become energy-independent. The US has regained its position as the world's largest natural gas producer and expanded the life of its reserves from 30 to 100 years due to hydraulic fracturing technology. Additional crude oil production through the use of "fracking" drilling technologies on difficult-to-reach oil deposits could result in a big reduction in the US net trade balance and improved overall economic growth. Debates over environmental concerns about fracturing, notably pollution of water sources, could derail such developments, however.

TECTONIC SHIFTS BETWEEN NOW AND 2030

Growth of the Global Middle Class	Middle classes most everywhere in the developing world are poised to expand substantially in terms of both absolute numbers and the percentage of the population that can claim middle-class status during the next 15-20 years.
Wider Access to Lethal and Disruptive Technologies	A wider spectrum of instruments of war—especially precision-strike capabilities, cyber instruments, and bioterror weaponry—will become accessible. Individuals and small groups will have the capability to perpetrate large-scale violence and disruption—a capability formerly the monopoly of states.
Definitive Shift of Economic Power to the East and South	The US, European, and Japanese share of global income is projected to fall from 56 percent today to well under half by 2030. In 2008, China overtook the US as the world's largest saver; by 2020, emerging markets' share of financial assets is projected to almost double.
Unprecedented and Widespread Aging	Whereas in 2012 only Japan and Germany have matured beyond a median age of 45 years, most European countries, South Korea, and Taiwan will have entered the post-mature age category by 2030. Migration will become more globalized as both rich and developing countries suffer from workforce shortages.
Urbanization	Today's roughly 50-percent urban population will climb to nearly 60 percent, or 4.9 billion people, in 2030. Africa will gradually replace Asia as the region with the highest urbanization growth rate. Urban centers are estimated to generate 80 percent of economic growth; the potential exists to apply modern technologies and infrastructure, promoting better use of scarce resources.
Food and Water Pressures	Demand for food is expected to rise at least 35 percent by 2030 while demand for water is expected to rise by 40 percent. Nearly half of the world's population will live in areas experiencing severe water stress. Fragile states in Africa and the Middle East are most at risk of experiencing food and water shortages, but China and India are also vulnerable.
US Energy Independence	With shale gas, the US will have sufficient natural gas to meet domestic needs and generate potential global exports for decades to come. Increased oil production from difficult-to-access oil deposits would result in a substantial reduction in the US net trade balance and faster economic expansion. Global spare capacity may exceed over 8 million barrels, at which point OPEC would lose price control and crude oil prices would collapse, causing a major negative impact on oil-export economies.

GAME-CHANGER 1: THE CRISIS-PRONE GLOBAL ECONOMY

The international economy almost certainly will continue to be characterized by various regional and national economies moving at significantly different speeds—a pattern reinforced by the 2008 global financial crisis. The contrasting speeds across different regional economies are exacerbating global imbalances and straining governments and the international system. The key question is whether the divergences and increased volatility will result in a global breakdown and collapse or whether the development of multiple growth centers will lead to resiliency. The absence of a clear hegemonic economic power could add to the volatility. Some experts have compared the relative decline in the economic weight of the US to the late 19th century when economic dominance by one player—Britain—receded into multipolarity.

A return to pre-2008 growth rates and previous patterns of rapid globalization looks increasingly unlikely, at least for the next decade. Across G-7 countries, total nonfinancial debt has doubled since 1980 to 300 percent of GDP, accumulating over a generation. Historical studies indicate that recessions involving financial crises tend to be deeper and require recoveries that take twice as long. Major Western economies—with some exceptions such as the US, Australia, and South Korea—have only just begun deleveraging (reducing their debts); previous episodes have taken close to a decade.

Another major global economic crisis cannot be ruled out. The McKinsey Global Institute estimates that the potential impact of an unruly Greek exit from the euro zone could cause eight times the collateral damage as the Lehman Brothers bankruptcy. Regardless of which solution is eventually chosen, progress will be needed on several fronts to restore euro zone stability. Doing so will take several years at a minimum, with many experts talking about a whole decade before stability returns.

Earlier economic crises, such as the 1930s' Great Depression, also hit when the age structures of many Western populations were relatively youthful, providing a demographic bonus during the postwar economic boom. However, such a bonus will not exist in any prospective recovery for Western countries. To compensate for drops in labor-force growth, hoped-for economic gains will have to come from growth in productivity. The United States is in a better position because its workforce is projected to increase during the next decade, but the US will still need to increase labor productivity to offset its slowly aging workforce. A critical question is whether technology can sufficiently boost economic productivity to prevent a long-term slowdown.

As we have noted, the world's economic prospects will increasingly depend on the fortunes of the East and South. The developing world already provides more than 50 percent of global economic growth and 40 percent of global investment. Its contribution to global investment growth is more than 70 percent. China's contribution is now one and a half times the size of the US contribution. In the World Bank's baseline modeling of future economic multipolarity, China—despite a likely slowing of its economic growth—will contribute about one-third of global growth by 2025, far more than any other economy. Emerging market demand for infrastructure, housing, consumer goods, and new plants and equipment will raise global investment to levels not seen in four decades. Global savings may not match this rise, resulting in upward pressure on long-term interest rates.

Despite their growing economic clout, developing countries will face their own challenges, especially in their efforts to continue the momentum behind their rapid economic growth. China has averaged 10-percent real growth during the past three decades; by 2020 its economy will probably be expanding by only 5 percent, according to several private-sector forecasts. The slower growth will mean downward pressure on per capita income growth. China faces the prospect of being trapped in middle-income status, with its per capita income not continuing to increase to the level of the world's advanced economies. India faces many of the same problems and traps accompanying rapid growth as China: large inequities between rural and urban sectors and within society; increasing constraints on resources such as water; and a need for greater investment in science and technology to continue to move its economy up the value chain.

GAME-CHANGER 2: THE GOVERNANCE GAP

During the next 15-20 years, as power becomes even more diffuse than today, a growing number of diverse state and nonstate actors, as well as subnational actors, such as cities, will play important governance roles. The increasing number of players needed to solve major transnational challenges—and their discordant values—will complicate decisionmaking. The lack of consensus between and among established and emerging powers suggests that multilateral governance to 2030 will be limited at best. The chronic deficit probably will reinforce the trend toward fragmentation. However, various developments—positive or negative—could push the world in different directions. Advances cannot be ruled out despite growing multipolarity, increased regionalism, and possible economic slowdowns. Prospects for achieving progress on global issues will vary across issues.

The governance gap will continue to be most pronounced at the domestic level and driven by rapid political and social changes. The advances during the past couple decades in health, education, and income—which we expect to continue, if not accelerate in some cases—will drive new governance structures. Transitions to democracy are much more stable and long-lasting when youth bulges begin to decline and incomes are higher. Currently about 50 countries are in the awkward stage between autocracy and democracy, with the greatest number concentrated in Sub-Saharan Africa, Southeast and Central Asia, and the Middle East and North Africa. Both social science theory and recent history—the Color Revolutions and the Arab Spring—support the idea that with maturing age structures and rising incomes, political liberalization and democracy will advance. However, many countries will still be zig-zagging their way through the complicated democratization process

during the next 15-20 years. Countries moving from autocracy to democracy have a proven track record of instability.

Other countries will continue to suffer from a democratic deficit: in these cases a country's developmental level is more advanced than its level of governance. Gulf countries and China account for a large number in this category. China, for example, is slated to pass the threshold of US $15,000 per capita purchasing power parity (PPP) in the next five years, which is often a trigger for democratization. Chinese democratization could constitute an immense "wave," increasing pressure for change on other authoritarian states.

The widespread use of new communications technologies will become a double-edged sword for governance. On the one hand, social networking will enable citizens to coalesce and challenge governments, as we have already seen in Middle East. On the other hand, such technologies will provide governments—both authoritarian and democratic—an unprecedented ability to monitor their citizens. It is unclear how the balance will be struck between greater IT-enabled individuals and networks and traditional political structures. In our interactions, technologists and political scientists have offered divergent views. Both sides agree, however, that the characteristics of IT use—multiple and simultaneous action, near instantaneous responses, mass organization across geographic boundaries, and technological dependence—increase the potential for more frequent discontinuous change in the international system.

The current, largely Western dominance of global structures such as the UN Security Council, World Bank, and IMF probably will have been transformed by 2030 to be more in line with the changing hierarchy of new economic players. Many second-tier emerging powers will be making their mark—at least as emerging regional leaders. Just as the larger G-20—rather than G-7/8—was energized to deal with the 2008 financial crisis, we expect that other institutions will be updated—probably also in response to crises.

GAME-CHANGER 3: POTENTIAL FOR INCREASED CONFLICT

Historical trends during the past two decades show fewer major armed conflicts and, where conflicts remain, fewer civilian and military casualties than in previous decades. Maturing age structures in many developing countries point to continuing declines in intrastate conflict. We believe the disincentives will remain strong against great power conflict: too much would be at stake. Nevertheless, we need to be cautious about the prospects for further declines in the number and intensity of intrastate conflicts, and interstate conflict remains a possibility.

Intrastate conflicts have gradually increased in countries with a mature overall population that contain a politically dissonant, youthful ethnic minority. Strife involving ethnic Kurds in Turkey, Shia in Lebanon, and Pattani Muslims in southern Thailand are examples of such situations. Looking forward, the potential for conflict to occur in Sub-Saharan Africa is likely to remain high even after some of the region's countries graduate into a more intermediate age structure because of the probable large number of ethnic and tribal minorities that will remain more youthful than the overall population. Insufficient natural resources—such as water and arable land—in many of the same countries that will have disproportionate levels of young men increase the risks of intrastate conflict breaking out, particularly in Sub-Saharan African and South and East Asian countries, including China and India. A number of these countries—Afghanistan, Bangladesh, Pakistan, and Somalia—also have faltering governance institutions.

Though by no means inevitable, the risks of interstate conflict are increasing owing to changes in the international system. The underpinnings of the post-Cold War equilibrium are beginning to shift. During the next 15-20 years, the US will be grappling with the degree to which it can continue to play the role of systemic guardian and guarantor of the global order. A declining US unwillingness and/or slipping capacity to serve as a global security provider would be a key factor contributing to instability, particularly in Asia and the Middle East. A more fragmented international system in which existing forms of cooperation are no longer seen as advantageous to many of the key global players would also increase the potential for competition and even great power conflict. However, if such a conflict occurs, it almost certainly will not be on the level of a world war with all major powers engaged.

Three different baskets of risks could conspire to increase the chances of an outbreak of interstate conflict: changing calculations of key players—particularly China, India, and Russia; increasing contention over resource issues; and a wider spectrum of more accessible instruments of war. With the potential for increased proliferation and growing concerns about nuclear security, risks are growing that future wars in South Asia and the Middle East would risk inclusion of a nuclear deterrent.

The current Islamist phase of terrorism might end by 2030, but terrorism is unlikely to die completely. Many states might continue to use terrorist group out of a strong sense of insecurity, although the costs to a regime of directly supporting terrorists looks set to become even greater as international cooperation increases. With more widespread access to lethal and disruptive technologies, individuals who are experts in such niche areas as cyber systems might sell their services to the highest bidder, including terrorists who would focus less on causing mass casualties and more on creating widespread economic and financial disruptions.

GAME-CHANGER 4: WIDER SCOPE OF REGIONAL INSTABILITY

Regional dynamics in several different theaters during the next couple decades will have the potential to spill over and create global insecurity. The **Middle East** and **South Asia** are the two regions most likely to trigger broader instability. In the Middle East, the youth bulge—a driving force of the recent Arab Spring—will give way to a gradually aging population. With new technologies beginning to provide the world with other sources of oil and gas, the region's economy will need to become increasingly diversified. But the Middle East's trajectory will depend on its political landscape. On the one hand, if the Islamic Republic maintains power in Iran and is able to develop nuclear weapons, the Middle East will face a highly unstable future. On the other hand, the emergence of moderate, democratic governments or a breakthrough agreement to resolve the Israeli-Palestinian conflict could have enormously positive consequences.

South Asia faces a series of internal and external shocks during the next 15-20 years. Low growth, rising food prices, and energy shortages will pose stiff challenges to governance in Pakistan and Afghanistan. Afghanistan's and Pakistan's youth bulges are large—similar in size to those found in many African countries. When these youth bulges are combined with a slow-growing economy, they portend increased instability. India is in a better position, benefiting from higher growth, but it will still be challenged to find jobs for its large youth population. Inequality, lack of infrastructure, and education deficiencies are key weaknesses in India. The neighborhood has always had a profound influence on internal developments, increasing the sense of insecurity and bolstering military outlays. Conflict could erupt and spread under numerous scenarios. Conflicting strategic goals, widespread distrust, and the hedging strategies by all the parties will make it difficult for them to develop a strong regional security framework.

An increasingly multipolar **Asia** lacking a well-anchored regional security framework able to arbitrate and mitigate rising tensions would constitute one of the largest global threats. Fear of Chinese power, the likelihood of growing Chinese nationalism, and possible questions about the US remaining involved in the region will increase insecurities. An unstable Asia would cause large-scale damage to the global economy.

Changing dynamics in other regions would also jeopardize global security. **Europe** has been a critical security provider, ensuring, for example, Central Europe's integration into the "West" after the end of the Cold War. A more inward-focused and less capable

Europe would provide a smaller stabilizing force for crises in neighboring regions. On the other hand, a Europe which overcomes its current intertwined political and economic crises could see its global role enhanced. Such a Europe could help to integrate its rapidly developing neighbors in the Middle East, Sub-Saharan Africa, and Central Asia into the global economy and broader international system. A modernizing Russia could integrate itself into a wider international community; at the same time, a Russia which fails to build a more diversified economy and more liberal domestic order could increasingly pose a regional and global threat.

Progress toward greater regional cohesion and integration in **Latin America** and **Sub-Saharan Africa** would promise increased stability in those regions and a reduced threat to global security. Countries in Sub-Saharan Africa, Central America, and the Caribbean will remain vulnerable, nevertheless, to state failure through 2030, providing safe havens for both global criminal and terrorist networks and local insurgents.

GAME-CHANGER 5: THE IMPACT OF NEW TECHNOLOGIES

Four technology arenas will shape global economic, social, and military developments as well as the world community's actions pertaining to the environment by 2030. **Information technology** is entering the big data era. Process power and data storage are becoming almost free; networks and the cloud will provide global access and pervasive services; social media and cybersecurity will be large new markets. This growth and diffusion will present significant challenges for governments and societies, which must find ways to capture the benefits of new IT technologies while dealing with the new threats that those technologies present. Fear of the growth of an Orwellian surveillance state may lead citizens particularly in the developed world to pressure their governments to restrict or dismantle big data systems.

Information technology-based solutions to maximize citizens' economic productivity and quality of life while minimizing resource consumption and environmental degradation will be critical to ensuring the viability of megacities. Some of the world's future megacities will essentially be built from scratch, enabling a blank-slate approach to infrastructure design and implementation that could allow for the most effective possible deployment of new urban technologies—or create urban nightmares, if such new technologies are not deployed effectively.

New manufacturing and automation technologies such as additive manufacturing (3D printing) and robotics have the potential to change work patterns in both the developing and developed worlds. In developed countries these technologies will improve productivity, address labor constraints, and diminish the need for outsourcing, especially if reducing the length of supply chains brings clear benefits. Nevertheless, such technologies could still have a similar effect as outsourcing: they could make more low- and semi-skilled manufacturing workers in developed economies redundant, exacerbating domestic inequalities. For developing economies, particularly Asian ones, the new technologies will stimulate new manufacturing capabilities and further increase the competitiveness of Asian manufacturers and suppliers.

Breakthroughs, especially for technologies pertaining to the **security of vital resources**—will be neccessary to meet the food, water, and energy needs of the world's population. Key technologies likely to be at the forefront of maintaining such resources in the next 15-20 years will include genetically modified crops, precision agriculture, water irrigation techniques, solar energy, advanced bio-based fuels, and enhanced oil and natural gas extraction via fracturing. Given the vulnerabilities of developing economies to key resource supplies and prices and the early impacts of climate change, key developing countries may realize substantial rewards in commercializing many next-generation resource technologies first. Aside from being cost competitive, any expansion or adoption of both existing and next-generation resource technologies over the next 20 years will largely depend

on social acceptance and the direction and resolution of any ensuing political issues.

Last but not least, new health technologies will continue to extend the average age of populations around the world, by ameliorating debilitating physical and mental conditions and improving overall well-being. The greatest gains in healthy longevity are likely to occur in those countries with developing economies as the size of their middle class populations swells. The health-care systems in these countries may be poor today, but by 2030 they will make substantial progress in the longevity potential of their populations; by 2030 many leading centers of innovation in disease management will be in the developing world.

GAME-CHANGER 6: THE ROLE OF THE UNITED STATES

How the United States' international role evolves during the next 15-20 years—a big uncertainty—and whether the US will be able to work with new partners to reinvent the international system will be among the most important variables in the future shape of the global order. Although the United States' (and the West's) relative decline vis-a-vis the rising states is inevitable, its future role in the international system is much harder to project: the degree to which the US continues to dominate the international system could vary widely.

The US most likely will remain "first among equals" among the other great powers in 2030 because of its preeminence across a range of power dimensions and legacies of its leadership role. More important than just its economic weight, the United States' dominant role in international politics has derived from its preponderance across the board in both hard and soft power. Nevertheless, with the rapid rise of other countries, the "unipolar moment" is over and Pax Americana—the era of American ascendancy in international politics that began in 1945—is fast winding down.

The context in which the US global power will operate will change dramatically. Most of Washington's historic

Severe Pandemic	No one can predict which pathogen will be the next to start spreading to humans, or when or where such a development will occur. An easily transmissible novel respiratory pathogen that kills or incapacitates more than one percent of its victims is among the most disruptive events possible. Such an outbreak could result in millions of people suffering and dying in every corner of the world in less than six months.
Much More Rapid Climate Change	Dramatic and unforeseen changes already are occurring at a faster rate than expected. Most scientists are not confident of being able to predict such events. Rapid changes in precipitation patterns—such as monsoons in India and the rest of Asia—could sharply disrupt that region's ability to feed its population.
Euro/EU Collapse	An unruly Greek exit from the euro zone could cause eight times the collateral damage as the Lehman Brothers bankruptcy, provoking a broader crisis regarding the EU's future.
A Democratic or Collapsed China	China is slated to pass the threshold of US$15,000 per capita purchasing power parity (PPP) in the next five years or so—a level that is often a trigger for democratization. Chinese "soft" power could be dramatically boosted, setting off a wave of democratic movements. Alternatively, many experts believe a democratic China could also become more nationalistic. An economically collapsed China would trigger political unrest and shock the global economy.
A Reformed Iran	A more liberal regime could come under growing public pressure to end the international sanctions and negotiate an end to Iran's isolation. An Iran that dropped its nuclear weapons aspirations and became focused on economic modernization would bolster the chances for a more stable Middle East.
Nuclear War or WMD/Cyber Attack	Nuclear powers such as Russia and Pakistan and potential aspirants such as Iran and North Korea see nuclear weapons as compensation for other political and security weaknesses, heightening the risk of their use. The chance of nonstate actors conducting a cyber attack—or using WMD— also is increasing.
Solar Geomagnetic Storms	Solar geomagnetic storms could knock out satellites, the electric grid, and many sensitive electronic devices. The recurrence intervals of crippling solar geomagnetic storms, which are less than a century, now pose a substantial threat because of the world's dependence on electricity.
US Disengagement	A collapse or sudden retreat of US power probably would result in an extended period of global anarchy; no leading power would be likely to replace the United States as guarantor of the international order.

Western partners have also suffered relative economic declines. The post-World-War-II-era was characterized by the G-7 countries leading both economically and politically. US projection of power was dependent on and amplified by its strong alliances. During the next 15-20 years, power will become more multifaceted—reflecting the diversity of issues—and more contextual—certain actors and power instruments will be germane to particular issues.

The United States' technological assets—including its leadership in piloting social networking and rapid communications—give it an advantage, but the Internet also will continue to boost the power of nonstate actors. In most cases, US power will need to be enhanced through relevant outside networks, friends, and affiliates that can coalesce on any particular issue. Leadership will be a function of position, enmeshment, diplomatic skill, and constructive demeanor.

The US position in the world also will be determined by how successful it is in helping to manage international crises—typically the role of great powers and, since 1945, the international community's expectation of the United States. Should Asia replicate Europe's 19th- and early 20th-century past, the United States will be called upon to be a balancer, ensuring regional stability. In contrast, the fall of the dollar as the global reserve currency and substitution by another or a basket of currencies would be one of the sharpest indications of a loss of US global economic position, strongly undermining Washington's political influence too.

The replacement of the United States by another global power and erection of a new international order seems the least likely outcome in this time period. No other power would be likely to achieve the same panoply of power in this time frame under any plausible scenario. The emerging powers are eager to take their place at the top table of key multilateral institutions such as UN, IMF, and World Bank, but they do not espouse any competing vision. Although ambivalent and even resentful of the US-led international order, they have benefited from it and are more interested

in continuing their economic development and political consolidation than contesting US leadership. In addition, the emerging powers are not a bloc; thus they do not have any unitary alternative vision. Their perspectives—even China's—are more keyed to shaping regional structures. A collapse or sudden retreat of US power would most likely result in an extended period of global anarchy.

ALTERNATIVE WORLDS

The present recalls past transition points—such as 1815, 1919, 1945, and 1989—when the path forward was not clear-cut and the world faced the possibility of different global futures. We have more than enough information to suggest that however rapid change has been over the past couple decades, the rate of change will accelerate in the future. Accordingly, we have created four scenarios that represent distinct pathways for the world out to 2030: *Stalled Engines, Fusion, Gini Out-of-the-Bottle, and Nonstate World*. As in previous volumes, we have fictionalized the scenario narratives to encourage all of us to think more creatively about the future. We have intentionally built in discontinuities, which will have a huge impact in inflecting otherwise straight linear projections of known trends. We hope that a better understanding of the dynamics, potential inflection points, and possible surprises will better equip decisionmakers to avoid the traps and enhance possible opportunities for positive developments.

STALLED ENGINES

Stalled Engines—a scenario in which the risk of interstate conflict rise owing to a new "great game" in Asia—was chosen as one of the book-ends, illustrating the most plausible "worst case." Arguably, darker scenarios are imaginable, including a complete breakdown and reversal of globalization due potentially to a large scale conflict on the order of a World War I or World War II, but such outcomes do not seem probable. Major powers might be drawn into conflict, but we do not see any such tensions or bilateral conflict igniting a full-scale conflagration. More likely, peripheral powers would step in to try to stop a conflict. Indeed, as we have stressed, major powers are conscious of the likely economic and political damage to engaging in any major conflict. Moreover, unlike in the interwar period, completely undoing economic interdependence or globalization would seem to be harder in this more advanced technological age with ubiquitous connections.

Stalled Engines is nevertheless a bleak future. Drivers behind such an outcome would be a US and Europe that turn inward, no longer interested in sustaining their global leadership. Under this scenario, the euro zone unravels quickly, causing Europe to be mired in recession. The US energy revolution fails to materialize, dimming prospects for an economic recovery. In the modeling which McKinsey Company did for us for this scenario, global economic growth falters and all players do relatively poorly.

FUSION

Fusion is the other book end, describing what we see as the most plausible "best case." This is a world in which the specter of a spreading conflict in South Asia triggers efforts by the US, Europe, and China to intervene and impose a ceasefire. China, the US, and Europe find other issues to collaborate on, leading to a major positive change in their bilateral relations, and more broadly leading to worldwide cooperation to deal with global challenges. This scenario relies on political leadership, with each side overruling its more cautious domestic constituencies to forge a partnership. Over time, trust is also built up as China begins a process of political reform, bolstered by the increasing role it is playing in the international system. With the growing collaboration among the major powers, global multilateral institutions are reformed and made more inclusive.

In this scenario, all boats rise substantially. Emerging economies continue to grow faster, but GDP growth in advanced economies also picks up. The global economy nearly doubles in real terms by 2030 to $132 trillion in today's dollars. The American Dream returns with per capita incomes rising $10,000 in ten years. Chinese per capita income also expands

rapidly, ensuring that China avoids the middle-income trap. Technological innovation—rooted in expanded exchanges and joint international efforts—is critical to the world staying ahead of the rising financial and resource constraints that would accompany a rapid boost in prosperity.

GINI OUT-OF-THE-BOTTLE[a]

This is a world of extremes. Within many countries, inequalities dominate—leading to increasing political and social tensions. Between countries, there are clear-cut winners and losers. For example, countries in the euro zone core which are globally competitive do well, while others on the periphery are forced to leave the EU. The EU single market barely functions. The US remains the preeminent power as it gains energy independence. Without completely disengaging, the US no longer tries to play "global policeman" on every security threat. Many of the energy producers suffer from declining energy prices, failing to diversify their economies in time, and are threatened by internal conflicts. Cities in China's coastal zone continue to thrive, but inequalities increase and split the Party. Social discontent spikes as middle-class expectations are not met except for the very "well-connected." The central government in Beijing, which has a difficult time governing, falls back on stirring nationalistic fervor.

In this scenario, economic performance in emerging and advanced economies leads to non-stellar global growth, far below that in our *Fusion* scenario, but not as bad as in *Stalled Engines*. The lack of societal cohesion domestically is mirrored at the international level. Major powers are at odds; the potential for conflicts rises. More countries fail, fueled in part by the dearth of international cooperation on assistance and development. In sum, the world is reasonably wealthy, but it is less secure as the dark side of globalization poses an increasing challenge in domestic and international politics.

---

[a] The "Gini" in this scenario title refers to the *Gini Coefficient*, which is a recognized statistical measurement of inequality of income.

NONSTATE WORLD

In this world, nonstate actors—nongovernmental organizations (NGOs), multinational businesses, academic institutions, and wealthy individuals—as well as subnational units (megacities, for example), flourish and take the lead in confronting global challenges. An increasing global public opinion consensus among elites and many of the growing middle classes on major global challenges—poverty, the environment, anti-corruption, rule-of-law, and peace—form the base of their support. The nation-state does not disappear, but countries increasingly organize and orchestrate "hybrid" coalitions of state and nonstate actors which shift depending on the issue.

Authoritarian regimes find it hardest to operate in this world, preoccupied with asserting political primacy at home and respect in an increasingly "fully democratized" world. Even democratic countries, which are wedded to the notion of sovereignty and independence, find it difficult to operate successfully in this complex and diverse world. Smaller, more agile countries in which elites are also more integrated are apt to do better than larger countries that lack social or political cohesion. Formal governance institutions that do not adapt to the more diverse and widespread distribution of power are also less likely to be successful. Multinational businesses, IT communications firms, international scientists, NGOs, and others that are used to cooperating across borders and as part of networks thrive in this hyper-globalized world where expertise, influence, and agility count for more than "weight" or "position."

This is nevertheless a "patchwork" and very uneven world. Some global problems get solved because networks manage to coalesce, and some cooperation occurs across state and nonstate divides. In other cases, nonstate actors might try to deal with a challenge, but they are stymied because of opposition from major powers. Security threats pose an increasing challenge: access to lethal and disruptive technologies expands, enabling individuals and small groups to perpetuate violence and disruption on a large scale. Economically, global growth does slightly better than in the *Gini Out-of-the-Bottle* scenario because more cooperation occurs on major global challenges in this world. The world is also more stable and socially cohesive.

TABLE OF CONTENTS

INTRODUCTION

The backdrop for *A Tale of Two Cities* was the French Revolution and dawn of the Industrial Age. We are living through a similar transformative period in which the breadth and scope of possible developments—both good and bad—are equal to if not greater than the aftermath of the political and economic revolutions of the late 18th century.

"It was the best of times, it was the worst of times . . . it was the spring of hope, it was the winter of despair . . . we were all going direct to Heaven, we were all going direct the other way . . ."

Charles Dickens, A Tale of Two Cities

The world is transforming at an unprecedented rate . . .

As the graph below shows, it took **Britain** 155 years to double GDP per capita, with about 9 million people in 1870 . . . The **US** and **Germany** took between 30 and 60 years with a few tens of million people . . . but **India** and **China** are doing this at a scale and pace not seen before: 100 times the people than Britain and in one tenth the time. By 2030 Asia will be well on its way to returning to being the world's powerhouse, just as it was before 1500.

Average increase in percentage point share of global GDP, per decade

UK, 1820-70	US, 1900-50	Japan, 1950-80	China, 2000-20	India, 2010-30

. . . but it is not totally back to the future.

The world has been transformed in other ways. By 2030, majorities in most countries will be middle-class, not poor, which has been the condition of most people throughout human history.

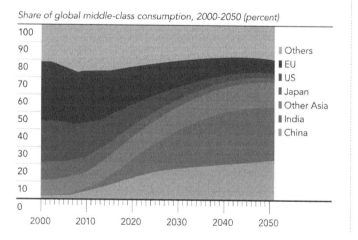

Share of global middle-class consumption, 2000-2050 (percent)

Others
EU
US
Japan
Other Asia
India
China

Global population in urban areas is expanding quickly . . .

Every year, 65 million people are added to the world's urban population, equivalent to adding seven cities the size of Chicago or five the size of London annually.

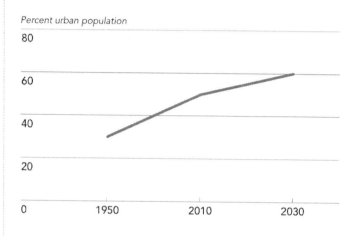

Percent urban population

. . . and the pace of technological change will accelerate.

Absorption of new technologies by Americans has become much more rapid. The absorption rate in developing states is also quickening, allowing these states to leapfrog stages of development that advanced economies had to pass through.

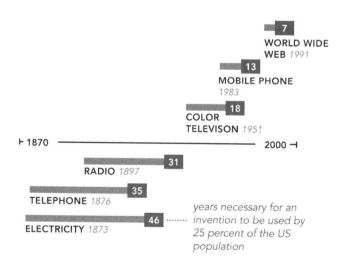

WORLD WIDE WEB *1991* — 7

MOBILE PHONE *1983* — 13

COLOR TELEVISON *1951* — 18

RADIO *1897* — 31

TELEPHONE *1876* — 35

ELECTRICITY *1873* — 46

years necessary for an invention to be used by 25 percent of the US population

INTRODUCTION

This report is intended to stimulate thinking about this rapid, vast array of geopolitical, economic, and technological changes transforming our world today and their potential trajectories over the next 15-20 years.

We begin by identifying what we see as the most important **megatrends** of our transforming world—individual empowerment, the diffusion of power to multifaceted networks and from West to East and South, demographic patterns highlighted by aging populations and exploding middle classes, and natural resource challenges. These megatrends are knowable. By themselves they point to a transformed world, but the world could transform itself in radically different ways. We are heading into uncharted waters.

We contend that the megatrends are interacting with six variables or **game-changers** that will determine what kind of transformed world we will inhabit in 2030. These game-changers—questions about the global economy, national and global governance, the nature of conflict, regional spillover, advancing technologies, and the United States' role in the international arena—are the raw elements that could sow the seeds of global disruption or incredible advances.

Based on what we know about the megatrends, and by positing the possible interactions between the megatrends and the game-changers, we envision four **potential worlds.** At one end of the spectrum is a **Stalled Engines** world in which the risks of interstate conflict increase and the US retrenches. At the other extreme is a newly rebalanced and **Fused** world in which social, economic, technological, and political progress is widespread. In the middle are two other possibilities: a **Gini-Out-of-the-Bottle** world in which inequalities dominate or a **Nonstate World** in which nonstate actors flourish both for good and ill.

None of these outcomes is inevitable. The future world order will be shaped by human agency as much as unfolding trends and unanticipated events.

In describing potential futures, we identify inflection points as well as opportunities and risks to help readers think about strategies for influencing the world's trajectory.

"These game-changers . . . are the raw elements that could sow the seeds of global disruption or incredible advances."

In looking out 15-20 years, we have sought not to be overly influenced by what has been in the West, at least, a gloomy outlook resulting from the 2008 financial crisis. Rather, we have taken a broad view of global developments at this historical juncture and of the forces that are working to sway them in one direction or another.

As with the NIC's previous Global Trends reports, we do not seek to predict the future—an impossible feat—but instead provide a framework for thinking about potential outcomes, their implications, and opportunities to influence the course of events.

INTERNATIONAL REACTIONS TO GLOBAL TRENDS 2030

We met with experts in nearly 20 countries on five continents to solicit reactions to the initial draft of Global Trends 2030. Governmental and nongovernmental institutions in several of the countries we visited also have undertaken similar studies. Thus we took the opportunity to gain a better understanding of how others view the future. Obviously, it would be impossible to capture all the reactions to our very wide-ranging draft covering a large number of topics. However, a number of common themes surfaced from the numerous discussions:

Too Much Optimism? To many, the draft appeared too optimistic about likely progress from trends like individual empowerment and technological advances. One critic stated, "I am puzzled about your optimistic view on the Internet because on one side the Internet could carry irrational things, not only ideology but crazy cults." One participant said that, "we tend to think that when people have access to more goods and services, they will calm down, but when they have more they have rising expectations. New generations do not have the patience to work for 20-30 years to get rich so they will be destructive."

"The World Looks More Like Hobbes than Kant:" Many felt that the initial draft did not adequately address identity politics. One reviewer opined, "individual power could be balanced by collective empowerment." Another said, "The growing rise of the politics of identity . . . leads to fragmentation including within states. This does not lead to convergence of values because the politics of identity is to differ with others rather than find common ground." Another thought that, "religious obscurantism, sectarianism and strife (could) throw entire regions to the past." Commenting on the section in the work about social media expanding the roles of Muslim women, one participant stated, "Muslim women who learn to read will read the Koran, not the Bill of Rights."

Arab Spring. Some Chinese analysts saw the Arab Spring "as the beginning of a very chaotic period and disorder, including unintended consequences." For Russian analysts, the emerging strategic environment was not just multipolar but also "multi-civilization." Our Russian interlocutors expressed concern about the potential for increased global instability created by extremists in the "Muslim civilization." Our UAE interlocutors thought there was no such thing as a "moderate jihadist," and some doubted whether the Arab uprisings would lead to democracy—even over the longer term.

Consumerism Run Amok? Most everyone agreed that the rising middle classes were a key megatrend with momentous implications. However, some participants, such as those from Brazil, cited the likely environmental stresses from growing resource consumption by the middle classes. One saw an "ecological disaster" happening simultaneously with the rise of the middle classes.

China. China was a key theme in all the discussions, as much outside China as inside. Some thought the initial text emphasized the country too much, but others wanted an even more fulsome treatment, seeing China as it own game-changer. For some Chinese analysts, "it is the best of times and the worst of times in China. Corruption is at its worst. In 2030, the situation will be better including in political reform." African analysts said that "as Africans, we need to decide what we want from China and be strategic, not leave it to them to set the rules of engagement." Indian analysts worried about their own position as the economic and technological gap with China widens. Most agreed with the point made in the text that the US-China relationship is perhaps the most important bilateral tie shaping the future.

Future of Europe. More than in reviews of previous Global Trends works, Europe was a lively topic for discussion. The Russians saw an even greater need for partnership with Europe and stronger US-Russian ties to ward off growing instability. Many European interlocutors saw "fragmentation" as summing up Europe's future, while some European businessmen stressed the likelihood of fiscal integration and the continued importance of transatlantic economic ties to the global economy. Outside of Europe, participants raised the possibility of decline with many in Africa worrying that Europe's decline would lead to too much dependence on China and other emerging powers.

Ambivalence Toward the US. Many saw the need for a strong power like US to uphold the international system: according to some of our Russian interlocutors, "the US never will stop being a world superpower guaranteeing the world order—there will not be isolationism . . ."Nevertheless, some disputed whether the US had been a good security provider." The US has been the instigator of conflicts like Iraq, and the US has been involved in more wars since World War II than anyone else."

The Governance Gap. The need for better leadership and governance was a universal theme, with most analysts bemoaning the lack of it in their regions. "The state is becoming bigger everywhere but less capable and powerful . . ." Some Chinese saw major disruptions: "if there is no global governance in 2030, we will still need to satisfy our economy with resources. As there is no global governance mechanism, it could be a crisis."

Increasing Risk of Conflicts. Participants worried that the number of conflicts could increase in the future. Some Russian analysts noted that future conflict will be characterized by new areas of military potential, including cyberweapons, the militarization of space, a precision global strike capability, and non-nuclear anti-ballistic missile defenses. Many anticipated further nuclear proliferation and questioned whether stable multipolar nuclear deterrence would be achieved. Indian analysts talked about the need to think about a "new extended commons" which would include cyberspace, outer space, and maritime space. Our African interlocutors particularly worried about climate change creating new social and economic tensions that could flare into civil conflict.

Continuity as well as Change in the International System. Most saw momentous, historic changes underway, sharing our view that the rapid change makes it difficult to forecast the future of the international system in 2030. One expert succinctly commented, "old is gone, new is not here yet." Many worried about a "chaotic situation in the future for the international system which would no longer be rules-based but interests-based. However, a number saw some continuity. As one said, "We think the system of international relations will be more polycentric, although with the same hierarchy of powers." Our Chinese interlocutors stressed that it would take decades for China to catch up to the US: China will not be the United States' "peer competitor" in 2030. Most agreed that nonstate actors were gaining power, but some disputed whether they will ever come close to wielding as much power as governments.

CHAPTER 1
MEGATRENDS

Four overarching megatrends will shape the world in 2030:

- **Individual Empowerment.**

- **The Diffusion of Power.**

- **Demographic Patterns.**

- **The Growing Nexus among Food, Water, and Energy** *in combination with climate change.*

These trends exist today, but during the next 15-20 years they will deepen and become more intertwined, producing a qualitatively different world. For example, the hundreds of millions of entrants into the middle classes throughout all regions of the world create the possibility of a global "citizenry" with a positive effect on the global economy and world politics. Equally, absent better management and technologies, growing resource constraints could limit further development, causing the world to stall its engines.

Underpinning the megatrends are **tectonic shifts**—critical changes to key features of our global environment that will affect how the world "works." (See table on page v.)

MEGATREND 1
INDIVIDUAL EMPOWERMENT

Individual empowerment is perhaps the most important megatrend because it is both a cause and effect of most other trends including the expanding global economy, rapid growth of the developing countries, and widespread exploitation of new communications and manufacturing technologies. On the one hand, we see the potential for greater individual initiative as key to solving the mounting global challenges during the next 15-20 years. On the other hand, in a tectonic shift, individuals and small groups will have greater access to lethal and disruptive technologies (particularly precision-strike capabilities, cyber instruments, and bioterror weaponry), enabling them to perpetrate large-scale violence—a capability formerly the monopoly of states. (See pages 67-70 for further discussion.)

Individual empowerment will accelerate substantially owing to poverty reduction and a huge growth of the global middle class, greater educational attainment, and better health care. The growth of the middle class constitutes a tectonic shift: for the first time, a majority of the world's population will not be impoverished, and the middle classes will be the most important social and economic sector in the vast majority of countries around the world. The ability of individuals to affect governance will be enabled by many existing and yet-to-be-developed communications technologies. Despite the greater empowerment of individuals, many will not feel secure owing to intensified competition for jobs.

POVERTY REDUCTION

Today about 1 billion people globally are living in extreme poverty, earning less than $1.25 a day,[a] and 1 billion are undernourished. The number of those living in extreme poverty globally has been relatively stable

[a] "Extreme poverty" is defined as earning less than $1 per day at purchasing power parity (PPP); most recently rebased to $1.25 per day.

for a long time, but the rate has been declining with population growth. Significant numbers of people have been moving from well below the poverty threshold to relatively closer to it due to widespread economic development. Absent a global recession, the number of those living in extreme poverty is poised to decline as incomes continue to rise in most parts of the world. The number could drop by about 50 percent between 2010 and 2030, according to some models.

Numerical declines of those living in extreme poverty in East Asia, notably China, have already been substantial, and the number is expected to drop further owing to rapid economic growth. The numbers are also expected to drop rapidly in South Asia and the Middle East as well as North Africa. In Sub-Saharan Africa, however, the average person living in extreme poverty will remain about 10 percent below the extreme poverty threshold during the next 15-20 years.

" . . . we see the potential for greater individual initiative as key to solving the mounting global challenges during the next 15-20 years."

Under most scenarios—except the most dire—significant strides in reducing extreme poverty will be achieved by 2030. However, if a long global recession occurred, the 50 percent reduction of those living in extreme poverty would be more than halved: as many as 300 million more people would remain in extreme poverty and experience malnutrition. Under low-growth scenarios, smaller reductions in the extreme poverty rate would occur and fewer new entrants would join the global middle class.

AN EXPANDING GLOBAL MIDDLE CLASS

Middle classes most everywhere in the developing world are poised to expand substantially in terms of both absolute numbers and the percentage of the population that can claim middle-class status during the next 15-20 years. Even the more conservative models see a rise in the global total of those living in the middle class from the current 1 billion or

Percent

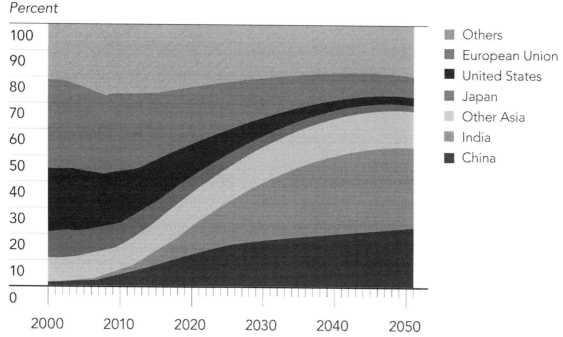

Source: OECD.

so to over 2 billion people.[a] Others see even more substantial rises with, for example, the global middle class reaching 3 billion people by 2030.[b] All the analyses we reviewed suggest that the most rapid growth of the middle class will occur in Asia, with India somewhat ahead of China over the long term. According to the Asian Development Bank, if China "achieves the new plan target of increasing household expenditures at least as rapidly as GDP, the size of its middle class will explode" with "75 percent of China's population enjoying middle-class standards and $2/day poverty will be substantially wiped out." Goldman Sachs in its study of the global middle class underlined that even not counting China and India, "new [middle class] entrants would still be larger than the world has seen for many decades." Multiple studies project that the rate of growth in the size of Africa's

middle class will be faster than elsewhere in the rapidly developing world, but the base is now very low.

Establishing the threshold for determining when someone is middle class versus climbing out of poverty is difficult, particularly because the calculations rely on the use of purchasing power parity. Most new members of the middle class in 2030 will be at the lower end of the spectrum. Their per capita incomes will be still rated as "poor" by Western standards even though they will have begun to acquire the trappings of middle-class status. Growth in the number of those living in the top half of the range of this new middle class—which is likely to be more in line with Western middle-class standards—will be substantial, rising from 330 million in 2010 to 679 million in 2030. Much of the future global leadership is likely to come from this segment.

The rapid growth of the middle class has important implications. Demand for consumer goods, including cars, rises sharply with the growth of the middle class. The Goldman Sachs study indicated that resource constraints are going to be "arguably tighter than they

---

[a] There are multiple applicable definitions of what constitutes membership in the middle class. The International Futures model that we use in this report focuses on per capita consumption expenditures rather than GDP per capita. In that model, middle-class membership is defined as per capita household expenditures of $10-50 per day at PPP. Goldman Sachs used a comparable GDP per capita of $6,000-30,000 per year, which yields a similar estimate of 1.2 billion middle-class people in the world in 2010. Kharas (OECD study) calculated the number of those in the middle class at 1.85 billion in 2009; Ravallion (World Bank) calculated that 2.64 billion people were in the middle class in 2005.
[b] The source for this estimate is a 2008 Goldman Sachs study.

were in late 19th-century Europe and the US" when the middle classes also made enormous gains.

More generally, values shift and demand for sociopolitical change rises as more individuals move up into the middle class. Historically, the rise of middle classes has led to populism and dictatorships as well as pressures for greater democracy. The value of $12,000 GDP per capita income is sometimes considered to be the level above which democracies do not revert to authoritarian systems.

With the expansion of the middle class, income inequalities—which have been a striking characteristic of the rising developing states—may begin to lessen in the developing world. Even if the Gini coefficients, which are used to measure inequalities, decline in many developing countries, they are still unlikely to approach the level of many current European countries like Germany and Finland where inequality is relatively low.

"All the analyses we reviewed suggest that the most rapid growth of the middle class will occur in Asia, with India somewhat ahead of China."

That said, a perception of great inequality will remain, particularly between urban- and rural-dwellers, motivating a growing number of rural-dwellers to migrate to the cities to seek economic opportunities. Their chances of becoming richer will be substantially greater in cities, but the increasing migration to urban areas will mean at least an initial expansion in the slums and the specter of poverty. If new middle-class entrants find it difficult to cling to their new status and are pulled back toward impoverishment, they will pressure governments for change. Rising expectations that are frustrated have historically been a powerful driver of political turmoil.

The increase in the overall numbers of the middle class worldwide disguises growing pressures on the middle class in Western economies. The share of global middle-class consumers from the US will decline and be dwarfed by the wave of new middle-class consumers (see graphic on page 10) in the developing world. Slower economic growth among many OECD countries will further ingrain the perception of a struggling Western middle class that also faces greater competition from an increasingly global employment market, including competition for jobs requiring higher skills. Some estimates, for example, see middle-class consumption in North America and Europe only rising by 0.6 percent a year over the next couple of decades. In contrast, spending by middle-class Asian consumers could rise 9 percent a year through 2030, according to Asian Development Bank estimates.

EDUCATION AND THE GENDER GAP

The educational sector is likely to be both the motor and beneficiary of expanding middle classes. The economic status of individuals and countries will greatly depend on their levels of education. The average years of completed formal education in the Middle East and North Africa are likely to rise from about 7.1 to more than 8.7 years. Moreover, the level for women in that region could rise from 5.0 to 7.0 years. Women throughout much of the world are steadily narrowing the gap with men in years of formal education and have moved ahead in enrollment and completion rates in upper-middle and higher-income countries.

The closing of the gender gap on educational attainment (and health outcomes as well) during the past couple decades has had limited effect, however, on narrowing differences on economic participation and political empowerment. Increased entry and retention of women in the workplace will be a key driver of success for many countries, boosting economic productivity and mitigating the impacts of aging. Better governance could also be a spinoff of greater political involvement of women, as some studies suggest participation of women in parliament or senior government positions correlates stronger with lower corruption.[a]

---

a   For more on the role of women as agents of change in the economic and political spheres, see previous Global Trends works—*Global Trends 2020: Mapping the Global Future*, pp 38-39 and *Global Trends 2025: A Transformed World*, pp 16-17.

According to the World Economic Forum's *Global Gender Gap Index*,[a] only 60 percent of the economic gap and only 20 percent of the political one have been closed globally in 2012. No country has completely closed the economic participation or the political empowerment gap, but the Nordic countries have come closest to gender equality. Their cases are instructive of the time and effort involved in achieving parity. Most Nordic countries enfranchised women relatively "early" (in the early 20th century), and many political parties introduced voluntary gender quotas in the 1970s. The quotas have led to a high number of women parliamentarians and political leaders in those societies. The Nordic countries also have promoted high female employment participation rates through generous childcare and maternity policies, which has contributed to higher birth rates.

Looking ahead to 2030 using the International Futures model suggests that pace of change will continue to be slow in all regions. The Middle East, South Asia, and Sub-Saharan, which start from a relatively low base of economic and political gender parity, will continue to lag other regions. The fastest pace in closing the gender gap is likely to be in East Asia and Latin America. The gap almost certainly will remain significantly narrower in high-income countries in North America and Europe in 2030, where the gap is already smaller than elsewhere.

ROLE OF COMMUNICATIONS TECHNOLOGIES

Emerging technologies such as second-generation wireless communications (smartphones) are also likely to accelerate the empowerment of individuals, introducing new capabilities to the developing world in particular. The second wave of wireless communications engenders a reduced need for developing countries to invest in and build expansive, costly communications infrastructures. Such technologies will reduce the urban-rural split that characterized first-wave technologies, especially in developing countries. (See pages 55-56 for discussion

---

a World Economic Forum Gender Gap Report 2012 is available at http://ww3.weforum.org/docs/WEF GenderGAP Report 2012.pdf.

How Social Media Are Accelerating the Process of Individual Empowerment

Muslim women have historically lagged in educational skills and integration into the market economy. More recently, they have become prolific users and consumers of social media. Although some data points to a connection between online participation and radicalization of Muslim women, indications of female empowerment and solidarity are far more plentiful. Muslim women are using online communities to reach beyond their everyday social networks into "safe spaces" to discuss such issues as women's rights, gender equity, and the role of women within Islamic law. Participation in online and social media platforms hinges on income, literacy, and access. As these expand by 2030, a growing number of Muslim women are likely to participate in online forums, potentially affecting their societies and governance.

of the impact of such technologies on governance.) The spread of smartphones in Africa during the past few years—65 percent of the continent's population now has access to them—has been particularly impressive. Now millions of Africans are connected to the Internet and the outside world, and they are using such technologies to mitigate deep-seated problems such as waterborne illness, which have slowed development. For example, an innovative program in western Kenya to distribute water filters and stop the use of contaminated water involved using smartphones to monitor changes in behavior.

IMPROVING HEALTH

By 2030 we expect to see continued progress on health—including extending the quality of life for those aging (see discussion on pages 98-102). Even in the face of the HIV/AIDS epidemic, the global disease burden has been shifting rapidly for several decades from communicable[a] to noncommunicable diseases. Absent a virulent pandemic (see box on page 14), global deaths from all communicable diseases—including AIDS, diarrhea, malaria, and respiratory infections—are projected to decline by nearly 30 percent by 2030, according to our modeling and other studies. AIDS appears to have hit its global peak—around 2 million deaths per year—in 2004. Great strides are being made toward wiping out malaria, but past periods of progress have sometimes given way in the face of donor fatigue and growing disease resistance to treatment. Nevertheless, in Sub-Saharan Africa, where the provision of health-care services has traditionally been weak, we believe the declining total deaths from communicable diseases and the increasing number from noncommunicable causes (such as from heart disease) will cross over in about 2030.

"By 2030 we expect to see continued progress on health—including extending the quality of life for those aging."

Elsewhere—even in other parts of the developing world—deaths from "chronic" maladies such as cardiovascular disease, cancer, and diabetes have been preponderant for some time, and the ongoing progress globally against noncommunicable or chronic diseases has resulted in longer life expectancy. With the dramatic reduction of infant and child mortality, due to the continued success against communicable diseases and maternal and perinatal diseases, life expectancy in the developing world almost certainly will improve. However, a significant gap in life expectancy will most likely remain between rich and poor countries.

A MORE CONFLICTED IDEOLOGICAL LANDSCAPE

A world of surging middle classes, varying economic potentials, and more diffuse power will also exhibit an increasingly diverse ideological landscape. The economics of globalization have spread the West's

ideas of scientific reason, individualism, secular government, and primacy of law to societies seeking the West's material progress but reluctant to sacrifice their cultural identites and political traditions. Managing the intensifying interaction of traditional political, religious, and cultural norms with the ideologies of the globalizing West will be a core challenge for many rapidly developing societies, affecting prospects for global and domestic governance and economic performance through 2030.

Amid this fluid ideological landscape, the West's conception of secular modernity will not necessarily provide the dominant underlying values of the international system. The persistence, if not growth and deepening, of religious identity, growing environmental concerns, and resource constraints, and the empowerment of individuals through new communications technologies are already providing alternative narratives for global politics. As non-Western societies continue their economic transformation, the prospect of a retrenchment along religious, ethnic, cultural, and nationalistic lines could fuel dysfunction and fragmentation within societies. Alternatively, the intersection of Western ideas with emerging states could generate—particularly over time—new hybrid ideologies that facilitate collaboration in an expanding number of areas, leading to increased economic output and greater consensus on global governance issues. The recent EU global trends study[b] using global survey data saw more "convergence" than "divergence" in norms and values as diverse peoples confront similar economic and political challenges.

The role assigned to religion by the state and society probably will be at the center of these ideological debates within and across societies. Religion—especially Islam—has strengthened as a key force in global politics owing to global increases in democratization and political freedoms that have allowed religious voices to be heard as well as advanced communications technologies and the

---

[a] Communicable diseases include maternal and perinatal conditions in addition to major communicable diseases such as AIDS, diarrhea, malaria, and respiratory diseases.

[b] European Strategy and Policy Analysis System (ESPAS) Report on Global Trends 2030, Institute for Security Studies, European Union, October, 2011.

PANDEMICS:
UNANSWERED QUESTIONS

Scientists are just beginning to recognize the amount of "viral chatter" that is occurring worldwide, discovering previously unknown pathogens in humans that sporadically make the jump from animals to humans. Examples include a prion disease in cattle that jumped in the 1980s to cause variant Creutzeldt-Jacob disease in humans, a bat henipavirus that in 1999 became known as Nipah Virus in humans, and a bat corona virus that jumped to humans in 2002 to cause SARS. Human and livestock population growth and encroachment into jungles increases human exposure to these previously rare crossovers. No one can predict which pathogen will be the next to start spreading to humans, or when or where such a development will occur, but humans will continue to be vulnerable to pandemics, most of which will probably originate in animals.

An easily transmissible novel respiratory pathogen that kills or incapacitates more than one percent of its victims is among the most disruptive events possible. Unlike other disruptive global events, such an outbreak would result in a global pandemic that directly causes suffering and death in every corner of the world, probably in less than six months.

Unfortunately, this is not a hypothetical threat. History is replete with examples of pathogens sweeping through populations that lack preexisting immunity, causing political and economic upheaval, and determining the outcomes of wars and civilizations. Examples include the Black Death that killed a third of Europeans; measles and smallpox in the Americas that may have killed 90 percent of the native population; and the 1918 influenza pandemic that decimated certain populations, including sickening more than 15 percent of German forces in June 1918. The WHO has described one such pandemic, an influenza pandemic, as "the epidemiological equivalent of a flash flood." The WHO states, "[pandemics] have started abruptly without warning, swept through populations globally with ferocious velocity, and left considerable damage in their wake."

Novel pandemic pathogens that spread more slowly but are just as deadly, if not more so, such as HIV/AIDS, are just as likely to emerge by 2030. In fact, such a slow-moving pathogen with pandemic potential may have already jumped into humans somewhere, but the pathogen and disease manifestations may not be recognized yet. This was the case for HIV/AIDS, which entered the human population more than a half century before it was recognized and the pathogen identified.

New discoveries in the biological sciences hold promise for more rapidly identifying pathogens and developing targeted therapeutics and vaccines; however, such advances may be inadequate to keep up with the threat. Drug-resistant forms of diseases previously considered conquered, such as tuberculosis, gonorrhea, and Staphylococcus aureus could become widespread, markedly increasing health-care costs and returning large segments of populations to the equivalent of the pre-antibiotic era. Advances in genetic engineering by 2030 may enable tens of thousands of individuals to synthesize and release novel pathogens, compounding the already formidable naturally occurring threat.

failure of governments to deliver services that religious groups can provide. The ability of religious organizations to define norms for governance in religious terms and to mobilize followers on economic and social justice issues during a period of global economic upheaval is likely to raise the prominence of religious ideas and beliefs in global politics. In this new era, religious ideas, actors, and institutions are likely to be increasingly influential among elites and publics globally.

Nationalism is another force that is likely to intensify, particularly in regions—such as East Asia—where there are unresolved territorial disputes and countries' fortunes may be rapidly changing. Moreover, many developing and fragile states—such as in Sub-Saharan Africa—face increasing strains from resource constraints and climate change, pitting different tribal and ethnic groups against one another and accentuating the separation of various identities. Ideology is likely to be particularly powerful and socially destructive when the need for basic resources exacerbates already existing tensions between tribal, ethnic, religious, and national groups. Urbanization—once expected to encourage secularization—is contributing instead, in some settings, to increased expressions of religious identity. Immigrants to cities—mostly Muslims in Europe and Russia, for example—are coalescing along religious lines. Urbanization is driving demands for social services provided by religious organizations—an opening that Islamic and Christian activists have been effective in using to bolster religious cohesion and leverage.

MEGATREND 2
DIFFUSION OF POWER

The diffusion of power among countries and from countries to informal networks will have a dramatic impact by 2030, largely reversing the historic rise of the West since 1750 and restoring Asia's weight in the global economy and world politics. In a tectonic shift, by 2030, Asia will have surpassed North America and Europe combined in terms of global power, based upon GDP, population size, military spending, and technological investment. China alone will probably have the largest economy, surpassing that of the United States a few years before 2030.[a] Meanwhile, the economies of Europe, Japan, and Russia are likely to continue their slow relative declines.

Just as important, the economies of other non-Western states such as Colombia, Egypt, Indonesia, Iran, South Africa, Mexico, Turkey, and others that are middle tier today could rise by 2030. Individually most of these countries will remain second-order players because China and India are so large. However, as a collective group, they will begin to surpass Europe, Japan, and Russia in terms of global power by 2030. Our modeling shows, for example, that this group of rapidly developing middle-tier countries—the Goldman Sachs "Next Eleven"[b]—will collectively overtake the EU-27 in global power by 2030. When this second tier is combined with the non-Western giants of China and India, the shift of power from the West to the emerging or non-Western world is even more pronounced. The enormity of this shift in national power is reflected in the number of regional power transitions that will be ongoing by 2030—some of the more dynamic will occur outside of Asia, where China and India are already consolidating their regional positions. In 2030

China's GDP,[c] for example, is likely to be about 140 percent larger than Japan's.

As the world's largest economic power, China is expected to remain ahead of India, but the gap could begin to close by 2030. India's rate of economic growth is likely to rise while China's slows. In 2030 India could be the rising economic powerhouse that China is seen to be today. China's current economic growth rate—8 to 10 percent—will probably be a distant memory by 2030.

The total size of the Chinese working-age population will peak in 2016 and decline from 994 million to about 961 million in 2030. In contrast, India's working-age population is unlikely to peak until about 2050. Also of significance, India will most likely continue to consolidate its power advantage relative to Pakistan. India's economy is already nearly eight times as large as Pakistan's; by 2030 that ratio could easily be more than 16-to-1.

In Africa, Egypt, Ethiopia, and Nigeria have the potential to approach or surpass South Africa in overall national power, but the key will be better governance to further economic growth and social and human development. In Southeast Asia, Vietnam's regional power will grow, approaching by 2030, Thailand. Vietnam benefits from a steady growth in GDP per capita while Thailand has been subject to erratic, drop-and-surge GDP per-capita-growth patterns. In Latin America, the next 15 years probably will confirm Brazil's position as the "colossus of the South," increasing its position relative to Mexico and Colombia—despite these countries' overall good growth prospects. In Europe, Germany is likely to remain the leader of the other 26 EU countries because of its economic growth prospects, but will be challenged by an aging population. By 2030 Russia faces a steep population drop—about 10 million people—a greater decline than any other country during that time frame. However, depending on its economic growth rates and immigration, Russia could retain its current global power share.

---

[a] Modeling suggests that China will surpass the US in 2022 if GDP is measured at purchasing power parity (PPP) and sometime near 2030 if GDP is measured at market exchange rates (MERs). Although MER-based measures are important for trade and financial analysis, PPP-based measures probably provide better insight into fundamental economic strength.

[b] Goldman Sachs' Next Eleven consists of Bangladesh, Egypt, Indonesia, Iran, Mexico, Nigeria, Pakistan, The Philippines, South Korea, Turkey, and Vietnam.

[c] This estimate is based on the Market Exchange Rate.

The main discussion refers to a global power index, based upon GDP, population size, military spending, and technology, which we have used in previous *Global Trends* works. Recently, we have contributed to the development of a new global power index, which incorporates a broader array of elements relevant to 21st-century power, including health, education, and governance. Using the new index, China's and India's shares of global power increase, but at a slower pace than projected by the other index. Using the earlier, four-pronged power index, China's share of national power equals the US share in 2030; using the new index, China's share is 4-5 percentage points below the US share. Using the new, broader power index, Europe (EU-27) ranks much closer to the US than in the previous index. Using either index, the aggregate power of developing states overtakes that of all developed states, including the US, by 2030. The share of global power held by the EU, Japan, and less so Russia decreases under both indices.

Traditional, Four-Component Power Forecast

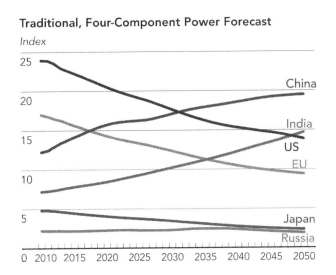

New Multi-Component Global Power Index Forecast

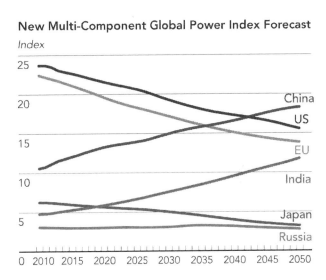

By 2030, no matter the power index, developing states (OECD) overtake developed states (non-OECD).

Traditional, Four-Component Power Forecast

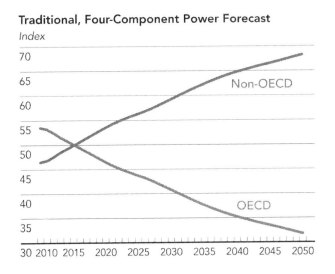

New Multi-Component Global Power Index Forecast

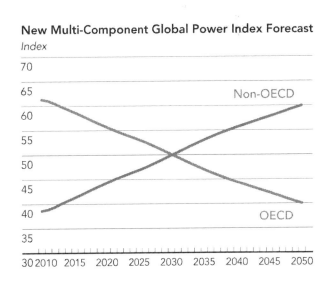

Our modeling also indicates that many of the currently vulnerable or fragile states—such as Afghanistan, Democratic Republic of Congo, and Somalia— are likely to remain highly vulnerable during the next 15-20 years. These countries will most likely continue to have weak governance, security, and economic performance while facing demographic and environmental challenges. (See chart on page 19.)

THE RISE AND FALL OF COUNTRIES: *NOT* THE SAME OLD STORY

The rapid change of various countries' fortunes—as much as the changes themselves—will put stresses both on countries' conduct with one another and internally as expectations about the position of one's country in the overall international setup are realized or dashed. A number of countries will pass through inflection points in the period out to 2030: their global power will either level off or the rate of increase of their global power will slow. Not only China and the United States, but also Europe, Japan, and Russia may be passing through inflection points, which will translate into added stress on the international system.

SELECTED COUNTRIES PUNCHING ABOVE THEIR WEIGHT IN 2010

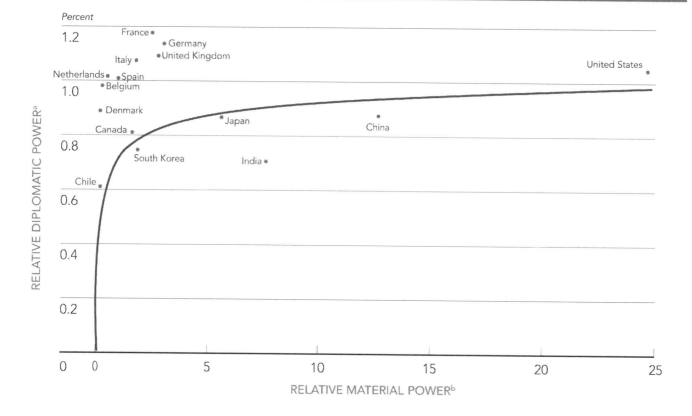

[a] Relative diplomatic power is the percentage of global diplomatic power held by each country. It is calculated by weighted country memberships in inter-governmental organization, the number of embassies that a country has in other countries and the number of treaties held by the UN seecretariat that a country has signed and ratified.

[b] Relative material power relates to the percentage of total global material held by each country. It is calculated from GDP, population size, military spending and technology.

Source: International Futures Model, University of Denver.

"Not only China and the United States, but also Europe, Japan, and Russia may be passing through major inflection points, which will translate into added stress on the international system."

For example, although China's global power will continue increasing, the rate of increase will slow. In the power cycle model developed by academics,[a] when the rate of a country's increasing power starts to slow or level off, countries are likely to become fearful and more assertive. Historically, the rate of change has been far slower for transitions in the power structure. China's and India's current economic rises, for example, dwarf all the previous ones of Britain (19th century) and the US and Japan (20th century).[b] Previously, only one or two countries have been rising at a time, shaking the international system rather than reordering it wholesale in a compressed time frame.

THE LIMITS OF HARD POWER[c] IN THE WORLD OF 2030

The shift in national power is only half the story and may be overshadowed by an even more fundamental shift in the nature of power. By 2030, no country—whether the US, China, or any other large country—will be a hegemonic power. Enabled by communications technologies, power almost certainly will shift more toward multifaceted and amorphous networks composed of state and nonstate actors that will form to influence global policies on various issues. Leadership of such networks will be a function of position, enmeshment, diplomatic skill, and constructive demeanor. Networks will constrain policymakers because multiple players will be able to block policymakers' actions at numerous points.

---

[a] For further detail regarding the theory and tests of its explanatory power using the historical record, see Charles F. Doran, *Systems in Crisis*, Cambridge University Press, 1991 and Jacob L. Heim, "Tapping the Power of Structural Change: Power Cycle Theory an Instrument in the Toolbox of National Security Decision-Making," SAIS Review, Vol 24, No 2, 113-27. RAND sponsored a workshop for the NIC on power cycle theory.
[b] See graphic opposite the Introduction on page 2.
[c] Hard power generally relates to military, economic, and technological prowess. Soft power relates to political, diplomatic, social, and cultural attainments and values that also garner influence and the capability to persuade.

COUNTRIES AT HIGH RISK OF STATE FAILURE

Rank	2008	2030
1	Burundi	Somalia
2	Yemen	Burundi
3	Somalia	Rwanada
4	Afghanistan	Yemen
5	Uganda	Uganda
6	Malawi	Afghanistan
7	Dem. Rep. of Congo	Malawi
8	Kenya	Dem. Rep. of Congo
9	Haiti	Nigeria
10	Ethiopia	Nigeria
11	Bangladesh	Niger
12	Pakistan	Pakistan
13	Nigeria	Chad
14	Niger	Haiti
15	Chad	Ethiopia

Source: Sandia National Laboratories.

Researchers at Sandia National Laboratories are developing a Human Resilience Index (HRI) to provide tools that help explore the links among human ecological conditions, human resilience, and conflict. Seven indicators are used to calculate the HRI: population growth rate, population density, caloric intake per capita, renewable fresh water per capita, arable land per capita, median age, and population health (including infant and child mortality and life expectancy). The table above lists countries that are projected to have a high risk of instability, conflict, or some other type of state failure in 2030 because of their poor human ecology and resilience.

Although we believe that worldwide norms may converge toward greater democratic governance, tackling global challenges might become more vexing because of the multiplicity of actors, including nonstate ones, and their dissimilar views.

Those countries to the northwest of the line (see graphic on page 18) are punching above their weight in hard power. In the next 20 years, we expect many of the middle powers to rise above the line as both their hard and soft powers increase. Factors used to determine diplomatic weight include intergovernmental and UN treaties to which the country is a party, and diplomatic connections and alliances. Considerable weight accrues to countries with both material and diplomatic power, such as the US and China, but such countries will be unlikely to get their way without state and nonstate partners.

Technology will continue to be the great leveler. The future Internet "moguls"—as with today's Google or Facebook—sit on mountains of data and have more real-time information at their fingertips than most governments. As these mountains of data are used to improve knowledge of human motivations, non state actors such as private companies will be able to influence behavior on as large a scale as state actors.

"The shift in national power is only half the story and may be overshadowed by an even more fundamental shift in the nature of power . . . Enabled by communications technologies, power almost certainly will shift more toward multifaceted and amorphous networks composed of state and nonstate actors . . . "

As the power of nonstate actors increases, achieving legitimacy will become a more important and crucial test for them—especially those seen to wield enormous power. Just as governments are likely to come under growing pressure to become more accountable from a more highly connected citizenry, nonstate actors will have to prove their worth to the public by pointing to positive outcomes resulting from the use of their power. Good intentions will not be enough. One could anticipate a dual-pronged movement of more state regulation on bad actors—such as hackers—while more political space opens up for individuals with positive motives.

MEGATREND 3
DEMOGRAPHIC PATTERNS

We believe that in the world of 2030—a world in which the growing global population will have reached somewhere close to 8.3 billion people (up from 7.1 billion in 2012)—four demographic trends will fundamentally shape, although not necessarily determine, most countries' economic and political conditions and relations among states. These trends are: aging both for the West and increasingly most developing states; a still significant but shrinking number of youthful societies and countries; migration, which will increasingly be a cross-border issue; and growing urbanization, which will spur economic growth but place new strains on food and water resources.

WIDESPREAD AGING

In 2030, age structures will range from extraordinarily youthful populations (median age 25 or younger) to populations that are longer lived than previously thought possible. The median age of almost all societies around the world is rising rapidly, except in Sub-Saharan Africa. Aging countries face an uphill battle in maintaining their living standards while more youthful ones have the potential, owing to the "demographic dividend," to gain an economic boost if they can put the extra numbers of youth to work.

OECD high-income countries will reach as a group a median age of 42.8 years by 2030, rising from an average of 37.9 years in 2010. Whereas in 2012 only the populations of Japan and Germany have matured beyond the median age of 45 years, by 2030, in a tectonic shift, a much larger group of countries is projected to have entered this post-mature category in Europe and East Asia (see map on page 22). The populations of these countries will feature a large proportion of people over 65 years of age—an unprecedented "pensioner bulge." At the same time, absent a large influx of youthful immigrants or an unlikely significant upturn in fertility, the working-age populations of these countries will decline in size and contain a relatively large proportion of middle-aged workers.

Countries that are amassing a large proportion of seniors face the possibility of slower aggregate GDP growth or stagnation. These post-mature states will be challenged to undertake cost-effective reforms of their retirement and health-care programs—and muster funding to adequately support needy retirees—while maintaining the living standards of those families and taxpayers who support them. The retreat from pay-as-you-go pension and health-care systems to more securely funded systems probably will create a political backlash as governments seek to reduce beneficiaries and benefits, increase workers' contributions, and extend the required number of working years. Governments of post-mature countries could be pressured to vastly restrain discretionary state spending and impose a higher tax burden.

"Countries that are amassing a large proportion of seniors face the possibility of a decline in economic productivity and slower aggregate GDP growth or stagnation."

Some analysts expect aging societies to be risk-averse and fiscally limited; these analysts contend that some European and rapidly aging East Asian states might conclude that they cannot afford to maintain a sizeable military or extend their power overseas. For some low-fertility Western European countries that have poorly integrated Asian and African immigrants, the rapid growth of these minorities could erode social cohesion and promote reactionary politics.

Most of these impacts are speculative, however. The magnitude of aging's effects and the ability of countries with well-developed institutions to minimize the negative impacts of aging are unknown. Advances in health care—which we examine on pages 98-102—are likely to improve the quality of life for some seniors, enabling them to work longer.

Youthful *(25 or younger)*
Intermediate *(over 25 to 35)*
Mature *(over 35 to 45)*
Post-mature *(over 45)*

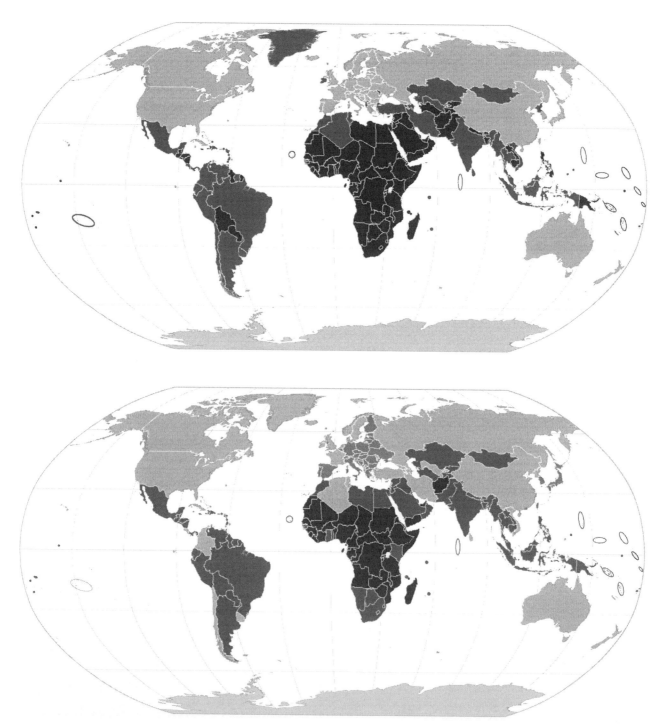

Source: US Census Bureau's International Database, June 2011. The median ages of Arab Gulf states (Bahrain, Kuwait, Oman, Qatar, Saudi Arabia, and UAE) reflect the age structure of resident citizens, omitting temporary labor migrants.

The group of countries with mature age structures (median age over 35 and less than or equal to 45 years) will also grow larger by 2030, gaining East Asian states and losing some European ones to the post-mature category. For countries in the mature category, such as China, the advantages and opportunities of the demographic bonus will have largely faded, though those that invested heavily in human capital may prolong that bonus. Despite the fading of their demographic advantages, these countries will not yet have large proportions of seniors. They will, however, need to pay closer attention to creating sustainable pension and health-care programs in order to avoid long-term risks to their development.

In the United States and Russia, the advance of the median age and an increase in the proportion of seniors will proceed slowly. In the US, a high rate of immigration and a fertility level that is near replacement are slowing aging. In Russia, the high rate of deaths among young men—because of tobacco use, alcohol abuse, and related accidents—means that instead of aging, males especially are dying at a relatively young age—in their 50s instead of living into their 60s and 70s as in other countries.

SHRINKING NUMBER OF YOUTHFUL COUNTRIES

Today more than 80 countries have populations with a median age of 25 years or less. As a group, these countries have an over-sized impact on world affairs—since the 1970s, roughly 80 percent of all armed civil and ethnic conflicts (with 25 or more battle-related deaths per year) have originated in countries with youthful populations. The "demographic arc of instability" outlined by these youthful populations ranges from clusters in the mid-section of Central America and the Central Andes, covers all of Sub-Saharan Africa, and stretches across the Middle East into South and Central Asia.

By 2030, this arc will have contracted (see map on page 22). Due to fertility declines that are well under way today, the tally of countries with youthful populations is projected to fall to about 50 by 2030.

The largest persistent cluster of youthful states is projected to be located along the equatorial belt of Sub-Saharan Africa. A second, more diffuse group of youthful countries is projected to persist in the Middle East—including the Palestinian Territories (West Bank and Gaza), and Jordan and Yemen in the region's south. In the Americas, only Bolivia, Guatemala, and Haiti are likely to retain their youthful populations. Along the Pacific Rim, this challenging condition is expected to persist in East Timor, Papua New Guinea, and the Solomon Islands.

Among the US Census Bureau's current projections for South Asia, only Afghanistan is projected to remain youthful by 2030. However, the aging that will occur among the large and growing populations in nearby Pakistan and India probably will mask youthful ethnic and regional populations that could remain a security concern. Youthful age structures are likely to persist for most of the next two decades among tribal populations in Pakistan's western provinces and territories. In Pakistan and Afghanistan, the rates of childbearing are probably greater than five children per woman among the Pushtun. In India, where the southern states and large cities have attained low fertility, youthfulness—which can contribute to instability in the absence of employment outlets—is likely to erode more slowly in the central northern states of Uttar Pradesh and Bihar.

Kurdish fertility in southeastern Turkey appears to be stalled at about four children per woman. In Israel, the fertility of the diverse Ultra-Orthodox Jewish minority remains above six children per woman. The persistence of high rates of fertility and population growth among dissonant minorities is bound to perturb the political order, particularly as these populations become much larger—although demography alone gives no clues as to how countries will adjust to these population shifts.

Age profiles of Japan illustrating the four categories of population age structures:

Youthful, 1935

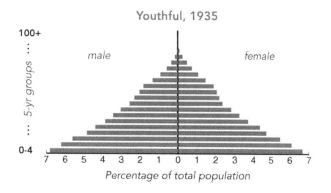

Percentage of total population

Intermediate, 1970

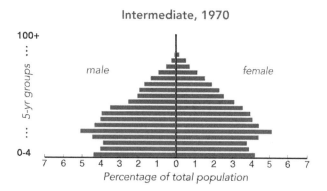

Percentage of total population

Mature, 1990

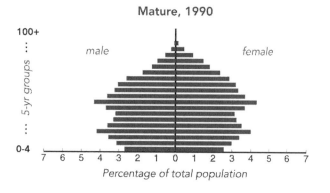

Percentage of total population

Post-mature, 2025 (projected)

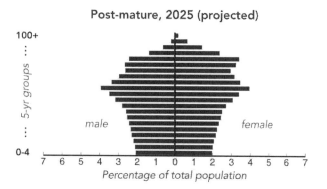

Percentage of total population

A NEW AGE OF MIGRATION?[a]

The first globalization of the late 19th and early 20th centuries saw a massive movement of people within the European continent and from Europe to the New World. We will not see the same high proportion of migrants as in the first industrial revolution, but international migration is set to grow even faster than it did in the past quarter-century. The factors promoting cross-border migration are likely to remain strong or intensify. These factors are globalization, disparate age structures across richer and poorer countries, income inequalities across regions and countries, and the presence of migrant networks linking sending and receiving countries.

Internal migration—which will be at even higher levels than international migration—will be driven by rapid urbanization in the developing world and, in some countries toward the end of our time frame, by environmental factors and the impact of climate change. Climate-change-driven migration is likely to affect Africa and Asia far more than other continents because of dependence on agriculture in Africa and parts of Asia and because of greater susceptibility in Asia to extreme weather events. Drought-driven migration will be a gradual phenomenon. Our interlocutors in Africa pointed to the growing numbers of migrants already spilling over from the Sahel region as it experiences increasingly drier conditions. Flood-driven migration will wipe out homes and infrastructures and significantly increase the perception of the risk of staying.

As with international migration, the specter of greater economic opportunities outside of local communities will be the biggest driver of internal migration. In China alone, nearly 250 million people are estimated to be internal migrants today; that number will continue to rise as more rural residents seek to raise their standard of living by moving to cities.

[a] See the joint NIC-EUISS work, *Global Governance 2025: At A Critical Juncture,* NIC 2010-08, September 2010, for further insights on migration and the lack of global governance oversight. We also benefited from an Atlantic Council-hosted workshop on migration in 2011. Data and insights from workshop papers were extensively used in the formulation of this section.

GLOBALIZED FLOWS OF WORKERS

Migration is likely to become more globalized as demand for both skilled and unskilled labor soars in traditional and new destination countries for migrants. Currently, the top ten countries hosting over half of the world's migrants are dominated by the G-8. Opportunities for migrants to fill gaps in rich countries' labor forces will continue to exist, even as these countries' economic growth slows. In Germany, the number of young people age 15-24 will fall by 25 percent, or about 2.5 million people by 2035; Japan's proportion of young people will decline by 25 percent or 3 million. Even in the US, although the number of young people will grow slightly, their percentage of the total population will decline from 14 to 12.8 percent in the next quarter century.

Age and income disparities create a paradox. One would normally expect fast-growing economies to attract migrant labor, not to send it. However, where economic growth enables more young people to acquire the knowledge and resources to take advantage of migration opportunities, and those young people can earn higher incomes abroad than at home, many will choose to migrate to richer countries.

The recently developed countries will offer numerous opportunities. Owing to rapid urbanization in the developing world, the volume of urban construction for housing, office space, and transport services over the next 40 years—concentrated in Asia and Africa—could roughly equal the entire volume of such construction to date in world history, creating enormous opportunities for both skilled and unskilled workers. Many emerging countries, such as Brazil, China, and Turkey—whose youthful populations are declining—will attract migrants from low-income countries with youthful populations, for example, countries in Sub-Saharan Africa and Southeast Asia. Brazil, China, and Turkey have already seen sharp drops in fertility: Brazil's youthful population is projected to decline by 5 million by 2030; China's will drop by 75 million; Turkey's is expected to decline slightly by 2030.

THE DEMOGRAPHIC WINDOW OF OPPORTUNITY

According to UN demographers, a country's demographic window of opportunity can be estimated by identifying those years in which the proportion of children (0 to 14 years of age) in the total population is less than 30 percent, and the proportion of seniors (65 years and older) is less than 15 percent.

Country	Median Age, 2010	Median Age, 2030	Demographic Window of Opportunity
Brazil	29	35	2000 to 2030
India	26	32	2015 to 2050
China	35	43	1990 to 2025
Russia	39	44	1950 to 2015
Iran	26	37	2005 to 2040
Japan	45	52	1965 to 1995
Germany	44	49	before 1950 to 1990
United Kingdom	40	42	before 1950 to 1980
United States	37	39	1970 to 2015

In theory, higher rates of migration would yield higher returns for global development. The World Bank estimates that a 3-percentage-point increase in the stock of migrants by 2025 would lead to a 0.6-percent increase in global income, a gain of $368 billion, with developing countries and migrants from those countries benefiting more than the natives of high-income countries. This is more than the gains from removing all remaining barriers to free trade.

Increasingly, elites in developed countries are likely to consider migration policy as part of an economic growth strategy, particularly as competition grows for highly skilled employees. China may see some increase in outmigration, as skilled workers seek opportunities in faster-growing countries while China's growth slows as its population ages. China could, however, see a much larger flow of in-migration as it seeks workers to care for and support its aging society.

"The World Bank estimates that a 3-percentage-point increase in the stock of migrants by 2025 would lead to a 0.6-percent increase in global income, a gain of $368 billion . . . more than the gains from removing all remaining barriers to free trade."

Over time, governments may need to increasingly manage mobility rather than simply immigration as more short-term movement occurs in addition to permanent migration. More people—particularly the highly skilled—will have their feet in more than one country's labor market. The rise of more global labor markets will create the need for international institutions to set new standards. For example, what happens to pensions and social and health benefits when people move: will they keep their entitlements in a country they formerly worked in? The growing number of even medium-sized companies with far-flung international interests and networks will be a pressure group for changing national policies. The dividing line between permanent residency, which most migrants can qualify for, and citizenship—

which is unattainable for many—could begin to blur. Countries may try to attract more highly skilled workers by offering permanent residents privileges, such as voting in local elections, formerly reserved for full citizens.

Technology—including widespread use of biometrics—will increase the capacity of countries to control entry, but greater information flows will enable more people to become aware of opportunities for work both nearby and in distant places. The Internet and social media can also provide increased information on conditions in receiving countries and ways to better integrate migrants. Migrants are likely to remain attracted to immigrant communities with similar ethnic, religious, or national backgrounds, but the IT revolution ensures greater and more real-time linkages to friends and family members in migrants' countries of origin.

The attractiveness of a broader number of both developed and rapidly emerging countries could become a serious blow to poor countries if it leads to an increased and one-way flow of highly skilled individuals. Migration generates a considerable flow of remittances, but a flood of skilled worker emigration has shown to harm development at home. Many countries in Sub-Saharan Africa, Central America, and the Caribbean show worrying levels of brain drain now, with some of these exceeding 30 percent of skilled workers. With the current exception of the Philippines, few "sending countries" are creating plans to protect migrants and enhance their abilities to succeed in recipient countries.

Nigeria is a good example of potential upside and downside risks from migration for many aspiring states. Nigeria's increasingly favorable demographic conditions offer it the opportunity to escape from the economic stagnation it has seen in the post-Independence period. If it collects its demographic dividend in full, it could see per capita incomes treble by 2030, lifting 80 million people out of poverty. Part of that economic success would involve experiencing continued high levels of migration as young Nigerians immigrate to acquire or hone their skills abroad before returning to join the growing middle class and contribute to the economic miracle at home. Policy failure, in contrast, could lead to a demographic disaster, with economic underperformance and enhanced risks of strife and conflict, creating substantially increased incentives to migrate.

"Owing to rapid urbanization in the developing world, the volume of urban construction for housing, office space, and transport services over the next 40 years could roughly equal the entire volume of such construction to date in world history, creating enormous opportunities for both skilled and unskilled workers."

In the developed world, migration has the potential to increase fertility and reshape the population's age structure. If current levels of migration continue, for example, most OECD countries can expect to see modest increases in their workforces. In only six OECD countries (the Czech Republic, Finland, Hungary, Japan, Poland, and the Slovak Republic) is the current level of immigration insufficient to compensate for a decline in the workforce. At the same time, the likely migration from Muslim countries with traditionally higher birth rates could create new political and social frictions. The Pew Foundation forecasts that Europe's Muslim population will double from 4.1 percent of Europe's total population today to 8 percent by 2030. France, Sweden, Austria, and Belgium, which already have the world's largest Muslim minorities, will have Muslim communities with 9-10 percent of their total populations.

History has repeatedly demonstrated the power of migration. At best, migration could help harmonize the very different economic and demographic conditions that will be experienced by countries as the world moves toward its peak population. At worst, migration could be driven primarily by economic failure, not success—reemerging as both a cause and result of conflict within and between countries. The

extent of the flows—potentially of tens of millions of people from the poorest developing countries to middle-income countries as well as to rich developed countries—creates the potential for huge human rights abuses and exploitation. Immigrant communities open up avenues for increased criminal activity such as drug smuggling. The rapidly growing age and gender imbalances across developed and developing countries also increase the potential for greater human trafficking.

Migration—unlike trade and other central features of increased globalization—is relatively unregulated by international agreements or cooperation. Immigration and border security is still largely—with the exception of the Schengen area in continental Europe—seen as coming under the purview of the country and not a subject for more international cooperation by most states in both the developing and developed worlds.

THE WORLD AS URBAN

In a tectonic shift, today's roughly 50-percent urban population (3.5 billion urban of the world's 7.1 billion people) will almost certainly climb to near 60 percent (4.9 billion of the world's projected 8.3 billion), a sharp contrast to the largely rural world of 1950, when roughly 30 percent (750 million) of the world's 2.5 billion were estimated to be urban residents. Between now and 2030, demographers expect urban population to grow most rapidly where rates of population growth are highest and where the urban proportion of the population remains relatively low, in Sub-Saharan Africa (now 37-percent urban) and Asia (near 50 percent)—two regions currently on disparate economic paths. According to the UN, between 2011 and 2030, there will be an additional urban population of 276 million in China and 218 million in India, which will together account for 37 percent of the total increase for urban population in 2030. Nine additional countries are projected to contribute 26 percent of the urban growth, with increases ranging from 22 million to 76 million. The countries are: Bangladesh, Brazil, Democratic Republic of the Congo, Indonesia, Mexico, Nigeria, Pakistan, the Philippines, and the US. In Africa, we expect urban formation and expansion

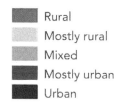

Rural
Mostly rural
Mixed
Mostly urban
Urban

The proportion of the population living in urban areas, 2010 estimates and 2030 projections. Data are drawn from the United Nations Population Division (2010). The criteria that define an urban area were selected by individual states.

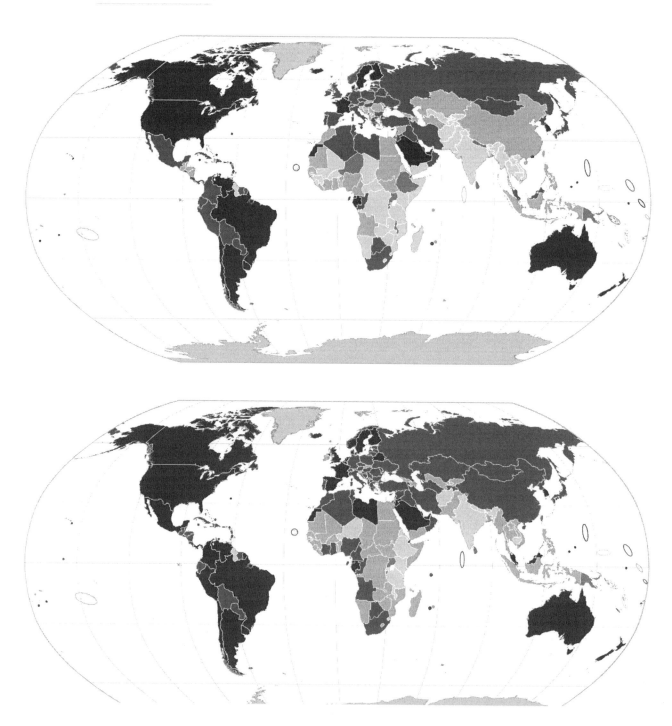

to help drive several constructive developmental trends, including urban-centered economic growth, smaller family sizes, and higher average educational attainment. Rapid urbanization could therefore give a boost to Asia's and Africa's long-term competitiveness and social and political stability, or, if not mastered, could become their Achilles' heels.

"The extent of the flows—potentially of tens of millions of people from the poorest developing countries to middle-income countries as well as to rich developed countries—creates the potential for huge human rights abuses and exploitation."

The next two decades' pattern of urban growth will look strikingly different from urban growth patterns of the late 20th century, dynamics that gave rise to most of today's 27 megacities (cities with a population greater than 10 million). Although UN demographers expect this count to continue to rise, these giants will, we believe, become further limited by physical land constraints and burdened by vehicular congestion and costly infrastructural legacies, entrenched criminal networks and political gridlock, and deteriorating sanitation and health conditions. The **peri-urban** or **"rurban"** areas will grow faster than city centers, as such areas provide cheaper land for housing and manufacturing. Metropolitan regions will spill over multiple jurisdictions creating mega-regions. By 2030, there will be at least 40 large bi-national and tri-national metro regions.

Cities have the potential to apply modern technologies and infrastructure: some of the world's largest cities are taking measures to reduce their carbon footprint and be more conservative consumers of energy. Still their growth will, we believe, promote substantial environmental and resource pressures. The growth of urban concentrations have, historically, led to dramatic reductions in forest cover, adverse shifts in the nutrient content and microbial composition of soils, alterations in the composition of higher plants and animals (including local extinctions), and changes in the availability and quality of fresh water. In some

studies these impacts have been detectable at distances sometimes exceeding 100 kilometers from the nearest urban center. Many urban centers are also vulnerable to potential shocks from flooding, particularly given inadequate drainage systems.

By 2030, few forested reserves, wetlands, and freshwater sources will be located on the perimeter of the impact zone of this fine-meshed urban network. Rapidly growing cities are likely to compete to secure freshwater catchment and land for housing growth, bringing greater prosperity to some nearby agriculturists, but setting up further tensions over freshwater rights, water quality, and urban expansion. These tensions will lead to legal battles, pressure for policy reforms, and public calls for state intervention (a situation already evident in China).

According to the McKinsey Global Institute (MGI), demand for power in China's cities will more than double from today's level, accounting for roughly 20 percent of global energy consumption. India's power targets are also ambitious—if present trends continue, India's carbon dioxide emissions will grow, and carbon emissions of South Asia as a whole will double by 2030. China's will also nearly double. Water is likely to be as much of a challenge as energy for both giants. India's cities will need 94 billion liters of potable water that MGI and others estimate will not be easily available. Sanitation also will need to be upgraded. In many poor mid-size cities, sewage collection coverage can be as low as 10-20 percent. Many transport infrastructures also are inadequate to absorb growth in mid-sized cities. Roads are neither wide enough nor sufficiently maintained to absorb expanding traffic.

Urban centers are engines of productivity, generating roughly 80 percent of economic growth. In much of Asia, Latin America, and Africa, large segments of the urban economy remain "informal"—outside the reach of business and labor laws, environmental regulation, and taxation. Similarly, only a fraction of utility consumption in these regions is metered and paid for directly. We expect the next two decades to witness unparalleled action by city governments in these regions to augment their power by taxing urban income flows and pricing utility use, an effort that will require the formalization of now-informal industries and service providers as well as the registration and taxation of consumers and land users.

"Rapid urbanization could therefore give a boost to Asia's and Africa's long-term competitiveness and social and political stability, or, if not mastered, could become their Achilles' heels."

In 2030 urban politics might feature confrontations between government authorities on the one hand and tax-evading entrepreneurs and informal markets on the other hand, as well as with squatters who maintain permanent residences. Local police are likely to escalate their efforts to extend their powers into established squatter settlements in some countries—particularly in Latin America and Sub-Saharan Africa. However, for formalization and policing to succeed, city governments in these regions will need to provide more services, hold police accountable for their actions, and extend representation to low-income residents. The confrontations of the coming decades will test the capacity of some urban governments.

The Asian Development Bank, in fact, warned in its study of Asia in 2050 that, "better financing and management of cities will require long-term planning and visionary leadership, further decentralization of responsibility to local governments, more local accountability and greater market financing of urban capital investments."

MEGATREND 4
GROWING FOOD, WATER, AND ENERGY NEXUS

The increasing nexus among food, water, and energy—in combination with climate change—will have far-reaching effects on global development over the next 15-20 years. In a tectonic shift, demand for these resources will grow substantially owing to an increase in the global population from 7.1 billion today to 8.3 billion by 2030. As we have discussed, an expanding middle class and swelling urban populations will increase pressures on critical resources—particularly food and water—but new technologies—such as "vertical" farming in high-rise structures which also reduce transportation costs —could help expand needed resources. Food and water security is being aggravated by changing weather conditions outside of expected norms.

" . . . expanding middle class and swelling urban populations will increase pressures on critical resources—particularly food and water—but shortages are not inevitable."

We are not necessarily headed into a world of scarcities, but policymakers and their private sector partners will need to be proactive to avoid scarcities in the future. Many countries probably won't have the wherewithal to avoid food and water shortages without massive help from the outside. The questions will be whether management of critical resources becomes more effective, the extent to which technologies mitigate resource challenges, and whether better governance mechanisms are employed to avoid the worst possible outcomes. Currently, no effective international frameworks exist for dealing with export controls, which often exacerbate food shortages. Increased promotion of food imports can help water-scarce countries to reduce pressure on their water sources. These "uncertainties" of largely human agency will be explored in the next chapters discussing game-changers and alternative worlds. This chapter focuses on the pressures on these resources.

Tackling problems pertaining to one commodity won't be possible without affecting supply and demand for the others. Agriculture is highly dependent on accessibility of adequate sources of water as well as on energy-rich fertilizers. Hydropower is a significant source of energy for some regions while new sources of energy—such as biofuels—threaten to exacerbate the potential for food shortages. There is as much scope for negative trade-offs as there is the potential for positive synergies.

The marketplace is also changing. State-backed Asian resource investment strategies are changing the business environment for competitors in extractive industries and other infrastructure investments in developing countries. Foreign direct investments by state-owned enterprises—largely based in emerging markets—have focused increasingly on mining, quarrying, and petroleum. Overall, commodities are now responsible for about two-thirds of foreign direct investment by state-owned enterprises. Asian countries already prioritize long-term bilateral resource supply deals for oil, gas, and coal, sealed with political and economic assistance packages.[a]

FOOD, WATER, AND CLIMATE

An extrapolation of current trends in per capita consumption patterns of food and water shows the projected extent of the problem during the next couple decades. Demand for food is set to rise by more than 35 percent by 2030, but global productivity gains have fallen from 2.0 percent between 1970 and 2000 to 1.1 percent today and are still declining. The world has consumed more food than it has produced in seven of the last eight years.[b] A major international study finds that annual global water requirements will reach 6,900 billion cubic meters (BCM) in 2030, 40 percent above current sustainable water supplies. Agriculture, which accounts for approximately 3,100 bcm, or just under 70 percent of global water withdrawals today, will

---

[a] This analysis is from a Chatham House study produced for the NIC in October, 2012, *National Security Impacts of Natural Resources by 2020, 2030, and 2040*. This study is forthcoming and will be available, when published, on the NIC's website, www.dni.gov/nic/globaltrends.
[b] This material is quoted from British researcher Alex Evans' unpublished paper on 2020 development futures.

CLIMATE CHANGE 2030: MORE EXTREME WEATHER

Empirical evidence alone—without reference to climate models—indicates that a general warming trend is affecting weather and ecosystems, causing increasing impacts on humans. Recent weather has been characterized by an increase in the frequency of extreme weather events—floods, droughts, tornadoes, glacial lake outbreaks, extreme coastal high-water levels, heat waves, etc.—and this pattern almost certainly will continue during the next 20 years.

According to the March 2012 ***Intergovernmental Panel on Climate Change (IPCC) Special Report on Managing the Risks of Extreme Events***[a], climate change is reinforcing extreme weather, making it more intense. Although the number of cyclones probably will not increase by 2030, the destructive power of tropical storms will intensify. Meanwhile, owing to population growth and the expansion of urban centers and rural agriculture, more people and infrastructures will be vulnerable to such extreme weather events. The key unknown is whether improved disaster risk-management measures will be adopted to effectively cope with these changing conditions by 2030.

Food security has been aggravated partly because during the past two decades the world's land masses have been experiencing weather conditions outside of expected norms. Observed temperature increases (though enhanced in the Arctic) are not solely a high-latitude phenomenon. Recent scientific work shows that temperature anomalies during growing seasons and persistent droughts have lessened agricultural productivity. Degraded agricultural productivity, when coupled with more protectionist national policies tightening global supply, undercuts food security, especially in impoverished regions.

Flows in the Nile, Tigris-Euphrates, Niger, Amazon, and Mekong river basins have been diminished by droughts that have persisted during the past decade. Although weather patterns in these regions are dominated by natural variability, these persistent droughts are consistent with the expected effects of warming from increased greenhouse gas concentrations in the atmosphere.

Dramatic and unforeseen changes are occurring at a faster rate than expected in regions with snow and ice. Observations show that Arctic summer sea ice is diminishing in area and volume faster than any models predicted and could vanish earlier than the original predictions of 2030-2050. Changes are also occurring in the major ice shelves (Greenland and Antarctica) that were unforeseen even five years ago. Future rates of change are currently unpredictable without better observations to improve the development of ice-prediction models. Sea-level rise could increase with the rapid melt of either the Greenland Ice Sheet or the West Antarctica Ice Shelf. With this melting, scientists now estimate that sea-level rise will be 1 meter or more by the end of the century and the rate will increase, making effective adaptation more difficult to achieve. Even modest sea-level rises, when coupled with potential storm surges from more intense storms and subsidence of delta lands, will have a significant adverse impact on coastal regions and Pacific small-island states.

The present emissions pathway is leading to a doubling of greenhouse gases by mid-century. Based on a better understanding of climate sensitivity and emissions, this concentration will lead to approximately 2°C warming by mid-century. Under the present emissions pathway, 6°C is more likely than 3°C by the end of the century, and will lead to even more significant impacts. By 2030 the emissions trajectory will be cast, determining this century's climate outcome.

---

[a] The complete title of the report is, ***Intergovernmental Panel on Climate Change (IPCC) Special Report on Managing the Risks of Extreme Events and Disasters to Advance Climate Change Adaptation***, IPCC, March 2012.

require 4,500 bcm without efficiency gains. About 40 percent of humanity lives in or near an international river basin; over 200 of these basins are shared by more than two countries, increasing the dependencies and vulnerabilities from changes in demand and availability of water. Based on current trajectories, the OECD estimates that by 2030 nearly half the world's population will live in areas with severe water stress.

Economic growth in developing countries has led to greater demands for a meat-based diet. The demand for meat places extra pressures on the grain market—because livestock feed on grain—and on water resources. The amount of water required to produce meat is far more than that required to produce an equivalent amount of grain or vegetables. In addition to population increases, rapid urbanization will increase pressure on land and water resources that are essential for food production. Biofuels also drive demand for agricultural commodities; 30-40 percent of the US corn crop is diverted to fuels in a given year.[a]

The most important short-term driver of crop supplies is weather. Of course, favorable weather can boost harvest outputs, but poor weather or large-scale weather-related disruptions can deal a serious setback. Poor harvests caused by bad weather, droughts, or crop infestations in major producing regions have already contributed to high food prices.

Climate change impacts on food and water availability will vary widely by region and probably will be more limited in the period out to 2030 than in the decades after that. In the medium-term, atmospheric carbon rise is expected to boost carbon fertilization and thereby crop yields; however, the impact of climate change on extreme weather events (see box on page 32) probably will offset the positive effect on farming. Moreover, climate change analysis suggests that average precipitation patterns will change such that wet areas will become wetter while dry, arid areas will become more so. Much of the decline in precipitation will occur in the Middle East and northern Africa,

as well as western Central Asia, southern Europe, southern Africa and the US Southwest. In places such as Algeria and Saudi Arabia, precipitation by 2050 is forecast to decline by 4.9 percent and 10.5 percent, respectively, while in Iran and Iraq, precipitation is forecast to decline by 15.6 percent and 13.3 percent, respectively. Average temperature change will be significant in many regions.

In the Andes, glacial meltwater supports river flow and water supply for tens of millions of people during the long dry season. Many small glaciers, e.g., in Bolivia, Ecuador, and Peru, will disappear within the next few decades, adversely affecting people and ecosystems. Hundreds of millions of people in China, India, and Pakistan depend upon glacier meltwater from the Hindu Kush and Himalaya Mountain regions.

Food supply will be strongly influenced by the availability of land and water as well as the use of emerging technologies. Given that agriculture uses 70 percent of global freshwater resources and livestock farming uses a disproportionate share of this, water management will become critical to long-term food security. However, water management practices—including regulating the price of water, which could incentivize investment and better management—would come with high political costs.

The world is already farming its most productive land. Given the limited availability of new agricultural land, improving crop efficiency will become especially important to meeting global food needs. High-growth economies in South and East Asia are expected to account for two-thirds of the increase in fertilizer use during the next five years. In poorer countries, underutilization of fertilizer due to low crop prices has eroded soil quality and imperiled the sustainability of crop production.

Our modeling suggests that the long-term trend of decreasing world food prices, which has already reversed itself, may have come to an end, with repercussions for consumers, especially poor ones. As long as the global economy continues to grow—which is also suggested by the modeling—increasing

---

[a] This was drawn from a NIC conference report, *Global Food Security to 2040*, NICR 2012-05, February, 2012. The report is available on the NIC's website.

food costs will not necessarily lead to greater child malnutrition. Tighter markets will result in higher prices and increased price volatility but not necessarily in a fundamental shortage of food. Continued reliance on maize as a biofuel feedstock will also increase the potential for volatility.

A stable supply of agricultural commodities to meet global food security needs and ensure trade flows can be achieved through supply-side management practices to boost crop production—including new technologies—to mitigate the potentially negative impacts of climate change.

However, a number of supply-and-demand factors could derail that outcome. These include extreme weather-related disruptions from unmitigated climate change, prolonged periods of poor management of water and soil, and inadequate use of modern agricultural technologies and fertilizer. If one or more of these factors came into play, a second, higher-risk outcome would emerge in which food production failed to keep pace with demand growth. Such a development would create shortages that could have dire geopolitical, social, and economic repercussions.

Increasing agricultural productivity in Africa would present a significant opportunity to boost and diversify global production and address regional poverty and food security. However, agricultural productivity in Africa will require major changes even to avoid shortages. Unlike Asia and South America, which have achieved significant improvements in production per capita, Africa only recently returned to 1970s' levels. Many African states have poor enabling environments for agricultural development, including lack of sufficient rural infrastructure and transportation to get seeds and fertilizer from the ports inland, and weak governance. Even a fairly marginal improvement in food supply chain management could translate into a significant reduction in waste, negating a significant amount of the pressures from growing populations and increased wealth.

Without rapid investment in adaptation, climate change is also expected to result in sharp declines in yields.[a] Increasing crop productivity on irrigated land could decrease the need to irrigate other land. This takes a disproportionately high amount of pressure off of water resources. The risk of failing to achieve increased crop productivity therefore could have a negative impact not only on food security but also on water security.

Cereal production in China and India faces significant challenges from environmental stresses relating to water scarcity, soil depletion, climate change, and pressures on land availability from urbanization. Both countries are major producers of wheat, and China is the second-largest producer and consumer of corn after the US. China, particularly, is investing heavily in agricultural technology and productivity. China and India are unlikely to abandon their efforts to achieve grain self-sufficiency through 2020. However, by 2030, demographic pressures and increasing environmental constraints may force both countries to increase imports, potentially triggering a significant price runup on international markets.[b]

The primary consequence of rising prices for agricultural commodities is the commensurate hike in staple food prices for average households. Although rich countries will also feel the pinch, the share of food spending in low-income households in poorer countries is far greater, and these families will be affected to a greater extent. As a result, food-price inflation probably will fuel social discontent over other economic issues such as low wages and poor governance.

Wheat is likely to exhibit particularly high price volatility. Significant production occurs in water-stressed and climate-vulnerable regions in China, India, Pakistan, and Australia, suggesting markets will remain tight and vulnerable to harvest shocks, including disease.

In general, the groups most vulnerable to the impacts of food-price inflation will be import-dependent

---

[a] The source for this information is a NIC-commissioned report from Chatham House, US National Security Impacts of Natural Resources by 2020, 2030, and 2040.
[b] Ibid.

"GOOD" AND "BAD" WILD CARDS

Technology is perhaps the most important wild card to ensuring global food security. Crop yield improvements due to better agricultural practices and technological improvements have accounted for nearly 78 percent of the increase in crop production between 1961 and 1999. (For more on possible future technological advances, see pages 91-93).

A nasty wild card, however, such as the spread of wheat rust could also have a long-lasting effect on food supplies. Wheat rust was largely eliminated by the genetic stock of the Green Revolution, but it reappeared in Uganda in 1998, spread to Kenya and Ethiopia, jumped to Iran in 2007, was confirmed in South Africa in 2010, and is likely to appear soon in Pakistan and the Punjab. In Kenya, it destroyed one fourth of the crop. The lesser biological diversity of wheat now than before the Green Revolution could make wheat rust a greater threat now than then. Efforts to combat it, even if they are successful, are likely to involve increasing genetic diversity again, with at least yield reductions.

poor countries, such as Bangladesh, Egypt, Djibouti, and Sudan. For this set of countries, the primary line of defense to stem food-price inflation will be to maintain, or, if necessary, expand existing subsidies on basic foodstuffs. This strategy will have its limits, however, as governments face budgetary constraints or cut funding for other programs in order to keep food prices down. Moreover, poor import-dependent countries are not in a position to undertake overseas investments to secure greater crop outputs elsewhere.

Large emerging markets such as China, India, and Russia—all of which are likely to see continuing spikes in food-price inflation—are less likely to see serious disruptive upticks in social unrest. Large grain-producing countries such as Russia and China will be better able to shield themselves domestically from rising food prices by imposing restrictions on the export of crops, although such policies will exacerbate food-price inflation and food scarcity globally. In addition to export curbs, these countries have more robust balance sheets to provide and maintain subsidies and domestic price controls and to use monetary policy tools to control inflation with more efficacy than smaller, less developed states. China, Saudi Arabia, the UAE, and others have been buying up overseas farming land. This trend will probably continue as food prices rise and the potential for scarcities increases.

A BRIGHTER ENERGY OUTLOOK

Experts are virtually certain that demand for energy will rise dramatically—about 50 percent—over the next 15-20 years largely in response to rapid economic growth in the developing world. The US Energy Information Agency anticipates steadily rising global production through 2035, driven primarily by a combination of OPEC production increases and larger unconventional sources. The main or reference scenario of the International Energy Agency also posits growing global production of key fossil fuels through 2030 (about 1 percent annually for oil).

Much of this increased production—and recent optimism—derives from unconventional oil and gas being developed in North America. The scale-up of two technologies, horizontal drilling and hydraulic fracturing, (see box on page 37) is driving this new energy boom. Producers have long known shale as "source rock"—rock from which oil and natural gas slowly migrated into traditional reservoirs over millions of years. Lacking the means economically to unlock the massive amounts of hydrocarbon in the source rock, producers devoted their attention to the conventional reservoirs. Once the industry discovered how to combine hydraulic fracturing and horizontal drilling, the vast gas resources trapped in shale deposits became accessible.

The economic and even political implications of this technological revolution, which won't be completely understood for some time, are already significant. In a

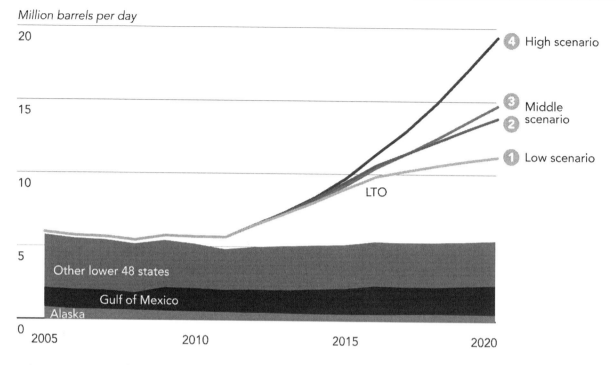

Source: HPDI; EIA; team analysis for NIC.

tectonic shift, energy independence is not unrealistic for the US in as short a period as 10-20 years. Increased oil production and the shale gas revolution could yield such independence. US production of shale gas has exploded with a nearly 50 percent annual increase between 2007 and 2011, and natural gas prices in the US have collapsed. US has sufficient natural gas to meet domestic needs for decades to come, and potentially substantial global exports. Service companies are developing new "super fracking" technologies that could dramatically increase recovery rates still further.

Shale oil production in the US is still in its early stages, and its full potential remains uncertain, but development is happening at a faster pace than shale gas. Preliminary estimates for 2020 range from 5-15 million barrels per day with a production breakeven price as low as $44-68 per barrel depending upon the fields. By the 2020, the US could emerge as a major energy exporter.

The greatest obstacle to the proliferation of new techniques to tap unconventional oil and gas

reserves both in North America and elsewhere is their environmental impact. Poor well construction and cementing, wastewater management and other above-ground risks will continue to cause accidents. Greater seismic activity around shale-producing areas has turned the public's attention in the US to possible seismic risks. Seismic activity can affect well integrity and construction, increasing the chances of methane entering drinking water supplies. Many environmental concerns could be mitigated by existing wastewater management techniques and technologies. A tighter regulatory environment—which is beginning to happen in some US states—could also close loopholes and reassure public safety. Nevertheless a major drilling-related accident could cause a public backlash, halting the fracking activity in key production areas.

The prospect of significantly lower energy prices will have significant positive ripple effect for the US economy, encouraging companies to taking advantage of lower energy prices to locate or relocate to the US. Preliminary analysis of the impact on the US economy suggests that these developments could

HYDRAULIC FRACTURING

Hydraulic fracturing, or fracking—a new technology to extract gas and oil from rock formations—is already making sizable differences in the ability of oil and gas companies to extract natural gas and oil from resources previously thought to be inaccessible. The technology will enable the release of natural gas and oil in sufficient quantities to drive down the cost of those energy resources and make substantial differences to the oil and gas import requirements of countries using fracking, as well as their dependence on coal. During the last five years the combined technologies of fracking and horizontal drilling have been an energy game-changer in the United States and other countries with large reserves of shale gas and oil.

Fracking technology was first developed and commercialized in the late 1940s. Since then over 2 million fracking stimulations of gas and oil have been completed. In fracking well operators pump a fluid (usually water) mixed with propping agent (usually sand) and a dozen or so chemical additives to control physical characteristics, such as viscosity, pH, surface tension, and scale prevention, at high pressure into a well bore. The pressure creates fractures that propagate through the rock formation; the propping holds the fractures open to allow the gas to flow through the opened porous formation once the well has been completed. The technology has evolved from its early days of using 750 gallons of fluid and 400 pounds of sand in a well to today's levels: fracking now uses over a million gallons of fluid and 5 million pounds of sand. The latest fracturing operations use computer simulations, modeling, and microseismic fracture mapping as well as tilt sensors, which monitor rock deformations. For fracking to be most efficient, the technology is coupled with horizontal drilling, a technique that became standard practice in the 1980s in oil and gas wells.

The coupling of fracking and horizontal drilling has provided oil and gas companies with access to numerous resources that were previously considered to be unusable. As a result, unconventional natural gas and oil have steadily become a larger portion of the gas and oil production in the United States. In the last five years, the increased supply and lower prices for natural gas have reduced the use of coal in the United States for power generation, thereby reducing carbon dioxide emissions.

The major hurdle that fracking faces in reaching its full potential to develop nonconventional gas and oil resources is the public concern that it will negatively impact the environment through water contamination, seismic inducement, and methane emissions. The fear of contamination of surface water and groundwater during site preparation, drilling, well completion, and operation and the risk to water resources for all users in the watershed are the primary environmental concerns of regulatory agencies.

Current research is focused on finding better ways to handle and treat the large quantities of water required and reducing significantly the amount of water used in fracking by using wastewater or mine water, liquids other than water, or compressed gases, including potentially carbon dioxide. Existing wastewater management techniques can mitigate water contamination by recycling the produced water or disposing it into deep wells. Deep-well disposal of produced water is the most common disposal technique, but at times it has been linked to seismic events in the area of a well site.

Fugitive emissions of methane, a potent greenhouse gas, are another environmental concern. Although the combustion of natural gas produces less carbon dioxide than that of coal or fuel oil, that advantage could be obviated by fugitive emissions of methane during drilling, completion, and operation of an unconventional gas well. If these emissions are kept small (~1 percent of production), a net advantage of natural gas remains, but if they are large (7-8 percent of production), natural gas loses its greenhouse gas advantage over coal.

deliver a 1.7-2.2 percent increase in GDP and 2.4-3.0 million additional jobs by 2030. Additional crude oil production would result in a significant reduction in US net trade balance. The US would import less or no crude oil from its current suppliers—Canada, Mexico, Saudi Arabia, Latin America and West Africa, forcing them to find alternative markets. A dramatic expansion of US production could also push global spare capacity to exceed 8 million barrels per day, at which point OPEC could lose price control and crude oil prices would drop, possibly sharply. Such a drop would take a heavy toll on many energy producers who are increasingly dependent on relatively high energy prices to balance their budgets.

Other regions and countries have significant shale reserves. According to its Ministry of Land and Resources' preliminary study, China has the world's largest reserves of nonconventional gas—double the estimated US reserves. China's relative lack of equipment, experience and potentially the necessary extraction resources—mainly water—may inhibit or slow down development there.

European leaders are uncertain about the geology, political and public acceptability, environmental impact, and financial viability of shale gas in Europe. For example, national authorization processes vary considerably by EU member-state and are generally stricter than for North America. The Polish Government sees shale gas as an important resource for diversification away from dependence on Russian gas and has been granting exploration licenses, while the French Government has banned hydraulic fracking.

ALTERNATIVES—THE WEAK PLAYER IN THE NATURAL GAS EXPLOSION

The potential for more abundant and cheaper supplies of natural gas to replace coal by 2030 would have undeniable benefits for curbing carbon emissions. Nevertheless, another consequence of an increased reliance on relatively cleaner natural gas as a source of energy could be the lack of a major push on alternative fuels such as hydropower, wind, and solar energy. Under most scenarios, alternative fuels continue

to provide a relatively small increase in the share of overall energy requirements. The IEA's baseline scenario shows the share of renewables rising just 4 percent during the 2007-2050 period. Hydropower accounts for the overwhelming majority of renewables in this scenario, with wind and solar energy providing 5 and 2 percent contributions in 2050 respectively. Their contributions in 2030 would be even less. IEA "blue" scenarios (built around ambitious goals for carbon emission reductions) show possible paths to solar power and wind power becoming much more appreciable shares by 2050—anywhere from 12 to 25 percent in the case of solar and 12 to 22 percent for wind, depending on the desired drop in CO_2 emissions under the various "blue" scenarios. Numbers for 2030 would be a lot smaller. Achieving 12-to-25 percent shares under the blue scenarios would also require, according to IEA calculations, substantial investment in alternatives compared to the baseline scenario.

CHAPTER 2
GAME-CHANGERS

The vast changes resulting from the megatrends alone ensure a transformed world by 2030. How the game-changers sketched below evolve and interact with each other and with the megatrends will determine what kind of transformed world we will inhabit in 2030. In this chapter, we drill down on **six key game-changers** *and their potential impacts:*

- **The Crisis-Prone Global Economy.** *Will divergences among players with different economic interests and global volatility result in a worldwide economic breakdown and collapse? Or will the development of multiple growth centers lead to increased resiliency in the global economic order?*

- **The Governance Gap.** *Will current governments and international institutions be able to adapt fast enough to harness change instead of being overwhelmed by it?*

- **The Potential for Increased Conflict.** *Will rapid changes and shifts in power lead to more intrastate and interstate conflicts?*

- **Wider Scope of Regional Instability.** *Will regional spillover, especially in the Middle East and South Asia, cause global instability?*

- **The Impact of New Technologies.** *Will technological breakthroughs be developed in time to boost economic productivity and solve the problems caused by the strain on natural resources and climate change as well as chronic disease, aging populations, and rapid urbanization?*

- **The Role of the United States.** *Will the US be able to work with new partners to reinvent the international system, carving out new roles in an expanded world order?*

THE CRISIS-PRONE GLOBAL ECONOMY

The international economy will most likely continue to be characterized by various regional and national economies moving at significantly different speeds—a pattern reinforced by the 2008 financial crisis. Although growth rates may converge as China's economy, in particular, begins to slow, the contrast between the current higher growth of the emerging economies and the slow or stagnating recoveries in the major developed economies exemplifies this trend—at least for the next decade or so. The contrasting speeds across different regional economies are exacerbating global imbalances—which were one of the contributing causes of the 2008 crisis—and straining governments and the international system. The key question is whether the divergences and increased volatility will result in a global breakdown and collapse or whether the development of multiple growth centers will lead to increased resiliency. Future political and economic crises are a real possibility in the absence of concerted policy adjustments in the major developed and developing economies.

"The 2008 crisis and its long 'tail' raise the prospect of an extended crisis that would undermine the social and political fabric in many Western countries and create long-term destabilizing effects."

Both developed and developing countries face stiff challenges to achieve a new "normalcy" or stability in the global economy. For the West, the challenge will be to ensure that the recent slow or stagnating growth since the 2008 financial crisis, driven by de-leveraging (paying down debt), does not lead to a prolonged slump or worse—more financial crises. In the case of many European countries and Japan, the challenge also will involve finding ways to sustain growth in the face of rapidly aging populations. For rising states such as China and India, the main challenge involves sustaining economic development and not falling into the "middle- income trap" (a situation in which per capita income does not increase to the level of the world's advanced economies). To avoid such an outcome, the rising powers will need to consider implementing wide-ranging changes to political and social institutions. Finally, the transition to a more multipolar global economy brings its own risks, which are likely to be particularly pronounced as the West's grip is loosening and the emerging powers are primarily focused on domestic development. In the interim, international management of the system could falter as players with diverging interests fail to cooperate with one another.

THE PLIGHT OF THE WEST

The 2008 crisis and its long "tail" raise the prospect of an extended crisis that would undermine the social and political fabric in many Western countries and create long-term destabilizing effects. Historical studies indicate that recessions involving financial crises tend to be deeper and require recoveries that take twice as long.[a]

McKinsey Global Institute's (MGI's) recent study of debt and deleveraging indicates that in the years since the onset of the financial crisis, "major [Western] economies have only just begun deleveraging." Total debt has actually grown for most major Western economies with the exception of the US, Australia, and South Korea, where the ratio of total debt to GDP has declined. Previous episodes of deleveraging have taken close to a decade. The report concludes that this pattern is likely to continue. "No single country has all the conditions in place to revive growth."[b] Most of the leading Western countries could therefore suffer the consequences of low economic growth that lasts longer than a decade.

---

[a] Mark Carney, "Growth in the Age of Deleveraging" speech to the Empire Club of Canada/Canadian Club of Toronto, 12 December 2011, available on Bank for International Settlements (BIS) website (www.bis.org); C.M. Reinhart and V.R.Reinhart, "After the Fall", Macroeconomic Challenges: The Decade Ahead, Federal Reserve Bank of Kansas City 2010, Economic Policy Symposium.
[b] See "Debt and Deleveraging: Uneven Progress on the Path to Growth," McKinsey Quarterly, January 2012.

Type	Present Status	Trendline	Impacts on Global Economy
Advanced Economies	The 2008 crisis and its long "tail" raise the prospect of an extended crisis undermining the social and political fabric in many Western countries, leading to potentially destabilizing effects.	To compensate for slowing labor force growth, Western countries will need to rely on growth in productivity. Even the slowly growing labor force may not be fully employed because of external competition, particularly among low-skill workers. One billion workers from developing countries are likely to be added to the global labor pool. In Europe, economic and fiscal issues are entwined with decisions on the EU's future, making potential solutions more complex because of the multiplicity of actors and political concerns.	The declining weight of US and other Western countries and growing multipolarity enhances fragility of the global economy. Absent a hegemonic power or strong global governance mechanisms, risks increase in this multipolar environment for major economic powers to focus on domestic imperatives without regarding the impact on others.
Emerging Powers	In the coming decades, not only will the big emerging powers like China, India, and Brazil make relative economic gains, but Colombia, Mexico, Indonesia, South Korea, Turkey, and potentially Nigeria also will make their marks.	To avoid the middle-income trap, China will need to transition to a more consumer-driven and knowledge-intensive economy, involving difficult political and social reforms. India faces similar problems and traps accompanying rapid growth, but New Delhi benefits from having democracy as a safety valve and a more youthful demographic profile. China and India are vulnerable to the volatility of key resources.	The health of the global economy will increasingly be linked to how well the developing world does—more so than the traditional West. The assumption of more global responsibilities in both political and economic spheres by emerging powers will be critical to ensure a stable global economic outlook.

A future rise in interest rates—highly likely under some scenarios—would see ballooning interest payments at a time when social entitlement payments are set to grow, making it more difficult to pay down the accumulated debt.[a] Many experts believe that, "drastic measures" will be necessary to check the rapid growth of current and future liability of governments and reduce their adverse consequences for long-term growth and monetary stability.

"Most of the leading Western countries could therefore suffer the consequences of low economic growth that lasts longer than a decade."

The key structural challenge—aging—underlying this negative economic outlook will impact Europe and Japan more but will have significant effects on the United States as well.

Previous financial and economic crises, such as the 1930s' Great Depression, hit when populations were youthful, providing a demographic bonus during the postwar economic boom. However, such a bonus will not exist in any prospective recovery. To compensate for significant drops in labor-force size, the hoped-for economic growth in countries such as Germany and Japan will have to come from growth in productivity. In spite of "baby boomer" retirements, the US is in a better position, with its working-age population projected to rise by 8 percent through 2030.

Ironically, even declining or **slowly growing labor forces**—which will dampen growth in richer, aging countries—may not be fully employed because of external competition, particularly at the low-skilled end. Western countries are likely to continue suffering from increasing global labor competition—a trend that began in the 1980s. A recent Oxford Economics study estimates that another one billion workers from developing countries are likely to be added to the global labor pool in the next several decades.

Labor force studies show that the twin impacts of globalization and technology lead to a two-tiered labor market of low- and high-skilled labor with a particular squeeze on workers at the low-to-middle end. If past experience, and economic theory holds, the increase in global labor supply will put additional downward pressure on low-skilled labor incomes, forcing low-skilled workers to accept lower wages or become redundant. The development of robotics and other emerging advanced manufacturing technologies is also likely to eliminate many jobs in the short-to-medium term (see pages 90-92 in technology section).

More advanced emerging market countries, such as China, with rising wages, also will face competition from other countries for low- and middle-skilled jobs unless they too move up the value chain to develop higher skilled workers. If they do, these countries will compete with more expensive skilled labor in advanced countries, increasing pressure on once-safe high-end employment. To level the playing field, developing countries will have to dramatically improve labor productivity, which in many cases means shedding low-skilled workers, increasing skills, and boosting automation.[b]

"A recent Oxford Economics study estimates that another one billion workers from developing countries are likely to be added to the global labor pool in the next several decades."

A relatively generous welfare system has cushioned the blow to the unemployed, particularly in Europe, for now. However, low economic growth rates, rising pension liabilities, and debt crises in European countries and the US place increased pressure on already strained budgets. With borrowing constrained because of high debts, these countries probably will not be able to afford to finance generous welfare systems unless they can significantly increase economic growth rates and labor productivity. Reducing borrowing risks political blowback,

---

[a] The source of this information is the Bank for International Settlements. BIS Working Papers No 300, Stephen G. Cecchetti, M.S. Mohanty and Fabrizio Zampolli, "The Future of Public Debt: Prospects and Implications," March 2010.

[b] Drawn from Bruce Jones' paper, "Labor and the Third Industrial Revolution: The Employment Challenge," 30 August 2011.

complicating and lengthening efforts to undertake structural economic reform. On the other hand, failure to take budgetary action risks the likelihood of more abrupt rises in government bond yields at medium and long maturities.

Europe is a special case: economic and fiscal issues are entwined with political decisions on the future of the EU, including more centralized powers for EU financial management. EU leaders want to avoid a breakup of the euro zone even though current efforts to avoid such an outcome have resulted in a crisis atmosphere, sowing uncertainty about Europe's future global markets. The current mode of crisis management is unsustainable over the long term. Possible solutions such as a multispeed Europe will spawn questions about Europe's capacity for unitary political action. Economic divergence and market volatility are likely to continue to characterize the EU throughout much of this period even if—as some expect—"Europe is well on its way to completing the original concept of a comprehensive economic and monetary union [and] . . . will emerge much stronger as a result."[a]

More than most Western countries, **Japan's** rapidly aging and dwindling population is putting the society in a bind, severely undercutting its long-term growth potential. The combination of a long-term deteriorating fiscal situation with a dramatically aging and declining population—roughly one elderly person per two working-age people by 2025—will limit the government's maneuvering room to consolidate its fiscal situation. (In Germany the population ages 15-65 will decline from 54 to 47 million between 2010 and 2030 and, in Japan, from 81.5 to 68.7 million.) The IMF has suggested that "strong policy adjustments" with adverse political repercussions will be required to put "public finances back on sustainable footing." Ambitious debt stabilization cannot be put in place without the risk of "substantial short-term output costs," posing a risk to economic recovery.[b]

Demographically, the **United States** is in the best position of all the major developed powers (and some developing ones like China) with a birth rate close to replacement level. However, the burden on the US to fund entitlement programs (Social Security and Medicare) will increase markedly, particularly without a slowdown in the rate of the United States' rising health-care costs. Economists also worry that the approaching transition of the "baby boomer" generation from workers to retirees will remove from the US labor force the cadre of its most educated, skilled, and experienced workers. The United States' declining educational base is not seen as adequately preparing younger workers for the more globally competitive environment. Moreover, most economists believe that, "a fundamental rebalancing of the composition of the US economy will be required" for the US to recover its former path of "buoyant and job-creating growth."[c]

CRUNCH TIME TOO FOR THE EMERGING POWERS

Most of the emerging economies weathered the 2008 financial crisis well. In the coming decade, we will probably witness not only relative economic gains by China, India, and Brazil, but also the increasing importance of emerging regional players such as Colombia, Indonesia, Nigeria, South Africa, South Korea, Mexico, and Turkey. However, developing countries will face their own challenges, especially in continuing the momentum behind their rapid growth.

The health of the global economy will be increasingly linked to how well the developing world does—more so than the traditional West. The developing world already provides more than 50 percent of global growth and 40 percent of global investment. Its contribution to global investment growth is more than 70 percent. **China's** contribution is now one and a half times the size of the US contribution. In the World Bank's baseline modeling of future economic multipolarity, China—despite a slowing of its economic

[a] For more discussion, see "The Coming Resolution of the European Crisis," C. Fred Bergsten and Jacob Funk Kirkegaard, Policy Brief PB12-1, Peterson Institution for International Economics.
[b] See *Japan: Population Again and the Fiscal Challenge*, IMF, (co-authored by Martin Muhleisen and Hamid Faruqee) Finance and Development, Volume 38, Number 1, March 2001.

[c] This analysis is from NIC-commissioned workshops and a report from McKinsey & Co, Global Economic Scenarios (December, 2010); C. Fred Bergsten, The United States in the World Economy, Peterson Institute for International Economics, August 12, 2011.

By 2020, emerging markets' share of financial assets is projected to almost double.[a]

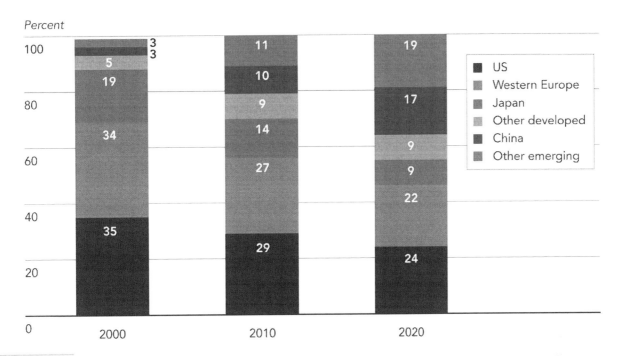

Percent

Legend:
- US
- Western Europe
- Japan
- Other developed
- China
- Other emerging

2000: 3, 3, 5, 19, 34, 35
2010: 11, 10, 9, 14, 27, 29
2020: 19, 17, 9, 9, 22, 24

[a] Assumes consensus GDP forecasts for individual countries and that emerging markets' currencies appreciate vis-à-vis the US dollar.

Source: McKinsey Global Institute, The Emerging Equity Gap: Growth And Stability In The New Investor Landscape (2011).

growth—will contribute about one-third of global growth by 2025, far more than any other economy. The world economy no longer depends on US consumers but on investment growth in emerging countries.

"The health of the global economy will be increasingly linked to how well the developing world does—more so than the traditional West."

Despite its bright prospects to become the world's economic growth engine, China probably faces some of the biggest hurdles to achieving that goal. The country's population will begin to age rapidly. Whereas 8 percent of the Chinese population is now 65 and older, that figure will exceed 16 percent in 2030. Meanwhile, the proportion of China's population in the normal working years (15-65), which recently peaked at 72 percent, will decline to about 68 percent by 2030.

In addition to the decline of its working-age population, a pending **youth dearth** is on the horizon for China.[b] The share of the population aged 15-29—now just over 30 percent—will fall to about 21 percent by 2030. University applications have declined for the past two years.[c] Presumably the early manifestation of a tightening labor market also is contributing to the rising labor unrest of the country.

China has averaged 10-percent real growth during the past three decades; by 2020 the economy will probably be expanding by only 5 percent, according to several private-sector forecasts. The slower growth—which will probably be twice the US average—will still ensure that China surpasses the US in overall economic size sometime during the next decade

[b] The Chinese youth dearth will not be the worst in the world in 2030; in fact, it will place the country 40th globally. Hong Kong and Japan will lead at just 15 percent of the population between ages 15 and 29, followed closely by Qatar, South Korea, Malta, Germany, Bosnia, and Austria (all under 17 percent).

[c] "The Next China," *The Economist*, July 31, 2010; pgs. 48-50.

or two. However, the slower growth will mean downward pressure on per capita income growth. China's per capita income in 2020 will have reached $17,000 in nominal terms, whereas Brazil's and Russia's will be more than $23,000 and $27,000 respectively. The G-7 economies are set to reach $64,000 per capita income (PPP) in 2020, more than three times China's.

China faces the prospect of being trapped in middle-income status. Many Latin American countries faced a similar situation in the 1980s and were unable to avoid the trap because of income inequality and their inability to restructure their economies. Understanding that the Chinese economy is likely to slow, China's leaders want to transition to a more consumer-driven economy and move China up the value-added industrial production chain. They are promoting S&T as the new economic growth driver, and China is already achieving progress in sectors such as nanotechnology, stem-cell research, materials research, and new applications of existing technologies.

"India—by contrast—will remain a relatively youthful country, continuing to benefit from a demographic dividend."

To achieve its goals, however, China will also need to develop its agricultural sector through establishment of fair and equitable land rights and build a banking sector that is more market-based and not geared to favor state-owned enterprises. There is also the question of whether a country can move to greater consumption if it does not have a social safety net. In the last 20 years, opening up brought capital and technology to China, enabling domestic industries to catch up with Western companies. In the next 20 years, Chinese firms will probably need to go outside China to obtain the next level of technological and managerial innovation and sophistication. To do so, China will have to engage in foreign direct investment in other countries— a logical step at this stage of development and possibly the only way for China to move up the value chain.

An economically difficult transition could mean an equally difficult political one in the case of China. Slower per capita growth will increase the difficulty of meeting rising expectations, potentially sparking discontent. A political crisis would make it harder for China to meet its economic goals. A prolonged political and economic crisis could cause China to turn inward, blaming external forces for its problems at home. Although the leadership and much of the middle class are now wedded to globalization because of China's success during the past 30 years, suspicion of the outside world lingers and, similar to historical cases elsewhere, could reemerge as a powerful political force if Chinese economic development stalls.

The World Bank assesses that **India** will join China as an "emerging economy growth pole" by 2025, which could help to strengthen the global economy. India's expected robust growth in the next 15-20 years means that its contribution to global growth will surpass that of any individual advanced economy except the United States. World Bank modeling suggests that together China and India will serve as nearly twice the engine for growth as of the United States and the euro zone combined by 2025.[a]

India, however, faces many of the same problems and traps accompanying rapid growth as China: large inequities between rural and urban sectors and within society, increasing constraints on resources such as food and water, and a need for greater investment in science and technology in order to continue to move its economy up a notch. India's democracy provides it with a safety valve for discontent in a way that China's one-party rule does not. At the same time, regional tensions between India and many of its neighbors could threaten India's rise should such tensions explode in conflict and confrontation. As with China, a sharp economic downturn—particularly propelled by a political or military crisis—could quickly have broader regional and global effects.

India—in contrast to China—will remain a relatively youthful country, continuing to benefit from a

---

[a] See *Global Development Horizons 2011: Multipolarity: The New Global Economy*, The World Bank 2011.

demographic dividend. The share of its population ages 15-65 will continue to rise from about 65 percent now to perhaps 69 percent by 2030. India's declining birth rate combined with a greater proportion of dependent seniors will not begin to create an economic burden before 2050. Consequently, long-term forecasts show Indian economic power growing steadily throughout the 21st century and overtaking China at the end of the century because of China's maturing age structure. To maximize its advantage from the greater proportion of youths, however, India will need to boost its educational system, both attainment and quality at lower levels; make substantial governance improvements, particularly in countering corruption; and undertake large-scale infrastructure program to keep pace with rapid urbanization and the needs of a more advanced economy.

Both China and India are also vulnerable to the **volatility in prices of key resources** and to the potential early impacts of climate change. The Asian Development Bank indicated in a 2011 report[a] that based on current trends Asia could become 90 percent dependent on imported oil by 2050. Rapid urbanization also enhances the vulnerabilities of Asian countries. Approximately 44 million people are being added to Asia's urban population every year; by 2025, the majority of Asia's population will be urban.

Currently many of China's and India's urban densities (unlike Tokyo, Seoul, and Singapore) are decreasing, creating urban sprawl, which is spurring growth in car ownership, higher energy use, and higher costs to provide utilities and transportation networks. Food and water demands also rise exponentially with urbanization. Asian cities are vulnerable to the severe weather connected to climate change, which amplifies storm surges and flooding of low-lying areas. This is particularly the case for many of these coastal cities: Kolkata (Calcutta), Mumbai (Bombay), Dhaka, Guangzhou, Ho Chi Minh City, Shanghai, Manila, Bangkok, Yangon and Hai Phong.

In light of these trends, emerging market demand for

---

[a] See *Asia 2050: Realizing the Asian Century*, Asian Development Bank, 2011.

infrastructure, housing, property, and manufacturing plants and equipment will raise global investment to levels not seen in four decades. Emerging market countries, with their faster growth rates and higher saving rates, will become the most important source of global finance, nearly doubling their share of the world's financial assets during the next decade or so. (See graphic on page 47.) However, the savings of emerging market countries may not be able to meet the increasing investment demands. McKinsey & Company estimates that the gap between potential capital supply and demand will reach between $0.8 and 2.4 trillion by 2030. This gap will result in upward pressure on long-term interest rates, particularly in regions without adequate savings. Such a secular trend would have negative implications for investments around the world.

A MULTIPOLAR GLOBAL ECONOMY: INHERENTLY MORE FRAGILE?

Some experts have compared the upcoming decline of US economic weight to the late 19th century when economic dominance by one player—Britain—receded into multipolarity. Other resemblances include an accelerating globalization, rapid technological development, and growing geopolitical competition among the great powers. The late 19th century was a time of relatively high real economic volatility with wide fluctuations in growth rates. The average growth rate of the leading country, the United Kingdom, in the 19th century was not high, while the growth rate of the rival—the US—was higher but variable. Just as now, intellectual property rights were in dispute with no government in a position to enforce them abroad. An added current complication are the differences over market liberalization and role of the state in the economy, which are likely to continue.

Other experts emphasize that the global economic system will become increasingly stressed. Up to now less than one billion people have accounted for three-quarters of global consumption; during the next two decades, new and expanded middle classes in the developing world could create as many as two billion additional consumers. Such an explosion will mean a scramble for raw materials and manufactured goods. With greater demand for products, economists worry that the number of bottlenecks will increase markedly and that supply of resources and goods will face at least temporary constraints. This could mean that the durations of business cycles will become significantly shorter and that they will be less smooth. Competition over resources might lead governments to become increasingly involved in managing them, ramping up tensions with other countries vying for the same resources.

"Up to now less than one billion people have accounted for three-quarters of global consumption; during the next two decades, new and expanded middle classes in the developing world could create as many as two billion additional consumers. Such an explosion will mean a scramble for raw materials and manufactured goods."

Effective global governance would be necessary to avoid such tensions escalating and to ensure against risks of mercantilism and protectionism infecting the global economy. Such risks are greater in a multipolar world marked by wide divergences in domestic forms of capitalism and differences regarding how to manage the international system. Any economic breakdowns in key countries such as China would be likely to spur political disruption, which would complicate recovery and potentially limit the ability of others to help.

Interest rates may increase with imbalances between easily available supplies and growing demand of raw materials. Upward movement in interest rates may also be pushed by a decline in global savings capacities as rising middle classes in the developing world consume more and aging populations in the developed world begin to draw down their savings. Some economists also expect growing incentives for investors to diversify. With long-run growth trends diverging, the relative attractiveness of Western bonds as opposed to emerging markets will begin to decline. As in the

late 19th century, a leading—though not dominant—global currency (the dollar) may remain, but alongside others. The absence of a clear hegemonic economic power—as represented by an unrivalled global currency—could in turn add to volatility as in the late 19th century. The various players pursued their special interests with little risk of any enforcement of common rules by an overwhelming power.

Of course, the future will not exactly repeat the past: there are both reasons to believe that the global economy will be stronger than in the late 19th century and also situations in which it could become more crisis-prone. We have a stronger global financial system for dealing with stresses than we did in earlier eras. The gold standard did not allow for a stabilization policy by central banks, accentuating the volatility. Bretton Woods institutions (the IMF and World Bank)—which reduce the risk of spillover from fiscal and other crises—did not exist. However, the degree to which the emerging powers would view these originally Western-established bodies with legitimacy and deference in a full-scale economic crisis is unclear.

The current institutional framework is not likely to withstand the unleashing of a major conflict between the big economic players. Despite all the economic integration during the late 19th century Belle Epoque, the first globalization spurt was undone by the First World War and 1930s' Great Depression. As we'll explore in a later section, in the next couple decades conflict involving great powers is not inconceivable, but if such a conflict does occur, it almost certainly will not be on the level of a world war with all major powers engaged.

Finally, we are assuming that the new normal—albeit more fragile and volatile than the Great Moderation of the pre-2008 period—would be based on active support of the emerging powers. As described above, one could envisage mercantilist and protectionist pressures growing to break down globalization, particularly if coupled with rising political tensions with neighbors and rivals.

Whether governments and international institutions will be able to adapt fast enough to harness change instead of being overwhelmed by it is a key question for future developments. The rapid advances in information, communications, and other technologies argue for publics and institutions that will be better able to tackle global and regional challenges. If the global middle class expands as many experts project, demand for rule of law and government accountability is likely to increase. Challenges associated with managing increasing urban conglomerations will tax governing structures, but such challenges also will prompt development of more effective governing structures and smarter technologies. However, the increasing number of players needed to solve major transnational challenges will complicate decisionmaking. A growing number of diverse and dissimilar state, subnational, and nonstate actors will play important governance roles in an increasingly multipolar world. Finally, the lack of consensus between and among established and emerging powers suggests that the baseline case for multilateral governance out to 2030 will be at best limited.

"The rapid advances in information, communications, and other technologies argue for publics and institutions that will be better able to tackle global and regional challenges . . . However, the increasing number of powers needed to solve a major transnational challenge will complicate decisionmaking."

GOVERNANCE STARTS AT HOME: RISKS AND OPPORTUNITIES

The governance gap will be most pronounced at the domestic level and driven by the rapid political and social changes. The advances over the past couple decades in health, educational levels, and income—

which we expect to continue, if not accelerate in some cases—are both affected by and drivers of new governance structures. Both social science theory and recent history—the Color Revolutions and the Arab Spring—support the idea that with maturing age structures, greater educational levels, and rising incomes, political liberalization and democracy are nurtured and advance. However, the extended transition to full democracy is much more stable and long-lasting when youth bulges begin to decline and incomes are higher.

Two conditions can increase the prospects for instability: First, studies have shown that countries moving through the mid-range between autocracy and democracy have a proven record of high instability. Second, countries that have a government system that is highly inconsistent with their level of development in other spheres, particularly their economic levels, tend to be less stable. These same two risk factors apply to a large number of the countries in the world.

COUNTRIES IN THE AWKWARD MID-RANGE

If we use Polity's 20-point scale[a] and define the awkward mid-range between autocracy and democracy as scores between five and 15 (with autocracy below five and democracy above 15), currently about 50 countries qualify as falling into this major risk group. Most countries remain below a more consolidated democratic level of 18 or above, suggesting that even in 2030, many countries will still be zig-zagging their way through the complicated democratization process.

The greatest number of countries in the mid-range in 2030 is likely to be in Sub-Saharan Africa (23 of 45 countries), followed by Asia (17 of 59 total, including five of the 11 Southeast Asian countries and four of the nine Central Asian ones), then the Middle East

---

[a] The Polity data series is a widely used data series in political science research. It measures along a 20-point scale regime authority characteristics and transitions for all independent states with greater than 500,000 total population and covers the years 1800–2006. Polity's conclusions about a state's level of democracy are based on an evaluation of that state's competitiveness of political participation, openness and competitiveness of executive recruitment, and constraints on the chief executive.

NATURAL DISASTERS THAT MIGHT CAUSE GOVERNMENTS TO COLLAPSE

In October 2011, the National Intelligence Council (NIC) partnered with Oak Ridge National Laboratory (ORNL) to identify and investigate natural disaster scenarios that would pose a severe threat to the US and other major nations.[a] Participants—which included subject-matter experts from universities in the US, Canada, and Europe in addition to NIC and ORNL officials—were asked to distinguish among various categories of natural disasters: extinction-level events; potentially fatal scenarios with medium recurrence intervals; and "ordinary" disasters with short recurrence intervals.

Scenarios in the extinction-level category are so rare that they were discounted. The impacts from these events—such as large volcanic eruptions or impacts of large asteroids or comets—are likely to be minimal because something else—such as major military defeat or economic collapse— is far more likely to bring down any great nation or civilization. At the other end, "ordinary" disasters—which typically cause high mortality and substantial human misery and therefore warrant major prevention and recovery efforts—do not present a major threat to the foundations of nations or human society.

Far more serious threats are those natural disasters that are both sufficiently severe to bring down nations and also sufficiently likely to occur. A short list of candidates fitting these criteria includes:

Staple-crop catastrophes, especially extreme and prolonged drought, crop plagues, and highly sulfurous long-duration but low-level volcanic eruptions. Although severe outbreaks of generalist pests (locusts and grasshoppers) are possible, many of the worst epidemics can be traced to the development of monocultures, which is increasingly the case in modern agriculture. (See page 35 where we talk about the potential for the spread of wheat rust to have a devastating effect because of the lesser biological diversity of wheat.) The "Laki" eruption in Iceland in 1783-84 only lasted eight months, but the "dry fog" that was produced by its sulfurous plumes resulted in a hemispheric temperature drop of 1.0-1.5 degree Centigrade and widespread crop failures.

Tsunamis in selected locations, especially Tokyo and the Atlantic Coast of the US. Tokyo—which is at a low elevation—is the largest global city at greatest risk. The largest tsunami that could hit the US East would be due to an earthquake in the Puerto Rico area. The travel time for the tsunami to the East Coast is only 1.5 hours. The probability of another massive earthquake occurring in Puerto Rico within this century is over 10 percent.

Erosion and depletion of soils. Modern agriculture is eroding soil at rates at least 10-to-20 times faster than soil forms. Worldwide soil erosion has caused farmers to abandon 430 million hectares of arable land since the Second World War, an area the size of India. Increases in oil prices and thus end of cheap fertilizers means that maintaining agricultural productivity without healthy soil will become increasingly expensive and difficult.

Solar geomagnetic storms that could knock out satellites, the electric grid, and many sensitive electronic devices. The recurrence intervals of crippling solar geomagnetic storms are less than a century and now pose a threat because of the world's dependence on electricity. Until "cures" are implemented, solar super-storms will pose a large-scale threat to the world's social and economic fabric.

---

[a] The full report will be available from the NIC.

and North Africa (11 out of 16).[a] Recent events in the Middle East/Levant confirm the region's vulnerability to the governance transition risk, which is likely to be playing out to 2030.

" . . . even in 2030, many countries will still be zig-zagging their way through the complicated democratization process."

COUNTRIES WITH A DEMOCRATIC DEFICIT

A "democratic surplus" is said to exist when a country's level of democratization is more advanced than its level of development. When democracy is present in the very poorest countries (India seems to be an exception) and autocracy exists in the most developed countries (those with not just high income, but high educational attainment), those countries are unstable. Regions that have somewhat higher levels of democracy than we might expect and therefore may be at some risk of reversal include Sub-Saharan Africa, Latin America, and the Caribbean and South Asia.

A "democratic deficit" is said to exist when a country's developmental level is more advanced than its level of governance. Democratic deficits are tinder that might be ignited by various sparks.

Our modeling—based on the International Futures model — highlights many of the Gulf, Middle East and Central Asia countries—Qatar, the UAE, Bahrain, Saudi Arabia, Oman, Kuwait, Iran, Kazakhstan, Azerbaijan— and Asian countries such as China and Vietnam. This set of countries is very different from the "usual suspects" lists provided by indices of state fragility or failure. These are not countries in which instability has manifested itself in violence or a breakdown of public services. Most of the standard indices of vulnerability do not include any measure of repression

or institutional incongruity, which almost certainly is a weakness.

Those countries with high levels of a democratic deficit—such as China and Gulf countries—present great risks because of their systemic importance to the international system. Under most scenarios, China is slated to pass the threshold of US$15,000 per capita (PPP) in the next five years or so. This level is often a trigger for democratization, especially when coupled with high levels of education and a mature age structure. Democratization is often accompanied by political and social disruptions. Many experts believe a more democratic China would unleash growing nationalistic sentiment, at least in the short-to-medium term, increasing already existing tensions with China's neighbors. Over the longer term, as rule-of-law institutions become more rooted and the political system stabilizes and and is perceived as non-threatening, Chinese "soft power" could be boosted. China's successful transition to democratization could increase pressure on other authoritarian states as well as further burnish China's economic development model as long as democratization did not permanently stem China's economic growth.

"The exponential increase in data, combined with emerging capabilities to analyze and correlate it, will give unprecedented capabilities to individuals and connected networks in nearly every part of the world well before 2030."

Several Gulf and Middle Eastern countries might be able to provide the economic well-being and lack of overt, violent repression that can hold back pressures for political change, as does Singapore today. It is very unlikely that many or all will. Although most risk analysis is heavily focused on Africa, the prominence of Middle Eastern countries, especially given the substantial dependence of the world on energy from the region, points to the need for continued attention on these Middle Eastern countries during the next 15-20 years.

---

[a] The full list of mid-range, vulnerable countries is Algeria, Angola, Azerbaijan, Belarus, Burkina Faso, Cambodia, Cameroon, Central African Republic, Chad, China, Cote d'Ivoire, Cuba, Djibouti, Egypt, Equatorial Guinea, Ethiopia, Fiji, Gabon, Gambia, Iran, Iraq, Jordan, Kazakhstan, Laos, Madagascar, Mauritania, Micronesia, Morocco, Myanmar, Niger, Nigeria, Palestine, Papua New Guinea, Republic of the Congo, Rwanda, Samoa, Sao Tome, Singapore, Sri Lanka, Sudan, Syria, Tajikistan, Tanzania, Togo, Tonga, Tunisia, Uganda, Vanuatu, Venezuela, Vietnam, Yemen, and Zimbabwe.

Governance Level	Present Status	Trendline	Drivers
Subnational	Spread of new communications technologies has broadened individual's sense of community, bridging national, regional, ethnic, and gender divides. More networks of cities are shaping policy debates and leading national and even global responses to governance challenges.	Cities will tap into growing public calls for more local control and decentralized government.	Some "global cities" will overshadow their central governments. Well-run cities will manage resources effectively; less efficient ones could fuel instability.
National	The governance gap is most pronounced at the domestic level. Currently 50 countries are in the "awkward" range between autocracy and democracy. Highly developed East Asian and Middle Eastern/Gulf countries have a "democratic deficit": a style of governance that does not match their economic levels.	Many countries are primed to move toward greater democracy by 2030, but the process is often destabilizing. China's democratization would have immense repercussions.	Rapid economic development—inasmuch as it leads to greater per capita income and higher educational levels—often accelerates democratization. A high correlation also exists between more mature age structures and a country's ability to achieve full democracy.
Regional	All regions have made great strides in regional institution- building, but integration has progressed at varying speeds and levels of comprehensiveness.	The likely growth of intraregional trade points to greater regional integration. Whether a regional collective security order can be established, particularly in Asia, is less clear.	Continuing distrust and economic competition and jockeying is likely to limit the extent of sovereignty-sharing.
Multilateral Institutions	Many are questioning their legitimacy because they do not reflect the changing economic hierarchy.	Even if global institutions better mirror the changing power setup, whether they can tackle growing global challenges is unclear.	A new concert among newer and established powers would enhance the workings of institutions and their effectiveness in tackling global challenges.

A number of Central Asian countries are on the democratic deficit list or close below the top 20. More generally, the region is another area beyond sub-Saharan Africa where countries (other than Afghanistan and Pakistan in South Central Asia or South Asia) seldom make the highest positions on risk lists when perhaps they should.

NEW TECHNOLOGIES SHIFTING ROLES OF CITIZEN AND STATE

The spread of IT use will give individuals and groups unprecedented capabilities to organize and collaborate in new ways. Networked movements enabled by IT already have demonstrated the capacity for disruption and the ability to quickly draw global attention to the need for political and social change. IT use enables individuals to organize around shared ideas in the virtual world and carry out sustained action. (See pages 86-90 for more on the future of IT technologies.)

Sub-Saharan Africa, rural India, and other traditionally isolated regions are being globally connected with positive economic impacts. Social networking will continue to be a potentially potent political weapon. The pressure of social networks, particularly on governmental power, almost certainly will grow even stronger. The fact that the immense choices on the Internet have not always led to a broadening of perspectives, but rather to a narrowing points to a potentially negative impact of social networking, such as increasing partisanship and nationalism.

The exponential increase in data, combined with emerging capabilities to analyze and correlate it, will give unprecedented capabilities to individuals and connected networks in nearly every part of the world well before 2030. The use of IT will accelerate due to three projected trends: a 95 percent drop in computer memory costs, a reduction in raw data storage costs to one hundredth of the current price, and a network efficiency increase by more than a factor of 200. In addition, four technological developments will provide individuals and groups with new capabilities as the use of IT proliferates:

- The shift to **cloud architecture** will improve utilization rates of computing infrastructure and optimize network use. The cloud also will put increased computing capability and meaningful analysis in the hands of 80 percent of the world's population.

- **Mobile devices** are becoming increasingly rich sensor platforms, enabling nearly all communication mediated by technology to be tracked and analyzed at a fine level of detail. More than 70 percent of the world's population already has at least one mobile device; global mobile data traffic in 2010 was three times the size of the entire Internet in 2000. By 2015—only three years away—in Sub-Saharan Africa, Southeast Asia, South Asia, and the Middle East more people will have mobile network access than with electricity at home.

- **Cheap digital storage** means nearly all data will be archived indefinitely. Information will be "smart" about itself—indexed, categorized, and richly tagged upon collection so that it can be easily analyzed later.

- **Bots**—programs that run automated tasks in the Internet-connected world—could become as prevalent as robotics in the industrial world. Although bots are best known for their use in hacking and disruptive activities, they can be used for any purpose. When combined with massive data, bots could manage complex and persistent tasks on behalf of individuals and networked groups.

This new environment of widespread and enabled IT use also will benefit illicit networks involved in crime, terrorism, human and drug trafficking, and the theft of intellectual property. IT devices will play an increasing role in the fight against corruption and government malfeasance and incompetence. However, at least for the moment, such illicit activities are outstripping the capacities of most countries and multilateral institutions to contain them.

AN EMPOWERED STATECRAFT?

The new expanding IT architectures and their use—whether by individuals and networks or states—are not deterministic. Governments and other traditional political institutions have the capacity to adapt and gain influence and clout.

Connective technologies will give governments—both authoritarian and democratic—an unprecedented ability to monitor their citizens. If threats and challenges to state control escalate, IT use in statecraft presents opportunities for middle and emerging powers to project soft power and increase their influence through new IT-enabled strategic communications relative to bigger countries. Over time, many experts we consulted believe that by 2020 or so, governments could begin to constrain the most threatening illicit activities by adapting their use of IT and partnering with nonstate actors and networks. Countries could root out the most threatening actors by going after places and organizations that support illicit activities. The 30 corporations that control around 90 percent of Internet traffic represent chokepoints that could be used to enforce bans on illicit activity.

"Both sides agreed . . . that the characteristics of IT use . . . increase the potential for more frequent discontinuous change in the international system."

Experts do not know how the balance will be struck between greater IT-enabled individuals and networks and traditional political structures. In our interactions, technologists and political scientists offered widely divergent views. Political scientists remained skeptical of IT-enabled alternatives to state power, while technologists viewed the IT as a global revolution that will make states and legacy institutions less influential in the next couple decades. Both sides agreed, however, that the characteristics of IT use—multiple and simultaneous action, near instantaneous responses, mass organization across geographic boundaries, and technological dependence—increase the potential for more frequent discontinuous change in the international system.

INCREASED FOCUS ON EQUALITY AND OPENNESS

Newly empowered citizens will demand equality, open access, transparency, and fairness. Authoritarian regimes, particularly, will face increasing pressures for greater accountability, openness, and citizen participation. Despite having some more powerful tools of their own, governments that fail to liberalize and open up are likely to face a losing battle.

Growing gaps in income and wealth within countries and between countries and regions has been a side effect of the rapid economic transformation for some time. During the next 15-20 years, some of this gap will be reduced with the rise of a growing middle class, although income inequalities in many societies both in the emerging and developed world will remain large. Other forms of inequality will become increasingly important.

First, owing to the likely growth of revenues dedicated to funding pensions, health-care, and other entitlements in the West to care for aging populations, younger generations will feel a growing sense of inter-generational inequality.

Second, the urban/rural divide, particularly in the rapidly developing world, will increase as the rising megacities become more important engines of regional and global growth. This may have an impact beyond the country in which the city is located. These new international cities will draw talent not only from the rest of the country, but also from less developed neighboring regions, complicating those regions' efforts to develop.

Third, awareness of inequalites between different actors of society, in particular between average citizens and international private economic actors, will grow. The focus on inequality will be due to individuals' sense of the impacts of globalization in consolidating wealth at the top of the global distribution of wealth (whether individuals, families, or corporations). Many are likely to fear that this highly mobile layer will be exempt from the same economic, political, and social constraints that affect other citizens, who are geographically constrained. Citizens will focus on misconduct and corruption of some of these actors, as well as governance gaps that arise from off-shore accounts, secrecy jurisdictions, and other aspects of the global taxation system.

The themes of equality and fairness are likely to have an impact in the international arena as well. For some time, the emerging powers have called for a more democratic process for international relations whereby the established powers are seen as setting the rules. Elites and publics in the emerging power countries believe the Post-World War II international system has been skewed to favor the West, disputing Western perceptions of an open, liberal order which has allowed emerging powers to prosper and rise. On the contrary, the impression of many of our interlocutors was that, "America's liberalism is selective and often in short supply." Examples cited include Western support for authoritarian regimes, a double standard toward states that acquire nuclear weapons, or actions that are perceived to undermine international law and human rights, particularly in the Middle East. Equality, openness, and fairness are not just values to be applied to domestic setups, but also pertain to the broader international order.

NEW GOVERNMENTAL FORMS

The political landscape will be much more complicated in 2030: megacities and regional groupings are likely to assume increasing powers whereas countries and global multilateral institutions will struggle to keep up with the rapid diffusion of power.

Cities' growing political role and clout already exists as witnessed by the growing number of networks of cities, increasing bilateral relationships between regions, and the role of cities in shaping policy debates and leading national and even global responses to governance challenges. The role of cities will be an even more important feature of the future as urban areas grow in wealth and economic power. In fact, McKinsey Global Institute calculates that, by 2025, emerging market cities will have more higher-end middle-income households than developed ones. Increasingly, cities are likely to take the initiative on resource management, environmental standards, migration, and even security because of their critical importance to the welfare of urban dwellers. Already many examples exist of grassroots innovation and creativity; in fact, within the territories of failed states, city and local governance structures are often the only ones that work. The growing calls for distributed governance networks and for legitimacy around different geographic and social contexts reinforce the importance of cities as actors within governance networks.

Localism is unlikely to be an unqualified positive trend. Historically, large-scale corruption has been a feature of rapid urbanization. Badly managed urban settings have also been a cauldron for political and civil strife, including revolution. Too narrow a community or local focus will prevent coordination or investment around high-level and strategic responses. Two critical issues for the future of the urban role in helping to tackle global challenges will be whether coherence can be built into local approaches to global issues and whether cities will coordinate their efforts with broader country and regional mechanisms. Within a more decentralized system, sharing mechanisms, joint framing, and more integration in planning processes will be critical. A key uncertainty is the extent to which effective approaches will be built for sharing innovative approaches across different cities and localities (especially from emerging economies and slums where pressures create extraordinary environments for innovation). The extent to which learning and linking up can take place to create global movements of local groups and communities will be important in addressing global challenges.

A NEW REGIONAL ORDER?

Economic trends, especially the likely growth of intraregional trade, point to greater regional integration, suggesting the possibility of a world order built more around regional structures. Asia has made great strides in starting a process of regional institution-building with a more diverse array of regional groups than anywhere else in the world. The scope will increase, especially for more functional groupings aimed at dealing with particular problems, such as environmental hazards—e.g., rising sea levels—and trade and financial regulations as regional integration advances.

It is less clear whether a regional collective security order can be established in Asia. Geopolitically, some Asian countries are drawn toward a Sino-centric system whereas many others strongly oppose the expansion of Chinese influence. This diversity means that it is difficult for Asian countries to agree on an answer to the most basic of questions: what is Asia? The United States is a key factor in whether Asia will move toward greater integration: the US has been influential elsewhere in encouraging regional multilateral institutions. China could be more reassuring and, in the event that it starts down the road of democracy, could be much more persuasive, particularly if Asians develop doubts about the credibility of the United States' staying power.

Regional integration elsewhere will progress, but at varying speeds and more for specific functional purposes, which over time could further increase demand for more integration. Regions such as South Asia and the Middle East are unlikely to build regional cooperation to the point of dealing with difficult regional peace and security issues in the period out to 2030. Scenarios we asked experts to construct for both regions point to continuing geopolitical rivalry and distrust even in the better cases. European integration—in the sense that Europe has succeeded in pooling sovereignty—is likely to remain the exception. Europe is increasingly not seen by other regions as a model for development.

GLOBAL MULTILATERAL COOPERATION

The current, largely Western dominance of global structures such as the UN Security Council, World Bank, and IMF probably will have been transformed by 2030 to be more in line with the changing hierarchy of new economic players. Besides the large emerging powers like Brazil, India (who are not permanent UNSC members), and China (has a veto in UNSC, but not IMF voting rights commensurate with its economic power), many second-tier emerging powers will be making their mark—at least as emerging regional leaders. Just as the larger G-20—rather than G-7/8—was energized to deal with the 2008 financial crisis, we expect that other institutions will be updated—most probably also in response to crises.

Even if global institutions by 2030 better mirror the changing power setup, however, the degree to which they will have tackled growing global challenges is unclear. A difficult tradeoff exists between legitimacy and efficiency: trying to ensure all the right countries are represented when a decision is taken—at the

GLOBAL POPULATION IN URBAN AREAS

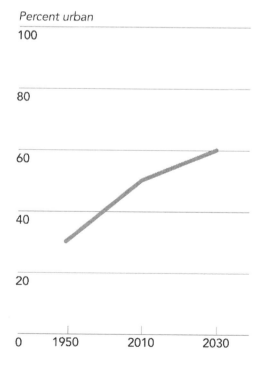

Percent urban

Source: McKinsey Company.

Challenge	Present Status	Worst-Case Outcome	Best-Case Outcome
Liberal Trade/ Economic Coordination	Between 1980 and 2005, world GDP growth increased 32 percent and world merchandise imports/exports increased more than sevenfold, but the Doha trade round has stalled.	Prospects for current and future international trade rounds dim. Selective multilateralism or regional arrangements are more likely than open trading. Destabilizing trade imbalances make multilateral coordination difficult, but 1930s'-style protectionism is unlikely absent a system breakdown from other causes.	Concessions by both developed and emerging powers lead to agreement in the Doha round. The G-20 role is solidified as the global forum for coordinated macro-economic coordination.
Climate Change	Annual meetings have failed to yield any new post-Kyoto comprehensive agreement.	Global economic slowdown makes it impossible for the US, China, and other major emitters to reach meaningful agreement. The result leaves UN-sponsored climate negotiations in a state of collapse, with greenhouse gas emissions unchecked.	Cheaper and more plentiful natural gas make emissions target easier to achieve, but so-called "two-degree" target would be unlikely to be met. As disparities between rich and poor countries decrease, rising powers may be more prepared to make economic sacrifices.
Nuclear Proliferation	Establishment and near-universal adoption of the Nuclear Non-Proliferation Treaty (NPT) has facilitated the emergence of a powerful international norm against nuclear proliferation. Unilateral action and military force has been employed to address non-compliance in some cases.	Iran and North Korea trigger others' active interest in acquiring or developing nuclear weapons. Terrorists or extremist elements also acquire WMD material. The erosion in NPT spills over, potentially triggering a total breakdown in the international system.	Iran and North Korea are dissuaded from further WMD development. Terrorist groups do not acquire WMD. The West may need to extend the nuclear umbrella to those countries feeling threatened by proliferation.
Responsibility to Protect (R2P)	Multilateral efforts to prevent violent political repression have been sporadic and partially successful, especially since the end of the Cold War.	Western countries become increasingly isolated. The lack of international consensus prevents UNSC from acting to impose sanctions, authorize military force, or make referrals to the International Criminal Court. Facing political and economic constraints, the US and Europe would only be capable of taking ad hoc actions to prevent atrocities.	Western engagement with India, Brazil, and other rising democracies would lead to greater consensus on R2P, particularly the basis for military intervention.
Failing States/ Ungoverned Spaces	Multilateral efforts to date have been sporadic, spotty, and under-resourced. Most have focused on acute security threats.	As a result of shrinking international commitments, criminal and terrorist networks flourish. UN and regional organizations find themselves further under-resourced to combat growing challenges. Resources in fragile states are squandered, adding to corruption and governance problems. Increase in number of failed states.	Emerging powers see their interests threatened by failing states. With a growing consensus, the G-20 facilitates burdensharing among major powers, the UN, and regional groups. Regional organizations assume greater responsibilities for fragile states in their neighborhoods.

same time trying to keep the numbers down to facilitate decisionmaking. The growing multipolarity and diffusion of power will make the process of updating global institutions difficult. However, no reform would mean the increasing loss of legitimacy in the eyes of many publics in the emerging world.

Governance will still be complicated by diversity and disparities between emerging and established powers, the growing clout of nonstate actors, and increasing capacities of subnational actors such as megacities. Moreover, discordant values among many of the key players and lingering suspicions are likely to be the norm throughout this transitional period. Longstanding worries by emerging powers about incursions on sovereignty by more powerful Western actors are deeply imbedded in popular as well as elite opinion and will only ease gradually as the emerging powers have to tackle growing transnational problems. China's recent movement away, for example, from strict noninterference toward greater involvement in peacekeeping and international military anti-piracy operations has surprised many observers. At the same time, China and many other emerging powers are likely to remain leery, if not hostile to direct interference, including sanctions aiming at forcing changes in other regimes' behavior. A democratic China that might be more nationalistic would be equally concerned about ceding sovereignty to others.

Future governance will not be either black or white: advances cannot be ruled out despite growing multipolarity, increased regionalism, and possible economic slowdowns. Prospects for achieving progress on global challenges will also vary across issues.

Technology and markets are likely to have a more important impact in reducing carbon emissions than efforts to negotiate any comprehensive or updated Kyoto-style agreement—the success of which looks questionable for the next decade or so. The expanded exploitation and use of cheaper and cleaner natural gas could overtake coal, resulting in significant emissions cuts for the US and other big emitters such as China. Other technological advances in renewable technologies would also shift the debate on climate

change by making mitigation efforts less burdensome on productivity. Such advances would also make a meaningful agreement to reduce carbon emissions more acceptable to both developing countries and the US, which worry that a carbon ceiling would impact economic growth prospects.

"Future governance will not be either black or white: advances cannot be ruled out despite growing multipolarity, increased regionalism, and possible economic slowdowns."

The future of nuclear proliferation hinges on the outcome of North Korean and Iranian efforts to develop nuclear weapons. Iran's success, especially, could trigger an arms race in the Middle East, undermining the nonproliferation regime. On the other hand, if the international community prevails in its efforts to stop both of them, multilateral cooperation would be bolstered and the Non-Proliferation Treaty strengthened. Similarly, use of nuclear weapons by state or nonstate actors could either encourage or discourage proliferation depending on how events unfolded.

Increased great power convergence in combating the challenges of weak and failing states is conceivable, particularly when the interests of all the powers is at stake. For example, the G-20 could be used to facilitate greater burdensharing among the major powers. With their large military manpower, emerging powers, including Brazil, India, and South Africa, have already played increasingly significant roles in supporting peacekeeping operations. Even China, a country that once criticized UN peacekeeping operations as interference with national sovereignty, now has more than 2,000 forces deployed.

Coalitions of the willing with the tacit acceptance or resignation of the other powers may still be able to get the job done in some cases. Although there is broad international support for "protecting populations from genocide, war crimes, ethnic cleansing, and crimes against humanity," the emerging powers may not want to take the initiative in order to avoid the appearance of interference. Of course, this would allow others to take action, including the use of force. With increased communications and more active global public opinion, the great powers will have increasing difficulty avoiding action for humanitarian relief or suppression of genocide.

The shared interests among the diverse collection of major countries mean that even if the best case is not achievable, multilateral and regional cooperation will not unravel completely. The recent example of the states avoiding 1930s'-style protectionism despite the large-scale financial crisis in 2008 and prolonged recession for most Western economies is a case in point. On the other hand, the fact that no single nation or bloc of countries will have the political or economic leverage to drive the international community toward collective action means that continued multilateral advances will be difficult to forge. Given this paradox, the table on page 59 provides clues as to how governance outcomes for key global challenges would fare under either the best or worst case.

Historical trends over the past two decades show fewer major armed conflicts and, where conflicts remain, fewer civilian and military casualties. Maturing age structures in many developing states point to the likelihood of continuing declines in the number of intrastate conflicts. In contrast, the chance of interstate conflict, including one that could draw in the great powers, although historically low, is rising. The great powers would not want to engage in interstate conflict because too much would be at stake. Their main objective is economic development, and they know that conflict could easily derail that. The nuclear context also makes the cost of war prohibitively high. Nevertheless, miscalculation by any one player remains a possibility.

The globalizing environment over the past several decades characterized by growing interdependence could change, particularly as economic growth slows in many countries and the global economy becomes more volatile and potentially crisis-prone. In a more competitive atmosphere, great power conflict may not be inconceivable. Several regions—the Middle East and South Asia—appear particularly susceptible to outbreaks of large-scale violence despite the costs to themselves and others. Many experts also have hypothesized that growing resource constraints combined with the possibility of increasing environmental degradation may be a tipping point for societies already struggling and lead to greater intra- or interstate conflict. Finally, unlike during previous periods, large-scale violence is increasingly no longer the monopoly of the state. Individuals and small groups will have access to WMD and cyber instruments capable of causing massive harm and widespread disruption.

INTRASTATE CONFLICT: CONTINUED DECLINE

As we have noted, since the 1970s, roughly 80 percent of all armed civil and ethnic conflicts (with 25 or more battle-related deaths per year) have originated in countries with youthful age structures—a population with a median age of 25 years or less. Wherever civil and ethnic wars have emerged, they have tended to persist. The average intrastate conflict that began between 1970 and 1999 continued without a one-year break in battle-associated fatalities for about six years. Some—including the Angolan civil war, Northern Ireland Troubles, Peru's war against the Shining Path, and the Afghan civil war—endured for decades. In contrast, interstate conflicts that began between 1970 and 1999 lasted, on average, less than two years.

Beginning in the early 1990s, there was a marked expansion in size and number of peace support operations (PSOs) deployed in the aftermath of intrastate conflicts. The PSOs, appear to have dampened the persistence of some conflicts and prevented the reemergence of others. The proportion of youthful countries experiencing one or more violent intrastate conflicts declined from 25 percent in 1995 to 15 percent in 2005. Peacemaking and nation-building—despite public ambivalence about such efforts—has also helped to keep down casualties.

Looking forward, the risk of intrastate conflict almost certainly will continue to decline in countries and regions with maturing age structures (median age above 25 years). Latin American countries and the Caribbean—with the exception of Bolivia, Guatemala, Haiti, and Paraguay—will be getting older and therefore lowering their risks. Similarly, the risk of intrastate conflicts will probably decline in continental East Asia—where many countries are aging quickly. However, the risk will remain high during the next two decades in western, central, and eastern portions of Sub-Saharan Africa; in parts of the Middle East and South Asia; and in several Asian-Pacific island hotspots: Timor Leste, Papua New Guinea, Philippines, and Solomon Islands. (See map on page 22.)

Type	Present Status	Trendline	Factors	Changes in Character
Intrastate	The proportion of youthful countries experiencing one or more violent intrastate conflicts declined from 25 percent in 1995 to 15 percent in 2005.	The risk of intrastate conflict will continue to decline in countries and regions—such as Latin America and Asia—with maturing age structures (median age above 25 years). The risk will remain high over the next two decades in western, central, and eastern portions of Sub-Saharan Africa; in parts of the Middle East and South Asia; and in several Asian-Pacific island hotspots.	Constrained natural resources—such as water and arable land—in many of the same countries that will have disproportionate levels of young men—particularly Sub-Saharan Africa, South Asia, and parts of the Middle East— increase the risks of intrastate conflict.	Most intrastate conflict will be characterized by irregular warfare— terrorism, subversion, sabotage, insurgency, and criminal activities. However, the spread of precision weaponry— such as standoff missiles—may make some conflicts more like traditional forms of warfare.
Interstate	Several interstate conflicts have occurred in the past decade, but the number is at a historical low.	New powers are rising, but they stand to benefit from the existing international order and are therefore status quo oriented. An increasing number of states has consciously or implicitly chosen to maintain military capabilities far below their inherent capabilities.	A more fragmented international system increases the risks. Additionally, increased resource competition, spread of lethal technologies, and spillover from regional conflicts increase the potential for interstate conflicts.	Future wars in Asia and the Middle East could include nuclear element. Information superiority will be increasingly vital. Proliferation of standoff missiles will increase the capacity of nonstate actors. Distinction between regular and irregular forms of warfare may fade as some state-based militaries adopt irregular tactics.

We need to be cautious about the prospects for a marked decline in the number and intensity of intrastate conflicts, however. First, such an outcome is probably dependent on continued global support for costly PSOs. Second, a gradual increase in intrastate conflict is occurring in countries with more mature country-level populations that contain a politically dissonant, youthful ethnic minority. Strife involving ethnic Kurds in Turkey, Shia in Lebanon, and Pattani Muslims in southern Thailand are examples of intrastate conflicts persisting in states that display an intermediate age structure (median age from about 25 to 35 years). A few of these conflicts have persisted after the country-level age structure turned mature (median age from 35 to 45 years). Examples include the Chechen conflict in southern Russia and the Northern Ireland Troubles. Looking forward, the potential in Sub-Saharan Africa for intrastate conflict is likely to remain high even after some of the region's countries graduate into a more intermediate age structure because of the probable large number of ethnic and tribal minorities who will remain much more youthful than various countries' overall populations.

Moreover, constrained natural resources—such as water and arable land—in many of the same countries that will have disproportionate levels of young men increase the risks of intrastate conflict breaking out. An index of countries facing growing resource scarcities and environmental risks highlights many Sub-Saharan African and South and East Asian countries, including India and China. Many of the wealthier countries are already dealing with the growing threats; however, a number of countries in these regions—Afghanistan, Bangladesh, Pakistan, and Somalia—also have faltering governance institutions and may not be able to cope with increasing environmental challenges and population pressures.

INTERSTATE CONFLICT: CHANCES RISING

Few interstate conflicts have occurred for almost a decade, and no major power war has erupted since 1939, constituting the longest era of major power peace during the past five centuries.[a] Scholars account for this in several ways. There have been few if any periods in the past when global power has been distributed as incongruously as it is today. US military capabilities are unmatched by any other plausible combination of powers and are likely to remain so for decades to come. New powers are rising, but they stand to benefit from the existing international order and are therefore status quo-oriented. An increasing number of countries has consciously or implicitly chosen to maintain military capabilities far below their inherent capabilities. This reflects their assessment of the modern utility of using force to achieve political objectives and perhaps their belief that they have little to fear regarding the threat of major war in the near future.

Nevertheless, we and other experts believe that the risks of interstate conflict are increasing owing to changes in the international system. The underpinnings of the current post-Cold War equilibrium are beginning to shift. If the United States is unwilling or less able to serve as a global security provider by 2030, the world will be less stable. If the international system becomes more fragmented and existing forms of cooperation are no longer as seen as advantageous to many of the key global players, the potential for competition and conflict also will increase.

Three different baskets of risks could conspire to increase the chances of an outbreak: changing calculations of key players, contention over resource issues, and a wider spectrum of more accessible instruments of war.

In addition, the chances are growing that regional conflicts—particularly in the Middle East and South Asia—will spill over and ignite a wider conflagration. The Middle East most likely will remain the most volatile region, even as it moves toward greater

<hr>

[a] This information is from the *Stockholm International Peace Research Institute (SIPRI) Yearbook 2011*. The SIPRI classifies a conflict that has a core intrastate dynamic and attracts outside actors as an intrastate conflict rather than an interstate one. Also see Bruno Tertrais' article, *The Demise of Ares: The End of War as We Know It?*, The Washington Quarterly, Summer 2012, 35:3 pp 7-22.

democratization. Fledgling democracies have a higher risk of backsliding and instability. Endemic rivalries—such as between Iran and its neighbors—would be inflamed if Iran decided to develop nuclear weapons. Many of these conflicts, once begun, would not be easily containable and would have global impacts. The increasing empowerment of nonstate actors, such as Hizballah, in the region has the potential to further escalate any conflicts. Instability in South Asia would also have strong global repercussions as the region increasingly becomes the driver for global economic growth. Indo-Pak tensions remain at the forefront: we are concerned, for example, about an escalation in tensions should another major terrorist attack occur on Indian soil emanating from territory under Pakistan's control. A conflict-ridden East Asia would constitute a key global threat and cause large-scale damage to the global economy. We address the possibility of regional conflicts with global consequences in Game-Changer Four, which begins on page 73.

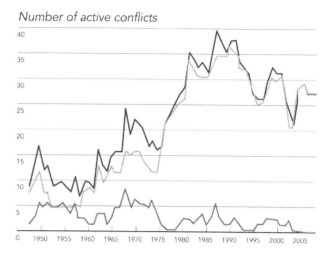

Source: Center for International Development and Conflict Management.

CHANGING CALCULATIONS OF KEY PLAYERS

The strategic calculations of the emerging powers—whose regional and global interests are in flux—are likely to change dramatically over the next 15-20 years. Heated debates are occurring among **China's** elites, for example, regarding whether China should move away from its traditional policies —not having overseas bases or major military alliances and not interfering in the internal affairs of other countries—as its overseas interests expand. The outcome of these debates will be critical indicators of whether China intends to become a global superpower, which in turn will have major implications for the prospect of future great power competition. Historical parallels with other great power rises suggest that Chinese assertiveness might increase as its economic growth slows and there is political need at home to demonstrate China's standing in the world.

With growing economic ties and dependencies in both the Persian Gulf region and Asia, **India's** worldview is expanding rapidly. Despite booming bilateral trade and economic relations between Beijing and New Delhi, the India-China relationship is clouded by

mistrust. This situation probably won't change as both powers grow simultaneously—a first for Asia, where one power has usually dominated. India's concern is fueled by what it perceives as a Chinese policy of containment that threatens India's rise. China's continuing cooperation with Pakistan on nuclear and missile developments, its growing assertiveness in its territorial claims, and opposition to New Delhi's participation in regional and global forums are likely to remain irritants and shape India's strategic outlook.

Russia's strategic calculations will depend to a great extent on whether Russian leaders decide to increase Russia's integration into the international system and mitigate the threat of future armed conflict or whether they choose to continue Russia's relative isolation and mistrust of others, exacerbating interstate tensions. Russia has serious concerns regarding the threat posed by a rapidly expanding China, particularly Beijing's growing appetite for natural resources which could eventually encroach upon the Russian Far East and Siberia. Russian leaders believe that they need to be wary of the potential for the US and NATO to intervene in a conflict involving Russia and one of the former Soviet republics.

Europe almost certainly will remain very cautious about the use of force and military intervention. The Europeans probably will continue to perceive that their primary security challenges result from globalization. These include threats that stem from WMD proliferation; cyber threats directed at critical infrastructures, including space assets; and threats resulting from the competition for resources or the influx of refugees from potential zones of instability. Severe budget constraints for the foreseeable future are likely to force European countries to integrate European defense resources, causing the military gap between Europe and the new global powers to be reduced over time. With more defense cooperation, the Europeans could play a greater role in future multilateral operations, particularly in humanitarian interventions.

The United States also is likely to face budgetary constraints at the same time that—like Europe—its global security challenges are multiplying. As such, the US overall will be grappling with how much it can continue to play the role of systemic guardian and guarantor of the international system. (For a fuller discussion of the US role see page 101) This may play out in several different arenas. The United States' historic role as security guarantor in Asia, including its substantial on-the-ground military presence, puts it in a competitive position with rising Asian states— particularly China—who desire greater regional roles for themselves. Continued US protection of the sea lanes—particularly in the Persian Gulf and extending both to Europe and through the Indian Ocean to East Asia—are likely to be welcomed by most countries in those regions. However, tensions—particularly with China—probably will grow over the US role. Chinese strategists worry that China's dependence on the US for sea lane security will be a strategic vulnerability for China in a future conflict, such as over Taiwan, where the US might impose an oil embargo. In response, China is building up its naval power and developing land-bound energy transportation routes to diversify its access to energy. With the potential for humanitarian

disasters to grow in scope, US military assets—such as lift and intelligence information—will be key for the success of broad-based global efforts.

NEW SOURCES OF FRICTION IN A RESOURCE-CONSTRAINED WORLD

Allied with the changing security outlooks are increasing tensions over resources. Access to key resources—minerals in addition to energy—will be vital to many developing states' continued rapid economic growth, and these states will be increasingly dependent on outside sources. The potential for disputes to grow over seabed rights is particularly striking in several regions—the South China Sea and the Indian, Arctic, and South Atlantic Oceans (see textbox on page 68). Not only are the territorial claims unsettled, but new technologies are increasingly able to tap deep seabed resources. Nevertheless, the relevant countries know that engaging in conflict over these resources would jeopardize their exploitation. This might prove to be a deterrent.

"Water may become a more significant source of contention than energy or minerals out to 2030 at both the intrastate and interstate levels."

Water may become a more significant source of contention than energy or minerals out to 2030 at both the intrastate and interstate levels. Although water stress[a] exists in the United States and Mexico and along the western coast of South America, the world's major belt of water stress lies across northern Africa, the Middle East, central and southern Asia, and northern China. These stresses are increasing because this is also the zone of the largest projected population growth during the next 15-20 years. Across this central belt, there are numerous well-known watersheds of significance, including the Nile, the Tigris and Euphrates, the Indus, the Ganges, the Mekong, the Yellow, and the Yangtze Rivers. Except for the Yangtze and Mekong, all of these are under moderate (the Nile

---

[a] Water stress is present when a country's or region's annual water supply is less than 1,700 cubic meters per person per year.

and Ganges) to high stress and the Mekong is at least temporarily under high stress as a result of drought and Chinese reservoir filling.

The lesser (and in many cases) less well-known watersheds across this belt—including the Jordan in Israel/Palestine, the Kura-Ural and Kizilimak (adjacent to the Tigris & Euphrates and largely in Turkey), Syr Darya and Amu Darya (at one time more substantial rivers feeding the Aral Sea), and Lake Balkhash and Tarim in Central Asia—are mostly under high stress. Across northern Africa, the Arabian Peninsula, and Iran, considerable territory has no notable watersheds and is therefore heavily dependent on fossil and imported water, including "virtual water" imports—such as agricultural goods like meat, fruit, and vegetables using high levels of water to produce.

Historically, water tensions have led to more water-sharing agreements than violent conflicts, but a number of risks could change this past pattern, including high levels of population growth in affected areas and rapid changes in the availability of water, such as, for example, from severe droughts. Intrastate disruptions and conflicts probably are more likely to be the immediate result as pressures build within countries for relief and migration from impacted areas puts added strains on other areas. However, the fact that many of the river basins in the most affected water-stressed areas are shared means that interstate conflict cannot be ruled out—especially in light of the other tensions ongoing between many of these countries.

SPREADING LETHAL TECHNOLOGIES

The next 15-20 years will see a wider spectrum of more accessible instruments of war, especially **precision-strike capabilities, cyber instruments, and bioterror weaponry.**

The commercial availability of key components, such as imagery, and almost universal access to precision navigation GPS data is accelerating the diffusion of **precision-strike capabilities** to state and nonstate actors, which we expect will be widespread by 2030.

The proliferation of precision-guided weapons would allow critical infrastructures to be put at risk by many more potential adversaries. This could create a fundamentally new security dynamic in regions like the Middle East with multiple contending forces. The proliferation of long-range precision weapons and antiship missile systems would pose significant challenges to US or NATO to forward deploy forces, limiting in-theater options for military action. It could discourage third parties from cooperating because of fears of becoming a victim of more precision targets with greater lethal consequences. More accurate weapons could lead attackers to become overconfident in their military capabilities and therefore more apt to employ such systems. Precision also may give attackers a false sense of their abilities to tailor attacks to create specific, narrow effects.

Cyberweapons can take various forms including viruses (self-replicating programs that require human action to spread), worms (a sub-class of viruses that can spread without human action), Trojan horses (malicious software hidden within a legitimate program), denial-of- service attacks (bombarding servers with messages to make them crash), and phishing (rogue emails and websites that trick people into revealing password information).

Potential cyberwarfare scenarios include coordinated cyberweapon attacks that sabotage multiple infrastructure assets simultaneously. One scenario involves a case where power, the Internet, cash machines, broadcast media, traffic lights, financial systems, and air traffic software simultaneously failed for a period of weeks. The trends in cyberattacks so far suggest that although some computer systems are more secure than others; few, if any, systems can claim to be completely secure against a determined attack. For some attackers, cyberwarfare offers other advantages that have seldom been the case for most warfare: anonymity and low buy-in costs. These attributes favor the employment by disaffected groups and individuals who want to sow mayhem.

Growing interconnectivity of devices and software, including greater use of the cloud and integration

A REDEFINED OCEAN GEOGRAPHY BY 2030

With the shift in economic power from West to East and South and changing climatic conditions, the world's geographic focus will also change. The Pacific and Indian Ocean basins are already the fastest-growing commercial hubs for the exchange of goods, services, and people—a trend that will intensify. With the growing competition for resources, the regions below, which are rich in natural resources, will also be of prime importance.

Indian Ocean. Although the Indian Ocean maritime region currently ranks fifth out of nine regions for global security (as classified by Lloyd's Maritime Intelligence Unit) behind northern Europe, the Pacific, the Far East, and the Mediterranean/Black Sea, the region is becoming an important avenue for global trade and arena for geopolitical competition. It has significant deposits of primary raw materials that are vital to the world's economy—such as bauxite, chromite, coal, copper, gold, iron ore, natural gas, nickel, oil, phosphates, titanium, tungsten, uranium, and zinc. The region's fisheries also are a key part of food security and regional livelihoods.

South China Sea. The difficulty of determining national jurisdiction has been exacerbated by coastal states' interest in the exploitation of fisheries and control of potential energy resources. Overlapping claims by China and several ASEAN states could lead to more confrontation, if not conflict. Coastal states' efforts to increase their maritime jurisdiction pose a cumulative threat to the military and commercial interests of all maritime states.

Arctic. By 2030 it will be possible to transit both the Northern and Northwest Passage for about 110 days per year, with about 45 days easily navigable. However, use of the Arctic for commercial purposes will depend on Arctic coastal infrastructure development, agreed safety standards for commercial vessels, and the availability of adequate search-and-rescue capabilities. The use by Arctic states of the Arctic Council to develop common policies reduces the potential for disagreements to lead to conflict. At the same time, climate change and related events, such as the melting of Arctic ice, will continue to propel a globalization of interest in the Arctic. The US Energy Information Administration estimates that the Arctic could hold about 22 percent of the world's undiscovered conventional oil and natural gas resources, but exploiting such resources involves greater expense, risk, and a longer timeline than elsewhere in the world. An array of interested parties plan to expand scientific research and invest in assets such as icebreakers that give themselves legitimacy as Arctic actors.

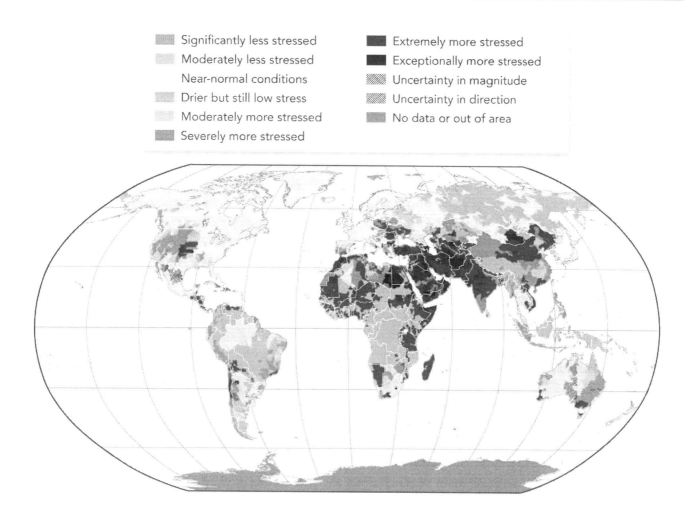

Significantly less stressed
Moderately less stressed
Near-normal conditions
Drier but still low stress
Moderately more stressed
Severely more stressed

Extremely more stressed
Exceptionally more stressed
Uncertainty in magnitude
Uncertainty in direction
No data or out of area

between systems, will increase the vulnerabilities of technology leaders, including the US, to attack. Current trends suggest that deep interconnectivity between different software systems and devices is likely to become the norm, enabling remote access to all kinds of systems that are offline today. More and more everyday actions will have a digital component—boarding a bus, buying groceries, entering a meeting room. As societies become more dependent on software and systems become more interconnected, the potential levels of damage that cyberweapons will be able to inflict will increase.

"Terrorists for the moment appear focused on causing mass casualties, but this could change as they understand the scope of the disruptions that can be caused by cyber warfare."

There are few alternatives to the Internet. One response would be to create disconnected networks, which would be less efficient but safer from cyber attacks. Authoritarian regimes are already taking such steps; for example, Iran has created a national Internet. Over the long term, however, organizations and individuals will likely have to work hard to get offline or carry out actions without leaving a digital trace.

As with the broad array of potential targets—everything from military systems to electricity grids, communications networks, and financial systems—so too are potential cyber saboteurs widely varied. So far the cyberweapons wielded by criminals and malicious individuals are unsophisticated in comparison to state actors, but this is likely to improve as criminal organizations become more adept and potentially sell their services to those state and nonstate actors with even more dangerous intentions. Terrorists for the moment appear focused on causing mass casualties, but this could change as they understand the scope of the disruptions that can be caused by cyber warfare.

Countries with nuclear weapons could be tempted to explode a nuclear device to wipe out their opponent's ability to maintain connectivity. Many current systems cannot operate in a hostile electromagnetic or radiated environment. In this instance, nuclear first use would not be used to harm humans as much as to deny opponents use of electronic systems. Space, ocean, and near coastal bottlenecks could be areas of nuclear use with little human collateral damage.

A cyber arms race is likely to occur as states seek to defend both public and private infrastructures against state and nonstate actors as well as to incorporate cyber and other debilitating physical attacks into their arsenals of strategy and weaponry. The degree to which cyber instruments will shape the future of warfare is unclear, however. Historians of war believe cyberpower may end up somewhat akin to early 20th century projections of the decisiveness of air power. Although air power played a significant role in 20th-century conflicts, it never achieved what its most ardent enthusiasts claimed it would: an independent, war-winning capability.

Cyber power may be as important off the battlefield in terms of the ability of information technology enabling the emergence of networked social movements that can create large economic, political, and security effects. The potential opened up by information technology is for future "do-it-yourself" revolutions conducted by networked social movements that employ information technologies which communicate and collaborate with like-minded individuals.

Advances in synthetic biology also have the potential to be a double-edged sword and become a source of lethal weaponry accessible to do-it-yourself biologists or biohackers. As costs decline and DNA sequencing and synthesis improve, researchers are capitalizing on such advances in ways that are laying important foundations for the field's development. Because early commercialization efforts have capitalized on the supply of tools and low-cost materials to academic and commercial researchers, the bio community has established an open-access repository of standardized and interchangeable building block or "biobrick" biological parts that researches can use. Such advances not only contribute to opportunities for exploring increasingly novel and valuable applications, they also raise the risk for unintended and intentional dual-use developments to occur. This will be particularly true as technology becomes more accessible on a global basis and, as a result, makes it harder to track, regulate, or mitigate bioterror if not "bioerror."

To date, policy initiatives have focused on introducing reporting requirements on suppliers of goods, but such efforts could become futile as research becomes more diffuse. Recent trends suggest applications of the technology will continue to advance ahead of understanding all the risks. Absent efforts to strengthen regulatory frameworks to proactively manage risks, the greater access to synthetic biology increases chances of the development and use of bioweaponry by individuals or terrorist groups or release unintentionally of dangerous material through "bioerror."

POTENTIAL NEW SHAPE OF WAR

If future state-on-state conflicts occur, they will most likely involve multiple forms of warfare. Future wars in Asia involving Russia, China, or India and Pakistan would risk use of a nuclear weapon in addition to conventional military capabilities. Future conflicts in the Middle East might also include nuclear aspects if the proliferation of nuclear weapons continues.

THE FUTURE OF TERRORISM

Several circumstances are ending the current Islamist phase of terrorism, which suggest that as with other terrorist waves—the Anarchists in the 1880s and 90s , the postwar anti-colonial terrorist movements, the New Left in 1970s—the recent religious wave is receding and could end by 2030. Terrorism is unlikely to die completely, however, because it has no single cause. The traditional use of the term "root cause" for understanding what drives terrorism is misleading. Rather, some experts point to the analogy of a forest fire: a mixture of conditions—such as dry heat, a spark, and wind—that lead to terrorism.

- **A Receding Enemy.** Although al-Qa'ida and others have focused on the United States a clear enemy, the appeal of the United States as the "great enemy" is declining. The impending withdrawal of US forces from Iraq and decreases in US forces in Afghanistan help to reduce the extent to which terrorists can draw on the United States as a lightning rod for anger. Soon, US support for Israel could be the last remaining major focus of Muslim anger.

- **Moral Resurgence of Secular Democracy.** The Arab uprisings have demonstrated the moral and strategic legitimacy of nonviolent struggle. Protestors acted in the name of democratic values, not in the name of religion.

- **Evaporation of Imagined War.** Although warfare is very real, it is also an imagined state, based on a narrative of an enemy and conflict between fundamental values. These perceptions can change—sometimes quickly. A new generation may simply view things differently and be less interested in an old narrative.

Al-Qa'ida core has been in decline for several years, as the kings of Muslims diminished the organization's broad appeal, the war in Afghanistan cost al-Qa'ida its initial base and forced it to move into the more difficult environment in the trial areas of Pakistan, and US attacks killed many senior leaders and key operatives. In the short term, the al-Qa'ida core might still be able to launch attacks; experts noted that organizations such as the Baader-Meinhof group in the 1970s still did damage even when facing similar problems as al-Qa'ida is today. Some al-Qa'ida affiliates and other types of Islamist terrorist organizations are likely to pose more serious threats, however. Shia groups such as Hizballah will continue to see terrorism as a means to achieve their objectives. Taking a global perspective, future terrorists could come from many different religions, including Christianity and Hinduism. Right-wing and left-wing ideological groups—some of the oldest users of terrorist tactics— also will pose threats.

STATES MANAGING TERRORISM

Many states might continue to use terrorist groups: states choose to exploit terrorist movements out of a strong sense of insecurity. States such as Pakistan and Iran feel threatened by what they perceive as stronger, threatening powers in their regions or globally. Therefore, they seek asymmetric options to assert power and deter attack; using terrorist groups as proxies and pursuing nuclear weapons are two such asymmetric tools. However, international disapproval of state support for terrorist movements has increased significantly, and the costs to a regime of directly supporting terrorists looks set to become even greater as international cooperation increases.

MORE WEAPONS AND TARGETS IN THE FUTURE

To date, most terrorists have focused on causing mass casualties, but this could change. The future will include very large vulnerabilities: only a small number of people might understand critical cyber systems, for example, creating a risk that they could sell their services to the highest bidder, including terrorists who would focus less on mass casualties and more on widespread economic and financial disruptions.

Conflicts with state-sponsored organizations, such as Hizballah and HAMAS, represent the middle ground in the spectrum of future warfare because such adversaries would probably combine irregular warfare tactics and organizational concepts with advanced standoff weaponry and air defenses.

The character of future wars will most likely be shaped ultimately by a number of ongoing and emerging military competitions. The dynamic created by these competitions, as well as the prospect of a clear winner eventually emerging, will help to define the character of the future security environment and any wars that take place within it.

Access vs. Anti-Access. The US ability to project air and maritime forces is in competition with China's burgeoning capabilities to deter and deny such force projection. The outcome of this competition will impact the ability of either side to control the maritime and air approaches to East Asia and the US ability to assure allies in the region.

Nuclear Disfavor vs. Nuclear Renaissance. Nuclear ambitions in the US and Russia over the last 20 years have evolved in opposite directions. Reducing the role of nuclear weapons in US security strategy is a US objective, while Russia is pursuing new concepts and capabilities for expanding the role of nuclear weapons in its security strategy. Other nuclear powers, such as Pakistan and potential aspirants Iran and North Korea, desire nuclear weapons as compensation for other security weaknesses.

Missile Defense vs. Missile Offense. The proliferation of standoff missiles to both state and nonstate actors has become a feature of modern warfare. The threat these missiles pose to critical infrastructures (economic, energy, political, etc) as well as to military forces will increase as their ability to be precisely targeted or carry weapons of mass destruction increases. In response, some countries are making significant efforts to counter the threat through multi-layed missile defenses. It remains to be seen whether technologically advanced and expensive missile defense systems can keep pace with the increasing numbers of ballistic and cruise missiles that can employed against them.

Information Superiority vs. Information Denial. The traditional way of war for the the US and NATO allies depends on achieving information superiority to identify targets, employ precision-guided weapons, and maintain effective command and control. The ability of a future adversary to deny or mitigate that information advantage—including through widening the combat to outer space—would have a dramatic impact on the future conduct of war. China's development of capabilities to counter US information superiority in a future conflict is an example of this type of competition.

Regular vs. Irregular Forms of Combat. The competition between regular, organized state-based military operations and decentralized, irregular warfighting exhibited recently in Afghanistan and Iraq almost certainly will continue. This competition is not new, but the evolution of "hybrid adversaries," who combine irregular tactics with advanced standoff weaponry, add new dimensions to it.

GAME-CHANGER 4
WIDER SCOPE OF REGIONAL INSTABILITY

Regional dynamics in several different theaters during the next couple decades will have the potential to spill over and create global insecurity. The **Middle East** and **South Asia** are the two regions most likely to trigger broader instability. The number of potential conflicts in these two regions is rising. Many of these, once begun, would not be easily containable and would have global impacts. Changing dynamics in other regions would prove equally important for global security. An increasingly multipolar **Asia** lacking a well-anchored regional security framework able to arbitrate and mitigate rising tensions constitutes a significant global threat; an unstable Asia would cause large-scale damage to the global economy. A more inward-focused and less capable **Europe** would provide a less stabilizing force for crises in neighboring regions. Countries in **Sub-Saharan Africa** and **Central America** and the **Caribbean** will remain vulnerable, nevertheless, to state failure through 2030, providing safe haven to both global criminal and terrorist networks and local insurgents.

THE MIDDLE EAST: AT A TIPPING POINT

By 2030, the Middle East will be a very different place, but the possibilities run a wide gamut from fragile growth and development to chronic instability and potential regional conflicts. Demographically, the youth bulge–a driving force for the recent Arab Spring–will give way to a gradually aging population, as the social and economic impacts of declining fertility rates begin to manifest. With new technologies beginning to provide the world with other sources of oil and gas, the region's economy will need to become increasingly diversified in order to continue to grow. Like other emerging powers around the globe, highly-populous Middle East countries could see their regional and potential global influence enhanced.

The future of the Middle East hinges primarily on political developments in the region. If the Islamic Republic maintains power in Iran and is able to acquire nuclear weapons, the Middle East will face a highly unstable future. The collapse of the House of Saud could wreak havoc on the region's economy, and the emergence of a radical Islamist government in Egypt could exacerbate regional tensions on a variety of fronts. Fragmentation along ethnic and religious lines in Iraq and Syria could lead to an unraveling of current borders. On the other hand, the emergence of moderate, democratic governments in these countries, or a breakthrough agreement to resolve the Israeli-Palestinian conflict, could have enormously positive consequences.

Our discussions with experts led us to identify six key determinants of the region's future, which we discuss below.

1. Will political Islam moderate as it assumes power? Political Islam, after the false start of the Islamic Salvation Front (FIS) election in Algeria over 20 years ago, is becoming empowered in the Sunni world. From the Justice and Development Party (AKP) in Turkey, to the Freedom and Justice Party (FJP) in Egypt, Ennahda in Tunisia, and Hamas in Gaza, and potential Islamic victories in Libya and Syria, the Middle East landscape is changing in profound ways. Islamic parties such as those in Egypt have responded with calls for expanding the safety net for the lower middle class; adding thousands of jobs to the public sector; and retaining subsidies on food and energy. These policies are not sustainable. Future ruling Islamic parties will become more market-oriented, empowering the more entrepreneurial younger Muslim Brotherhood "new guard" and others who can grow the economy.

Over time political pragmatism could trump ideology helped by a growing civil society that will begin to produce a new cadre of pragmatic, entrepreneurial and social leaders—something that authoritarian regimes consistently stifled.

Islamic democracy almost certainly will mutate into a variety of political hues. Tunisian Islamic parties will be different from one another, but all of them will be intent on establishing their legitimacy in this new post-authoritarian era. In post-Assad Syria, it is likely that an urban Sunni would take power in a coalition comprising the Muslim Brotherhood, religious minorities, Druze, Kurds, and others. Before Hafez Assad took power over 40 years ago, urban Sunni parties ruled Damascus in frequent and unstable governments. It may be back to the 1960s in Syria. In Iraq, the government is already showing signs of reverting to factionalism, in this case the Shia are willing to share power with the Sunni Arabs or Kurds.

If corruption and chronic unemployment persists, or if large segments of the working poor feel their lives have failed to improve with the election of democratic governments, they may choose to turn to political leaders who offer a more radical approach. Hardline Islamists may have greater popular appeal given their commitment to conservative religious principles, providing a clearly identified alternative to Western capitalism and democracy.

2. Will governments in transition prevent civil strife?
Chronic instability will be a feature of the region because of the growing weakness of the state and the rise of sectarianism, Islam, and tribalism. The challenge will be particularly acute in states such as Iraq, Libya, Yemen, and Syria where sectarian tensions were often simmering below the surface as autocratic regimes co-opted minority groups and imposed harsh measures to keep ethnic rivalries in check. In event of a more fragmented Iraq or Syria, a Kurdistan would not be inconceivable. Having split up before, Yemen—with a weak central government—may do so again. Under any scenario, Yemen is likely to be a security concern with weak central government, poverty, unemployment with a young population that will go from 28 million today to 50 million in 2025. Bahrain could also become a cockpit for growing Sunni-Shia rivalry, which could be destabilizing for the Gulf region.

Over time, ongoing violence could undermine support for democratic governance and lead to the emergence of strongman dictators—propelling these countries away from liberal democracy. Regionally,

weak governments mired in domestic violence and civil strife are unlikely to play a strong role, leaving non-Arab powers, especially Turkey, Iran, and Israel, as the major players.

3. Can Middle Eastern countries fix their economies and ride the globalization wave?
The fertility rate is coming down, but the youth bulge will last until 2030. At the same time, an aging population by 2030 may face a health-care crisis absent a better-provisioned welfare system. Only 2 percent of global foreign direct investment (FDI) is currently going to the Middle East, and there is little to attract FDI apart from energy, tourism, and real estate. Many Middle Eastern countries are also far behind on technology, and the region is one of the least integrated in trade and finance. The Middle East's traditional trade partner—Europe—is facing slower growth, although Sub-Saharan Africa, whose economy is expanding could present increased opportunities.

"If the Islamic Republic maintains power in Iran and is able to acquire nuclear weapons, the Middle East will face a highly unstable future."

The richer Gulf Cooperation Council (GCC) countries are in a good position to help: GCC sovereign wealth funds have built up sizable assets in recent years and a growing share of petrodollar wealth is likely to be invested in local and regional markets, including Egypt, Libya, and Tunisia. In addition, GCC states are turning more of their oil into refined products or petrochemicals to create value-added commodities. The Gulf is a magnet for investments from Asia, Europe, and elsewhere.

Still, Gulf countries could face stiff challenges if oil supplies increase substantially from the exploitation of shale gas and oil deposits, which will undercut high energy prices. The fiscal breakeven price of oil for Saudi Arabia keeps rising from $67 a barrel to more recent government figure of $100, suggesting spiraling budget expenditures that could outpace oil price rises. Without hikes in the internal oil price, which would reduce rising domestic consumption, Saudi Arabia is on course to become a net oil importer by 2037.

4. How will Iran project regional power? Iran's influence is linked to its nuclear aspirations. A number of our interlocutors believe that Iran will stop short of developing a nuclear weapon— but will retain the ability to develop such a weapon. In this scenario, a breakdown of the nonproliferation system would be inevitable, with Saudi Arabia obtaining nuclear weapons or capabilities from Pakistan. Turkey might react to a nuclear Iran by seeking its own nuclear capability or relying instead on the NATO defensive shield. The UAE, Egypt, and possibly Jordan almost certainly would begin nuclear programs in the energy field as hedges that enabled them to go forward if Iran, Saudi Arabia, or others in the region became overt nuclear powers. If this occurred, the region would be in constant crisis. Sunni-Shia and Arab-Persian antagonisms would increase, spilling over to create far-reaching instability outside the region.

A second scenario would involve the Iranian regime coming under growing pressure from its public, which could desire economic gains rather than nuclear weapons, and might not want to pay the price in terms of international isolation. Eventually, the regime could be toppled by elite infighting and mass demonstrations. Under this scenario in which Tehran focused more on economic modernization, a more pro-Western, democratic Iran—and a more stable region—would emerge.

5. Can an Israeli-Palestinian settlement be reached, enhancing the region's prospects for stability? At home, Israel faces increasing political and social divisions between those who still cherish a vision harking back to its 1948 founding of a sectarian, liberal republic or an Israel characterized by the growing demographic weight of the religiously conservative Haredim and settler movement. Some of our interlocutors thought the divisions would come to a head before 2030. Israel will remain the strongest military power, but face continuing threats from low intensity warfare in addition to any nuclear one from Iran. Growing Arab public opinion could constrain Israeli room for maneuver, however, if it wants to avoid an escalating conflict with Arab opponents.

Resolution of the Israeli-Palestinian conflict would have dramatic consequences for the region over the next two decades. For Israel, a permanent resolution to the conflict could open the door to regional relationships unthinkable today. The end of Palestinian conflict would provide a strategic setback to Iran and its resistance camp and over time undermine public support for militant groups such as Hizballah and Hamas. Without some sort of resolution, Israel would be increasingly absorbed with trying to control a burgeoning Palestinian population with limited political rights and a restive Gaza next door.

Many of our interlocutors saw a Palestine emerging from Arab-Israeli exhaustion and an unwillingness of Israelis and Palestinians to engage in endless conflict. Issues like 'right of return', demilitarization and Jerusalem will not be fully resolved by 2030, and there will be no complete end of conflict. The way forward toward a Palestinian state will be through a series of unofficial independent actions known as 'coordinated unilateralism,' incrementally leading to statehood. As Hamas moves away from Syria and Iran to the Sunni Arab fold, the potential for reconciliation between the Palestinian Authority in Ramallah and Hamas in Gaza would increase. Palestine's borders will be roughly along the 1967 borders with adjustments or land swaps along the Green Line, but other issues will remain unresolved.

6. Will Saudi Arabia and other Sunni Gulf monarchies—beyond Bahrain—remain immune from regime-threatening protest movements that have transformed the Arab world? Whether or not oil spare capacity develops elsewhere, political turmoil in Saudi Arabia could trigger widespread economic and political uncertainty. Within the country, competing groups probably would vie for power, including Muslim-Brotherhood-affiliated groups, radical Islamic extremists, secularists, and Shiite actors. As in Egypt, a future political transition could be messy and complicated. Other Sunni monarchies may soon find themselves under pressure to embrace far-reaching

Type	Present Status	Trendline	Drivers
Middle East	At a tipping point, the Middle East faces a wide gamut of possibilities from fragile growth to chronic instability and regional conflicts.	The youth bulge—a driving force for the recent Arab Spring—almost certainly will give way to a gradually aging population. New energy technologies and production elsewhere will mean Middle East economies will need to diversify.	If Iran develops nuclear weapons, the Middle East faces a highly unstable future. Other critical variables include the stability of the House of Saud; the emergence of a radical Islamist government in Egypt; and fragmentation in Iraq and Syria, which could lead to the unraveling of current borders.
South Asia	Low economic growth, large youth bulges, rising food prices, and energy shortages pose stiff challenges in Pakistan and Afghanistan. Inequality, lack of infrastructure, and educational deficiencies are key weaknesses in India.	Three possible scenarios include a *Turn-the-Corner* scenario, which many experts believe is unlikely. In an *Islamistan* scenario, the influence of radical Islamists grows. In an *Unraveling* scenario, destructive forces would come to the fore, resulting in a social and political fracturing of Pakistan and Afghanistan.	Intra-regional trade would be important in building trust between India and Pakistan. A Mumbai-style terrorist attack perpetrated by militants backed by Pakistan could spark an open conflict with India. Conflicting strategic goals and widespread distrust will make it difficult to develop a strong regional security framework for Afghanistan.
East Asia	Surging economic growth, dramatic power shifts, nationalism, and aggressive military modernization—not just in China but India and elsewhere—have amplified rather than diminished regional competition.	Regional trends will pull countries in two directions: toward China economically but toward the US and each other for security.	Rule of law and more transparency on its military modernization would assuage security concerns about China. China's weaknesses, however, could make Beijing more unpredictable or even highly aggressive.
Europe	By any measure—GDP, trade volume, number of transnational companies, or technological capabilities—Europe will remain a great power.	Economic logic—which argues for more integration—conflicts with the desire of publics to hold onto separate national affiliations, limiting greater integration.	Massive transfers of sovereignty may be a bridge too far. On the other hand, EU members may stick together to avoid major political and economic disruptions.

Type	Present Status	Trendline	Drivers
Sub-Saharan Africa	The megatrends of population growth without aging, rapid urbanization, and middle class expansion will shape the trajectories of most African countries. At least a few—particularly in the Sahel and the Horn—will be sharply challenged by resource scarcities.	Most African states already face moderate-to-high threats of instability, but improved governance, resource management, and economic diversification offer the chance to move to more stable ground. The Sahel region, Congo/DROC, and Somalia will be the most vulnerable.	Africans will be able to choose from best-proven approaches and technologies in the developed world without needing to adapt and reform legacy systems, but rent-seeking, patronage, populism, and corruption may tempt many and challenge long-term planning.
Latin America	Latin America and the Caribbean have undergone far-reaching change during the past decade, including sustained economic growth, but the distribution of the benefits still remains uneven.	With annual real GDP growth averaging 4 percent, the middle class ranks have swelled. The region has also seen greater economic and political participation by women, indigenous peoples, and minority groups, many of whom have benefited from greater access to education and health-care services.	The pace of world economic growth will be a key factor affecting the demand for Latin American commodities, labor, and other services. The second key factor is the extent to which Latin Americans position themselves to capture economic gains through investments in education, market-opening reforms, and enhanced rule of law and governing capacity.
Russia	Russia's economy is its Achilles' heel. Its budget is heavily dependent on energy revenue; efforts to modernize the economy have made little progress; and its aging workforce will be a drag on economic growth.	Russia will need to improve the environment for foreign investment and create opportunities for Russian exports of manufactured goods.	Russia's posture towards the West and China will help determine whether it moves to becoming a more stable, constructive global player. A negative role is more likely with sagging living standards which would spur more nationalist sentiments.

political reforms or face a similar uprising in their own countries. In Lebanon, the Palestinian Territories, Iraq, and other places where the Saudis have used their influence to support Sunni allies, groups that have long relied on such support may be considerably weakened, perhaps to the benefit of Shiite and pro-Iranian rivals.

If the GCC monarchies are able to successfully ride out the Arab Spring, the greatest beneficiaries regionally might be Jordan and Morocco—the most vulnerable Sunni monarchies. Such a result would also ensure GCC regional influence, providing Gulf countries with continued economic leverage in Arab countries in transition, including Egypt and potentially Syria. Finally, the status quo scenario would preserve and perhaps deepen the cold war dynamic between the Gulf states and Iran, especially as Iran nears the nuclear threshold.

SOUTH ASIA: SHOCKS ON THE HORIZON

Like the Middle East, South Asia will face a series of internal and external shocks during the next 15-20 years. Impacts from climate change, including water stress, in addition to low economic growth, rising food prices, and energy shortages will pose stiff challenges to governance in Pakistan and Afghanistan. Afghanistan's and Pakistan's youth bulges are large—similar in size to those found in many African countries—and when combined with slow-growing economies portend increased social instability. India is in a better position, benefiting from higher growth, but New Delhi will still be challenged to find jobs for its large youthful population. Inequality, lack of infrastructure, and educational deficiencies are key weaknesses in India. India also faces an intransigent rural insurgency—the Naxalites—which constitutes an internal security challenge. Rapid urbanization in India and Pakistan almost certainly will transform their political landscapes from more traditional control by rural elites to one shaped by a growing pool of urban poor and middle class.

The neighborhood has always had a profound influence on internal developments in all the countries in the region, increasing the sense of insecurity and bolstering military outlays. Pakistan's large and fast-growing nuclear arsenal in addition to its doctrine of "first use" is intended to deter and balance against India's conventional military advantages. India worries about a second Mumbai-style terrorist attack from militants backed by Pakistan. A major incident with many casualties and Pakistani fingerprints would put a weakened Indian Government under tremendous pressure to respond with force, with the attendant risk of nuclear miscalculation. Afghanistan could become the focus of future Indian-Pakistani competition, particularly after the drawdown in US and NATO forces post-2014. Both countries want to deny giving the other a strategy advantage, making regional cooperation difficult. More broadly, conflicting strategic goals, widespread distrust, and hedging strategies of all Afghanistan's neighbors—not just India and Pakistan—will make it difficult to develop a strong regional security framework.

Increasingly China is also driving India threat perceptions, partly because of China's role in supporting Pakistan, but mostly because of China's increasing global and regional profile. Indian elites worry about the potential for a widening economic gap between China and India if Indian growth does not rebound from its recent slowdown and India does not put more emphasis on rapid economic and technological development. Intensifying competition between India and China could lead to great-power conflict that would not be limited to the South Asian theatre, drawing in the US and others.

Three possible scenarios include:

In a *Turn-the-Corner* scenario, sustained economic growth in Pakistan based on the gradual normalization of trade with a rising India would be a critical factor. An improved economic environment would produce more opportunities for youth entering the workforce, lessening the attractiveness of militancy and containing the spread of Islamic violence. Intra-regional trade would also be important in building trust between India and Pakistan, slowly changing threat perceptions and anchoring sectors with vested interests in continuing economic cooperation. Just as China's economic engine transformed its relations with neighbors from the early 1990s, so a strong economic engine in India could lay down new foundations for prosperity and regional cooperation in South Asia. Over several decades, Pakistan would grow into a relatively stable economy, no longer requiring foreign assistance and IMF tutelage. Suspicions of India would persist in military circles; even so, both nuclear-armed countries could find means to coexist in order to avoid threatening the growing economic ties.

> "Just as China's economic engine transformed its relations with neighbors from the early 1990s, so a strong economic engine in India could lay down new foundations for prosperity and regional cooperation in South Asia."

Many of our interlocutors saw this scenario as unlikely. Critical to the scenario would be the establishment of a more capable civilian government in Pakistan and improved governance, such as better tax and investment policies that spurred new industries, jobs and more resources for modern education. A collapse in neighboring Afghanistan would probably set back any such civilian-led agenda, reinforcing security fears and retrenchment. On the other hand, Indian policies to open up trade and visa access with its neighbor could serve as a countervailing fore, building up new Pakistani constituencies for reform.

In an *Islamistan* scenario, the influence of radical Islamists in Pakistan and Talibans in Afghanistan would grow. In Pakistan, a weak government would continue to lose ground to Islamists over the next decade. Signs of growing influence of radical Islamists would include more broadly held extreme interpretations of sharia law, proliferation of jihad-oriented militant bases in settled areas, and greater control of local government by Islamists. A symbiotic relationship would deepen between the military and the Islamists. As Pakistan became more Islamicized, the army would become more sympathetic to the Islamic cause. Consequently, the military would likely cede control of territory

to Islamist insurgents and would be more willing to engage in negotiations with these Islamists.

In an *Unraveling* scenario, all the destructive forces lurking in the region—such as weak government, large numbers of unemployed youths, and food and water crises—would come to the fore and result in the social and political fracturing of Pakistan and Afghanistan. India would be left trying to defend against the spillover of militancy, increased tensions in Kashmir, and potential radicalization of its Muslim populations. Rather than uplifting its neighbors as in the *Turn-the-Corner* scenario, India would be dragged down by them, challenging its ability to play a more global role.

EAST ASIA: MULTIPLE STRATEGIC FUTURES

Surging economic growth, dramatic power shifts, nationalism, and aggressive military modernization—not just in China but India and elsewhere—have amplified rather than diminished tensions and competition among the rising powers and with Japan. Owing to the unusual nature of the post-World War II settlement in Asia—and the persistence of conflicts on the Korean Peninsula and Taiwan Strait as a result of that settlement—historical grievances have festered and intensified in Asia. Fear of Chinese power, growing nationalism across the region, and possible questions about US staying power will fuel these tensions over the coming decades. Economic growth and interdependence have not diminished Asians' grievances, as seen in the difficult relations today between Japan-China, Japan-Korea, China-Korea, India-China and Vietnam-China.

Regional trends probably will continue to pull countries in two directions: toward China economically but toward the United States and each other for security. Since 1995, Asian powers — including Japan, Korea, Australia, and India—have gradually swapped the United States for China as their top trading partner but have coupled growing economic interdependence with the continued "insurance" of close US security ties. This pattern is likely to continue through 2030, although political liberalization in China—such as rule of law and more transparency on its military modernization program—would likely assuage security concerns in ways that would make the regional "hedge" less necessary. Better-than-expected Chinese economic growth and Beijing's ability to manage the challenging transition to an innovation-and-consumer-based economy could increase Beijing's magnetic pull on regional trade and investment, increasing China's status as the leading provider of Asian foreign direct investment.

Alternatively, a serious or prolonged Chinese economic slump could take the steam out of China's regional clout and reinforce latent fears about the potential regional implications of internal unrest there. Other important variables include the potential for a unified Korea and a subsequent strategic alignment away from the US.

"Regional trends probably will continue to pull countries in two directions: toward China economically but toward the United States and each other for security."

As global economic power has shifted to Asia, the Indo-Pacific is emerging as the dominant international waterway of the 21st century, as the Mediterranean was in the ancient world and the Atlantic in the 20th century. US naval hegemony over the world's key sea lanes, in this and other oceans, will fade as China's blue-water navy strengthens. This could beg the question of which power is best-positioned to construct maritime coalitions to police the commons and secure universal freedom of passage.

At the macro level, four broad pathways for Asian order are possible during the coming decades:

1. A continuation of the **present order** that mixes rules-based cooperation and quiet competition within a regional framework structured around existing alignments sustained by US leadership. Continued US maritime preeminence and the US alliance system sustain a security order in which China's "militarization," North Korea's nuclear mischief, and other potential security dilemmas in Asia are mitigated

by the preponderance of power enjoyed by the United States and its allies, thereby deterring aggressive action by Beijing or Pyongyang. Asian institutions continue to develop roots and economic integration continues to be oriented around a Pacific rather than an exclusively Asian axis.

2. A **balance-of-power order** of unconstrained great power competition fueled by dynamic shifts in relative power and a reduced US role. A US retreat into isolationism or economic decline would lead to the weakening of Washington's alliance commitments in East Asia and its willingness to remain the region's security guarantor. Such a regional order would be "ripe for rivalry." Some Asian powers might develop and seek to acquire nuclear weapons as the only means of compensating for less US security.

3. A **consolidated regional order** in which an East Asian community develops along the lines of Europe's democratic peace, with China's political liberalization a precondition for such a regional evolution. Such a pathway for regional order presumes that Asian regionalism will develop in a pluralistic way that preserves the autonomy of smaller Asian states. A pluralistic and peace-loving East Asian community might require the continued role of the United States as the region's security guarantor.

4. A **Sinocentric order** centered on Beijing that sustains a different kind of East Asian community on the basis of China's extension of a sphere of influence across the region. An Asian system in which China sat at the summit of a hierarchical regional order presumes that Asian institution-building develops along closed lines of Asian exclusivity, rather than through the open transpacific regionalism that has been the dominant impulse behind Asian community-building since the early 1990s.

NUMEROUS WILD CARDS

Should India fail to rise or Japan temper its relative decline, the Sinocentric order become more likely. Should the United States' core Asian partners possess less capability or willingness to balance Chinese power themselves, the US may need to step up involvement as a counterbalance, risking a direct contest with China.

Chinese weakness is perhaps the biggest uncertainty. If Beijing fails to transition to a more sustainable, innovation-based economic model, it will remain a top-tier player in Asia, but the influence surrounding what has been a remarkable ascendance will dissipate. In an extreme case, China would collapse with deep divisions opening up between rich coastal area and the impoverished interior and also growing separatism in China's far-flung areas of Tibet and Xinjiang. Under these circumstances, China may become a more unpredictable or even highly aggressive power with the leadership trying to divert attention away from its domestic problems. A conflict with one of its neighbors and/or the US that China lost could also puncture its standing. On the other hand, a victory would increase the chances of a Sinocentric order.

EUROPE: TRANSFORMING ITSELF

By most any measure—GDP, trade volume, number of transnational companies, or technological capabilities—Europe will remain, in the aggregate, a great power in 2030. The key question is whether it will punch its collective weight in the future. The stakes are high both politically and economically—and Europe's future is very uncertain.

Even before the recent unprecedented sovereign debt crisis, the conflicting forces of fragmentation and integration made Europe an inherently unpredictable actor. Constructed as a union of "peoples," the EU has not aimed at merging European peoples into a single identity. The euro zone crisis has laid bare the tensions and divisions between member states and, for the first time in decades, raised fundamental questions about Europe's future. Although there is no consensus on the region's future shape or role, our experts agree that it will not resemble today's Europe.

On top of the current crisis, the European economy is suffering from enormous structural woes. Productivity has been declining vis-à-vis other developed economies in the last 15 years, spending on R&D remains low,

European governments have grown very large relative to their economies, and demographic trends point to a shrinking labor force as well as increased age imbalance between active and non-active citizens.

Because the euro zone lacks many of the features economists deem necessary to a well-functioning optimal currency area (including labor mobility, fiscal transfers, similar economic culture, and solidarity), the first decade of the euro has seen considerable divergence in the economies of the core euro zone and its periphery. The former generally thrived while the latter experienced massive capital influx leading to market bubbles while losing competitiveness, which led to sovereign debt crises. Beginning in 2010, euro zone leaders have been introducing reforms and new instruments to address the crisis, but more integration probably will be required to overcome the crisis and address structural problems. A genuine "leap forward" in integration would imply massive transfers of sovereignty to central authorities, with the accompanying loss of autonomy which is increasingly unpopular with European publics. Popular feelings against the EU have gained traction with populist anti-EU parties gaining strength even in traditionally pro-EU member states. Economic logic—which argues for more integration—conflicts with the logic of those publics who want to hold onto separate national affiliations and limit greater integration.

Below we outline three scenarios for Europe and its international role in 2030:

A *Collapse* scenario has a low probability of occuring but would entail very high international risks. In this scenario, domestic firms and households respond to indications of an imminent currency regime change by rapidly accelerating withdrawal of euro deposits from domestic financial institutions. Following contagion to other member states and economic damage to the core countries, the euro would be the first casualty. The EU as an institution would be a likely collateral victim because the single market and freedom of movement across Europe would be jeopardized by the reinstatement of capital and border controls. Under such a scenario, severe economic dislocation and political fracture would lead to a breakdown in civil society. If the collapse were sudden and unexpected, it would very likely trigger a global recession or another Great Depression.

"Even before the recent unprecedented sovereign debt crisis, the conflicting forces of fragmentation and integration made Europe an inherently unpredictable actor."

In a *Slow Decline* scenario, Europe manages to escape from the worst aspects of the current crisis, but fails to undertake the necessary structural reforms. As member states endure years of low economic growth, they stick together in order to avoid major political and economic disruptions. EU institutions hang on, but public discontent remains high. The euro survives, but it does not become a rival to the dollar or the renminbi. Given years of low economic growth, Europe's international presence is diminished; countries re-nationalize their foreign policies.

Our third scenario, *Renaissance,* is based on the familiar pattern of crisis and renewal, which Europe has experienced many times in the past. After staring at the abyss, most European leaders agree on a "federalist leap." Publics support such a step, given the imminent risks involved maintaining the status quo. A more federal Europe might begin with only a core group of euro zone countries with some choosing to opt out or adopt a wait-and-see policy. Over time, despite the existence of a multispeed Europe, the single market would still be completed and a more united foreign and security policy agreed upon with enhanced elements of European democracy. European influence would increase, strengthening Europe's role and that of multilateral institutions on the world stage.

SUB-SAHARAN AFRICA: TURNING A CORNER BY 2030?

Many African countries have the opportunity to greatly advance while others are likely to be left behind, creating a more diverse Africa in 2030. African countries will be able to choose from the best-proven approaches and technologies in the developed world without needing to adapt and reform legacy systems, but rent-seeking, patronage, populism, and corruption may tempt many and challenge long-term planning. Elections are now frequent in Africa, but the quality and rooting of democracy is often shallow and subject to regression.

The megatrends of population growth without aging, rapid urbanization, and, to some extent, middle class expansion will significantly shape the trajectories of most African countries and at least a few—particularly in the climate change-threatened Sahel and Sahara regions—will be sharply challenged by resource scarcities. With other regions rapidly aging, increasingly a disproportionate number of Africans will make up the global working age population. However, the trend of individual empowerment will only slowly be evidenced in the most impoverished regions, and Africa will be catching up to the world in introduction of existing and new technologies.

Countries that improve governance and management of their economies will harness higher productivity from relatively youthful and urban populations, spurring economic growth. New technologies, legal frameworks, and trade and investment incentives can lead to more efficient food and energy production and water and resource management. Governments that do not respond to demographic change and meet popular expectations face increased destabilization, criminality, and emigration—particularly by the most skilled. Education will be a game-changer for those African countries that not only offer nominally widespread schooling but ensure that qualified teachers are in classrooms—currently lacking across the continent. Providing electricy and building infrastructures, creating better and more stable policy regimes, raising the skill levels of workers, maintaining security, opening space for private sector development and entrepreneurship, and closing opportunities for corruption will also be critical.

Commodity-exporting countries need to be wary that increased volatility in global markets is probably ahead and will challenge their fiscal viability and stability

RUSSIA: POTENTIAL GLOBAL FUTURES

Russia's role in the world during the next two decades will be shaped by the rising challenges it faces at home as well as in the global environment. Russia's economy is its Achilles' heel. Its budget is heavily dependent on energy revenue; efforts to modernize the economy have made little progress; and its aging of the workforce will be a drag on economic growth.

Russia's population is projected to decline from almost 143 million in 2010 to about 130 million in 2030. Although Russia's fertility rate is similar to that of many European countries and aging populations are also a drag of European economies, life expectancy is about 15 years lower for Russians than for Europeans: since 2007 the size of the Russian workforce has been declining and it will continue to do so for the next two decades.

However, Russia's greatest demographic challenge could well be integrating its rapidly growing ethnic Muslim population in the face of a shrinking ethnic Russian population. There are now about 20 million Muslims in Russia, comprising about 14 percent of the population. By 2030, that share is projected to grow to about 19 percent. Russia's changing ethnic mix already appears to be a source of growing social tensions.

To enhance its economic outlook, Russia will need to improve the environment for foreign investment and create opportunities for Russian exports of manufactured goods. Russia's entry into World Trade Organization (WTO) should provide a boost to these efforts and help Moscow to diversify the economy: by one estimate Russia's membership in the WTO could provide a substantial boost to the economy, adding 3 percent to GDP in the short term and 11 percent over the longer term.

Russia's relations with the West and China are also likely to be a critical factor in determining whether Russia moves toward becoming a more stable, constructive global player during the next two decades. We see three possibilities:

1. Russia could become more of a partner with others, most probably, in a marriage of convenience, not of values. Russia's centuries-long ambivalence about its relationship with the West and outside is still at the heart of the struggle over Russia's strategic direction.

2. Russia might continue in a more or less ambivalent relationship with the other powers, but over the next 20 years this path would likely be a more troublesome one for international cooperation if Russia rebuilds its military strength and must contend with an increasingly powerful China.

3. Russia could become a very troublesome country, trying to use its military advantage over its neighbors to intimidate and dominate. This outcome would be most likely if a Russian leader were facing rising public discontent over sagging living standards and darkening economic prospects and is looking to rally nationalist sentiments by becoming much more assertive in the Near Abroad.

if they do not work to diversify their economies. Technological advances in the developed world might reduce demand for African hydrocarbons and other minerals. The high petroleum prices of recent years enjoyed by oil-dependent economies such as Angola and Nigeria might not continue. On the other hand, Africa was largely insulated from the shock of recent international financial crises because African borrowing from private lenders is limited.

The diffusion of power in the international system toward multipolarity is unlikely to give Africa a much stronger voice in global forums by 2030, given its weaker economic weight in the international system. Global powers will most likely be less able to forge consensus to address African crises if the United States and Europe are less able to assert leadership and provide assistance. Consequently, Africa will need to become more independently able to address regional threats. Opportunities exist to strengthen the African Union and subregional organizations to this end.

Africa will be at risk of conflict and increased violence as development proceeds unevenly among and within African countries. Most African states already face moderate-to-high threats of instability but improved governance, resource management, and economic diversification offer the chance to move to more stable ground. The Sahel region, Congo/DROC, and Somalia will be the most vulnerable and challenged to improve governance and resource management. In some instances, individual empowerment and disillusionment with the unmet promises of modern democracy, education, and medicine will highlight ethnic and religious divisions at the expense of national unity. Beyond traditional conflict, criminal networks and extremist groups will be able to expand their reach within countries and across borders if the capabilities of national governments do not keep pace.

Despite the strides toward greater stability in Sub-Saharan Africa, substantial outside humanitarian and economic assistance will be needed to ensure these continuing conflicts do not spill over into broader regional and global conflagrations.

LATIN AMERICA: MORE PROSPEROUS BUT INHERENTLY FRAGILE

Latin America and the Caribbean have undergone far-reaching change during the past decade, including sustained economic growth and a reduction in poverty. The greater integration of the Americas through free trade agreements (FTAs) with the North American Free Trade Agreement (NAFTA) has expanded to multiple regional and extra-regional FTAs, especially by Canada, Chile, Colombia, Mexico, and Peru. With annual real GDP growth averaging 4 percent, the ranks of the middle classes have swelled, along with greater economic and political participation by women, indigenous peoples, and minority groups, many of whom have benefited from greater access to education and health services. However, the distribution of these political and economic benefits remains uneven across Latin America and the Caribbean, even though income inequality has been reduced in recent years.

Other trends, such as the spread of criminal violence associated with drug trafficking and criminal gangs have hurt the region. Two primary factors, one external and the other internal, will drive the economic growth rate and quality of life in Latin America over the next 18 years. The first factor is the pace of world economic growth, which affects the demand for Latin American commodities, goods, labor and other services. China has led in ramping up demand for Latin American commodities to the point that many experts in Brazil and elsewhere worry about an overdependence on commodity exports. Cheap Chinese imports have also undercut the competitiveness of industrial goods, and some of our interlocutors worry about the future of the manufacturing sector.

The second key factor is the extent to which Latin American countries position themselves to capture potential economic gains through investments in education, market-opening reforms, and enhanced rule of law and governing capacity. Assuming that average GDP growth in the region declines to 3.5 with the lower global growth projections, aggregate Latin American GDP will total $9 trillion by 2030, possibly approaching half the size of the US economy. Given reduced population growth rates, Latin America's per capital income could reach $14,000—almost 50 per cent more than current levels. At the same time, the emergence of an even larger middle class in Latin America will fuel additional political and economic expectations with which governments must be prepared to cope.

Under more adverse global circumstances, vulnerabilities in some Latin American countries could generate strategically significant crisis if stability is jeopardized amid spiking insecurity and transnational criminal activity; institutions are undermined by populist politics; and integration, trade, and growth drop precipitously with the contagion spreading more broadly throughout the region. In such a scenario, outside actors such as the US may be confronted with a range of politically and economically costly dilemmas that impose substantial trade-offs for the United States' and others' abilities to cope with emergencies in Latin America and elsewhere. Natural disasters—frequent already in Central America and the Caribbean—could have fundamental stability implications in a weaker global economic environment.

Even in the case of a relatively robust global economy, subregions such as Central America and Caribbean will find it harder to cope with security and governance challenges. Rising food and fuel costs are likely to add further strain on the more fragile governance structures in Central America and the Caribbean. In recent years, Mexican drug cartels have increasingly used Central America for transshipment, which also undermines governance and rule of law. Unlike elsewhere in the region, Central America's lack of competitiveness and continuing sole reliance on US markets means that its economy has not grown at the rate it needs to to attract investment and generate jobs for its large youth population.

Brazil will play an outsized role on the region's future. Its resources and scale could offer benefits and insulation others lack. However, the country could be challenged if global trade and growth declines, instability grows on its periphery, megacities are overwhelmed by crime and infrastructure strain, and there is no greater investment in education. The environment could play a critical role in Brazil's fortunes during the next 15-20 years—the Amazon Basin produces about 20 percent of the Earth's fresh water flows into the oceans and has a major impact on global weather. An Amazon die-back or deforestation could alter the region's water cycle in a way that would devastate Brazilian and much of Argentinian agriculture. Recent models suggest a die-back tipping point could be when deforestation reaches 20 percent; it presently stands at 18 percent.

Economic growth in emerging market countries will stimulate increased technological innovation around the world during the next 15-20 years.

A shift in the technological center of gravity from West to East and South, which has already begun, almost certainly will continue as the flows of companies, ideas, entrepreneurs, and capital from the developed to the developing markets increase. During the next 15-20 years, more technological activity is likely to move to developing world as multinationals focus on the fastest-growing emerging markets and as Chinese, Indian, Brazilian, and other emerging-economy corporations rapidly become internationally competitive. The speed of this movement will depend on the availability of risk capital in the developing countries, rules of law to protect intellectual property rights, and the desire of developing-economy companies to grow and be globally competitive.

Four technology arenas will shape global economic, social, and military developments by 2030: information technologies, automation and manufacturing technologies, resource technologies, and health technologies.

Information technology is entering the big data era. Process power and data storage are becoming almost free; networks and the cloud will provide global access and pervasive services; social media and cybersecurity will be large new markets.

Automation and advanced manufacturing technologies are changing the business model of mass production and how future products and services will be delivered to the increasingly important middle classes in both developed and developing countries. Asian manufacturing enterprises have already built the competencies to develop novel automation and advanced manufacturing applications from their current capabilities, and they are poised to dominate many emerging markets, like China has recently done in photovoltaic panels.

Technological breakthroughs pertaining to the security of **vital resources** will be necessary to meet the food, water, and energy needs of the world's population. Key technologies likely to be at the forefront in this arena will include genetically modified crops, precision agriculture, water-irrigation techniques, solar energy, advanced bio-based fuels, and enhanced oil and natural gas extraction via fracturing (see box on page 35).

" . . . a shift in the technology center of gravity from West to East and South . . . almost certainly will continue . . . "

Last but not least, new **health technologies** will continue to extend the average age of populations around the world, ameliorate debilitating physical and mental conditions, and improve overall well-being.

INFORMATION TECHNOLOGIES

During the next 15-20 years, the hardware, software, and connectivity aspects of IT will experience massive growth in capability and complexity as well as more widespread diffusion. This growth and diffusion will present significant challenges for governments and societies, which must find ways to capture the benefits of new IT technologies while dealing with the new threats that those technologies present.

Three technology developments with an IT focus have the power to change the way we will live, do business, and protect ourselves before 2030: solutions for storage and processing large quantities of data, social networking technologies, and "smart cities" encompassing a host of urban technologies enabled by enhanced and secure IT systems. Advances in data storage and analysis herald a coming economic boom in North America; advances in a host of urban technologies will be shaped by the giant investments in smart-cities infrastructures in the developing world.

Technology Focus	Current Status	Potential for 2030	Issues	Impact
Data Solutions	Large data sorting and analysis is applied in various large industries, but the quantity of data accumulating is outstripping the ability of systems to leverage it efficiently.	As software and hardware developments continue, new solutions will emerge to allow considerably more data to be collected, analyzed and acted on.	The greatest areas of uncertainty are the speed with which big data can be usefully and securely utilized by organizations.	Opportunities for commercial organizations and governments to "know" their customers better will increase. These customers may object to the collection of so much data.
Social Networking	Large numbers of people have embraced social networking and found innovative uses of the networks.	Social networks will evolve as new uses are found.	Service providers must find successful business models to support their growth. Network users have to make tradeoffs between privacy and utility.	Social networks enable both useful and dangerous communications across diverse user groups and geopolitical boundaries.
Smart City Technologies	The IT components of a smart city are today poorly integrated and not very efficient.	New and developing cities will have installed semi-integrated IT infrastructures to sustain the myriad of services they provide.	Only an integrated system can maximize the full value of smart city visions. The scale, complexity and high costs of implementing such a system may be too expensive for most cities.	Gains are huge in terms of improved quality of life, increased commercial activity, and lower resource consumption.

DATA SOLUTIONS

Data solutions comprise a range of emerging technologies that help organizations accumulate, store, manage, and extract value from "big data"—extremely large data sets that are difficult to manage using conventional tools. On the one hand, new solutions for data storage and processing could help policymakers address difficult economic and governance problems, enable more intuitive and humanlike interaction with computers, enhance the accessibility and usability of knowledge, and greatly improve the accuracy of predictive models. On the other hand, advanced data solutions could become a channel for information overload, a tool of oppressive governments, a high-maintenance burden that is nevertheless necessary for ubiquitous infrastructures, and a battleground for multipolar information warfare.

Current applications of data solutions are already important to commerce, large-scale scientific efforts, and government services, including intelligence and law enforcement. For example, large retailers use data solutions to fuse information about their customers' in-store spending habits, credit histories, web-surfing histories, social network postings, demographic information, and so on. From such fusion, data solutions allow retailers to extract valuable insights about their customers' preferences, allowing for very precisely targeted advertising, among other things.

Retailers and other businesses also commonly use data solutions technologies for supply-chain management and logistics. Internet companies are also heavy users of data solutions technologies, which are essential to enabling web search, targeted advertising, image recognition, language translation, natural language processing, and similar features and functions. Scientific applications of data solutions include weather prediction, physics research, and space exploration, with the potential for new domains including computational ecology.

Government services rely on very large databases and information-delivery systems and are beginning to use data solutions to fuse those databases and systems. Government collectors, who are major customers and users of advanced large-scale IT systems, currently handle some of the largest, most unstructured, and most heterogeneous data sets. Current data solutions rely on conventional computation, but quantum computing is a technology wild card that could begin to have an impact by 2030, with implications for basic scientific discovery, search, and cryptography. Formidable technical challenges remain, but progress by several different routes has occurred.

Since modern data solutions have emerged, big data sets have grown exponentially in size. At the same time, the various building blocks of knowledge discovery, as well as the software tools and best practices available to organizations that handle big data sets, have not kept pace with such growth. As a result, a large—and very rapidly growing—gap exists between the amount of data that organizations can accumulate and organizations' abilities to leverage those data in a way that is useful. Ideally, artificial intelligence, data visualization technologies, and organizational best practices will evolve to the point where data solutions

ensure that people who need the information get access to the right information at the right time—and don't become overloaded with confusing or irrelevant information. How rapidly—or even whether—such an evolution occurs is highly uncertain.

"Fear of the growth of an Orwellian surveillance state may lead citizens . . . to pressure their governments to restrict or dismantle big data systems."

Equally uncertain is the way in which governments or individuals will shape the future growth of data solutions. Fear of the growth of an Orwellian surveillance state may lead citizens, particularly in the developed world, to pressure their governments to restrict or dismantle big data systems. Similarly, individuals' distaste for overly intrusive advertising that exploits personal details may lead to a backlash against many kinds of commercial uses of data solutions technologies. On the other hand, the governments of many authoritarian countries probably will try to use big data systems to further control opposition forces.

SOCIAL NETWORKING TECHNOLOGIES

Today's social networking technologies help individual users form online social networks with other users, based on factors that can include shared interests, common backgrounds, relationships, geographic locations, and so on. In many respects, social networks are becoming part of the fabric of online existence, as leading services integrate social functions into everything else an individual might do online. The kinds of networks and interactions that social network services foster varies greatly. In many cases, members have developed uses for their social network services that go far beyond what the service providers themselves may have intended. Innovative uses for such services range from controlling home appliances remotely to managing restaurant reservations in real time, and analysts widely cite Twitter (along with other social network services) as having been a significant contributor to the Arab Spring protests. Protestors used social network services to organize themselves, disseminate information, and bypass government censorship efforts. Some governments are already deploying aggressive countermeasures, while simultaneously using social networks as a means of gathering information on dissidents. Social networking technologies could allow groups of people to easily communicate outside traditional media and government channels in order to pursue progressive, disruptive, and criminal agendas that can have impact across geopolitical boundaries.

Because social networking technologies are becoming the fabric of online existence, they could become an important tool for providing corporations and governments with valuable information about individuals and groups, facilitating development of robust human social predictive models that can have applications ranging from targeted advertising to counterterrorism. Social networks could also displace services that existing corporations and government agencies now provide, substituting instead new classes of services that are inherently resistant to centralized oversight and control. For example, social networks could help drive the use of alternative and virtual monetary currencies.

A significant uncertainty regarding the future development of social networking technologies involves the complex tradeoffs that users must make between privacy and utility. In general, the more open one is on a social network service, the more utility the service can provide. Thus far, users seem to have voted overwhelmingly in favor of utility over privacy, but future events might make large numbers of users change their preferences, thereby depriving social network services of the information they need to stay relevant to users. Another significant uncertainty involves the business of social networking itself. Historically, social network services have been relatively short lived, as users have tired of one service and flocked to another or as service providers have failed to develop ways to make money and grow. Facebook has emerged as the dominant social network worldwide, with nearly a billion users, but its continued dominance during the next 15-20 years (or even the next five) is not guaranteed. The dominant

social networks of the future may not even be formal organizations, but rather anarchic collectives built on sophisticated variants of peer-to-peer file-sharing technologies, against which developed- and many developing-world governments might have no meaningful negotiating leverage. However, the Chinese Government and several others will likely severely restrict any services that threaten their control over information flow.

SMART CITIES

Smart cities are urban environments that leverage information technology-based solutions to maximize citizens' economic productivity and quality of life while minimizing resource consumption and environmental degradation. In smart cities, advanced IT capabilities are the foundation of urban planning, governance, resource-management, physical infrastructure, communications infrastructure, building design, transportation systems, security services, emergency services, and disaster response systems. Many of those capabilities deliver maximum value only in the context of an integrated system. For example, emerging "city dashboard" solutions provide city managers with real-time comprehensive situational awareness of the state of their cities. City dashboards integrate data from a wide range of sources distributed throughout the city, potentially including cameras and distributed sensor arrays that monitor the health of critical infrastructures such as transportation and power and water supplies. Dashboards will also provide valuable insights and input for modeling and simulation activities that can help cities grow more smoothly. Smart city technologies also support and are connected to private infrastructures. For example, citizens will increasingly interact with smart city infrastructure via their smartphones, which are already beginning to see use as sensor platforms to feed data back into smart city systems.

"Such an approach could allow for the most effective possible deployment of new urban technologies—or create urban nightmares, if new technologies are not deployed effectively."

Governments around the world, especially in developing countries, could spend as much as $35 trillion in public-works projects in the next two decades. To do so in a manner that maximizes sustainability, quality of life, and economic competitiveness they will need a mix of novel approaches to security, energy and water conservation, resource distribution, waste management, disaster management, construction, and transportation. These areas represent massive market opportunities for information technology, systems-integration, and sustainable-technology providers and integrators—to ensure that the megacities develop. Some of the world's future megacities will essentially be built from scratch, enabling a blank-slate approach to infrastructure design and implementation. Such an approach could allow for the most effective possible deployment of new urban technologies—or create urban nightmares, if new technologies are not deployed effectively. Most megacities will need to integrate new technologies and approaches into existing physical, social, and government infrastructures, a process that may not always yield good results—or may not happen at all. In any event, for both cities built from scratch and cities needing to integrate new technologies into existing infrastructures, the major challenges will be the enormous scale, complexity, and costs of new technologies. With this heavy investment in smart-city infrastructure in African, Latin American, and especially Asian urban centers, the epicenter of smart-city innovation will begin by 2030 to move away from Europe and North America.

AUTOMATION AND MANUFACTURING TECHNOLOGIES

As manufacturing has gone global in the last two decades, a global ecosystem of manufacturers, suppliers, and logistics companies has formed. New manufacturing and automation technologies such as additive manufacturing (3D printing) and robotics have the potential to change work patterns in both the developing and developed worlds. However, relative to existing trends, any transition may be relatively slow. In developed countries these technologies have the potential to improve productivity, address labor constraints, and diminish the need for outsourcing, especially if reducing the length of supply chains brings clear benefits. Nevertheless, such technologies could still have a similar effect to outsourcing in making more low- and semi-skilled manufacturing workers in developed economies redundant, which would exacerbate domestic inequalities. For developing economies, particularly Asian ones, the new technologies will stimulate new manufacturing capabilities and further increase the competitiveness of manufacturers and suppliers.

ROBOTICS

Robotics is in use in a range of civil and military applications today. Robotic systems perform physical manipulations similar to humans; such manipulations are programmable and can be carried out autonomously or by teleoperation. Robots have better sensory and mechanical capabilities than humans do, making them ideal for routine tasks. Industrial robots have transformed many manufacturing environments; over 1.2 million industrial robots are already in daily operation around the world. Home robots vacuum homes and cut lawns; hospital robots patrol corridors and distribute supplies; the US military has thousands of robots operating on battlefields; and a new generation of robots is emerging for service-sector applications, including cleaning, public relations, and maintenance.

Developers are extending the capabilities of robots, crossing the boundary between industrial robots and nonindustrial robots. Although much development is still required to improve robots' cognitive abilities, many of the building blocks for futuristic and highly disruptive systems could be in place by 2030. Such robotics could eliminate the need for human labor entirely in some manufacturing environments, with

Technology Focus	Current Status	Potential for 2030	Issues	Impact
Robotics	Robotics is already in wide use in defense and manufacturing.	Robotics will eliminate human labor in some applications. Blurring between industrial and service robots will occur.	Researchers must reduce the cost of robots and improve their intelligence. As robots spread they will face much greater public scrutiny.	Total automation may become more cost effective than using large levels of labor or outsourcing to developing countries.
Remote and Autonomous Vehicles	Remote and autonomous vehicles are in use in defense and mining and exploration.	UAVs will routinely monitor intrastate and interstate conflicts, enforce no-fly zones and survey national borders.	Ensuring autonomous vehicles operate safely and reliably in populated areas will be crucial.	Increased disruption is possible from terrorists' use of UAVs.
Additive Manufacturing/3D Printing	Additive manufacturing is in use for creating models and for rapid prototyping in the automotive and aerospace industries.	Additive manufacturing begins to replace some conventional mass-produced products, especially high value products.	Material quality and cost are the limiting factors for the acceptance of additive manufacturing by industry.	Both advanced and developing economies will benefit from the flexibility, speed, and customization of additive manufacturing.

total automation becoming more cost effective than outsourcing manufacturing to developing economies. Even in developing countries, robots might supplant some local manual labor in sectors such as electronics, potentially holding down local wages.

The military is expected to increase its use of robots to reduce human exposure in high-risk situations and environments as well as the number of troops necessary for certain operations. The ability to deploy such robots rapidly, for particular tasks, could help military planners address the wider resource demands present in a more fragmented, multipolar world. Health-care and elder-care robots will become more autonomous and be able to interact with humans. However, they will be able to perform only specialized functions such as surgical support or certain tasks to

assist with daily living. Robotics addresses some of the impacts of an aging society, but in the next 20 years the effect is likely to be most pronounced in specific countries like Japan and South Korea.

Cost is both a driver and barrier to the implementation of robotics technologies. Robots are often expensive to buy, but their ability to repeat tasks efficiently and quickly, reduce waste, or minimize labor costs can save companies money. Manufacturers could lease expensive robots to users, but the cost per unit must decrease significantly before widespread applications emerge. Technology development is the biggest single constraint for nonindustrial robotics, because researchers must overcome major barriers in the development of robots' intelligence, including their understanding of the world around them, coping with unanticipated events, and interacting with humans. Nevertheless, with many enabling technologies now available off the shelf, a new generation of developers and enthusiasts may be able to construct new robotic products, some with potentially dangerous capabilities. Many of these non-industrial applications will be conceived and commercialized initially in today's developed countries, but such applications will face unprecedented scrutiny by the media. The public's reaction also could affect the development of nonindustrial robotics.

"Health-care and elder-care robots will become more autonomous and be able to interact with humans. However, they will be able to perform only specialized functions . . . "

AUTONOMOUS VEHICLES

Today, remote and autonomous vehicles are mostly in use in the military and for specific industrial tasks in remote locations. Mining companies are using remote and/or autonomous vehicles to improve safety, reduce cost, increase efficiency, and address skilled labor shortages. A remote vehicle refers either to remote-operated versions of traditional land, sea, and air vehicles, or to specialized mobile telerobotic platforms such as bomb-disposal robots and tethered submersibles. Remote vehicles are controlled using radiofrequency transmission or via a tether and incorporate electric or hydraulic actuators for manipulation, as well as cameras and other sensors for surveillance. Autonomous vehicles, which are mobile platforms that can operate without any direct human control, incorporate sensors and control software to orient the vehicle and avoid obstacles. Autonomous vehicles may also use radar or laser-based rangefinders to detect objects and data from global navigation satellite systems and geographic information systems to facilitate navigation and maneuvering.

Autonomous vehicles could transform military operations, conflict resolution, transportation, and geo-prospecting, while simultaneously presenting

novel security risks that could be difficult to address. Unmanned aerial vehicles (UAVs) are already being used to spy or launch missiles. By 2030, UAVs could be in common use to monitor intrastate and interstate conflicts, enforce no-fly zones, or survey national borders. Low-cost UAVs with cameras and other types of sensors could support wide-area geo-prospecting, support precision farming, or inspect remote power lines. Autonomous vehicles could spawn a new era of industrialization in mining and agriculture, addressing heightened demand from developing economies. Self-driving cars could begin to address the worsening congestion in urban areas, reduce roadway accidents and improve individuals' productivity (by allowing drivers the freedom to work through their commutes). Mass-transit innovations will likely emerge from the fastest-growing urban areas of Asia. Nevertheless, more disruption could result from terrorists' use of civilian UAVs as platforms to deliver explosives or unconventional weapons.

The key problem for autonomous vehicles—and, to some extent, remote vehicles—is the concern regarding whether such vehicles can operate safely and reliably, especially when operating in—or over—populated areas. For this reason, most regulatory agencies worldwide greatly restrict operation of UAVs in civilian airspace. Self-driving cars currently being tested on public roads still rely on an attentive human driver who can take the wheel at a moment's notice. An additional barrier for UAVs is the question of acceptance: Users appears to have had little trouble adapting to office-workplace telepresence robots, but facilitating a transition between human-piloted and autonomous vehicles may be more difficult.

"Autonomous vehicles could transform military operations, conflict resolution, transportation, and geo-prospecting, while simultaneously presenting novel security risks that could be difficult to address."

ADDITIVE MANUFACTURING

Additive manufacturing is a group of technologies that allows a machine to build an object by adding one layer of material at a time. Additive manufacturing, or 3D printing, is already in use to make models from plastics in sectors such as consumer products and the automotive and aerospace industries, but by 2030, additive manufacturing could replace some conventional mass-production, particularly for short production runs or where mass customization has high value. Additive machines use computer-aided design (CAD) and a computer-guided laser, extruder, or printer head to construct an object one layer at a time. They can generate geometrically complex objects, with internal cavities or moving parts inside an object, which traditional machines cannot manufacture. With additive manufacturing, manufacturers can avoid the high initial setup costs for specialty tooling and molds and can also build geometrically complex objects that cannot easily be fabricated by other means. The CAD file can be a laser scan of the surface of another object or a person or can even be medical data, such as computed tomography (CT) or magnetic resonance imaging (MRI) scans, which makes it possible to build objects in the shape and with the functionality of bones or internal organs.

A combination of low-cost machines and online stores of 3D object files could democratize manufacturing and empower individuals, resembling the early days of personal computers and the Internet, when small companies were able to make a large impact. Additive manufacturing could lead to large numbers of micro-factories akin to preindustrial revolution craft guilds, but with modern manufacturing capabilities. Such local micro-factories could manufacture significant amounts of products, especially those for which transportation costs are traditionally high or delivery times are long, and in the process shorten and simplify supply chains.

The developing world could be a major beneficiary because additive manufacturing allows products to be designed and printed for local consumption, reducing the reliance on expensive imports. Additive manufacturing could also level the playing field for those countries or organizations that missed out in earlier periods—because additive manufacturing requires less industrial infrastructure than conventional manufacturing. At the same time, additive manufacturing could reduce the need for some conventional manufacturing jobs in many regions of the world.

The relatively less sophisticated quality of the materials produced by additive manufacturing limits the acceptance of additive manufacturing by industry. The ability of developers to produce parts with sufficient strength in high volume and at low cost is still highly uncertain. Inexpensive 3D printing machines are now available for $500, but they produce relatively low-quality objects, suitable as novelties, but not yet viable for many applications. Industrial machines cost upwards of $30,000, and laser-based machines that make high-quality metal products can cost as much as $1 million. Some machines improve the performance of metal or ceramic objects, but greater knowledge and skill is required than for the objects that come out of cheaper 3D printing machines. Additive manufacturing is currently limited to structural components that have no electronic, optical, or other functional capabilities. By 2030, manufacturers may be able to combine some electrical components (such as electrical circuits, antennae, batteries, and memory) with structural components in one build, but integration with printed electronics manufacturing equipment will be necessary. Though printing of arteries or simple organs may be possible by 2030, bioprinting of complex organs will require significant technological breakthroughs.

RESOURCE TECHNOLOGIES

Technology advances will be required to accommodate increasing demand for resources owing to global population growth and economic advances in today's underdeveloped countries. Such advances can affect the food, water, and energy nexus by improving agricultural productivity through a broad range of technologies encompassing precision farming and genetically modified (GM) crops for food and fuel.

Technology Focus	Current Status	Potential for 2030	Issues	Impact
Food and Water				
GM Crops	Successful but limited applications are economically successful.	GM crop technology will expand the types of crops able to be modified and the traits able to be transferred to these crops.	Time to market for each transferred trait into each crop is the major hurdle. Many governments have reservations about the safety of GM crops.	GM crop deployments will enable higher yields and address climate-change driven food scarcities.
Precision Agriculture	Automation of equipment is suitable only for large-scale farming.	Feasible reductions in scale and price will enable greater application of automated systems and higher yields per hectare.	The cost of equipment and the scalability to small farms is the major barrier.	Major impact will be continued yield and quality improvements for large-scale agricultural operations in developed countries.
Water Management	Microirrigation techniques deliver water to roots with 90% efficiency.	Water demand will be high. Cheaper subsurface drip-irrigation together with precision agriculture is likely. Commercial drought-tolerant crops are a possibility.	Microirrigation will be too expensive for widespread use in developing countries.	Insufficient water supplies for residential, industrial and agricultural use will affect a large proportion of the world's population living in water-stressed areas.
Energy				
Bio-Based Energy	Technology of delivering energy from non-food biomass is proven but non-competitive.	Non-food biomass will be a growing alternative source for energy and chemical feedstocks.	Widespread deployment depends on government policies.	If cost-competitive, the technology would provide a useful alternative to fossil fuels.
Solar Energy	Photovoltaics has substantial growth potential, but has its limitations.	Advances in photovoltaics, storage technologies, and smart grid solutions needed for solar to be competitive with carbon-sourced energy production.	Research focuses on dealing with negative environmental consequences of the technology.	Successful extension of accessible natural gas and oil reserves will stymie arguments for aggressive climate-change mitigation strategies.

Technology Focus	Current Status	Potential for 2030	Issues	Impact
Disease Management	Molecular diagnostics technologies identify some disease predispositions or presence.	Genetic sequencing enables more personalized healthcare.	Costs per individual diagnostic tests must be reduced to enable widespread adoption.	Will lead to increased life quality, life expectancy, and aging societies.
Human Augmentation	Contemporary prosthetic limbs and exoskeletons provide limited functionality to users.	Fully functional limb replacements, enhanced eyesight, and hearing augmentations will be widely available.	Improved understanding of human, brain function, and enhanced portable power sources are necessary.	Very high technology costs could limit availability to the well off, professional athletes, and military.

New resource technologies can also enhance water management through desalination and irrigation efficiencies. In addition, they can increase the availability of energy, not only through highly successful enhanced oil and natural gas extractions resulting from use of hydraulic fracturing (see box on page 37), but also through alternative energy sources such as solar and wind power and biofuels. Widespread communication technologies will make the potential effects of these technologies on the environment, climate, and health well known to increasingly educated populations.

China, India, and Russia—countries that have critical needs for key resources—are expected to realize substantial rewards in being the first countries to commercialize next-generation resource technologies. Being first may allow private and state-owned Chinese, Indian, and Russian resource companies to establish strong global competitive positions. Aside from being cost competitive, any expansion or adoption of both existing and next-generation resource technologies during the next 15-20 years will largely depend on social acceptance and the direction and resolution of any ensuing political issues.

GENETICALLY MODIFIED CROPS

Genetically modified crops are key to meeting the challenge of providing sufficient and affordable food and fuel from plant crops for a world with an expanding population and a changing climate. The rapidly evolving genetic knowledge of plant cells, enabled by the tools of molecular biology, is likely to accelerate during the next 15-20 years, providing the means to increase the yield of major food crops. The promising results of ongoing research to relate key plant traits to a plant's genetic structure indicate that the application of modern molecular plant breeding and transgenic technologies have the potential to significantly enhance global food security in the next 15-20 years. However, this group of plant technologies faces some of the most intense regulatory and public pressures of any new technologies, which makes widespread adoption of any of these potential advances uncertain.

Advances in molecular biology applied to crop development have enabled scientists to identify genes that express important agronomic traits in crop plants. Transgenic technologies—which enable the transfer of genes from one plant species to another to produce a plant with new or improved traits—hold the most promise for achieving food security in the next 15-20 years.

Through transgenic technologies, researchers have identified hundreds of genes with corresponding useful traits in crop plants that could eventually be commercialized. However, in spite of the rapid growth of transgenic technology, only a few traits in three plant species exist on a commercial scale: herbicide- and insect-resistant soybeans, cotton, and maize. Modified potato crops are new additions to this list; in the next five years commercial plantings of genetically modified canola and rice are also likely. The development of nitrogen fixation by non-legume plants and drought-tolerant maize are examples of the goals and advances of scientists using today's GM crop technology know-how. Drought-tolerant maize received regulatory approval in 2012 and is in the beginning stages of commercialization.

"Transgenic technologies—which enable the transfer of genes from one plant species to another to produce a plant with new or improved traits—hold the most promise for achieving food security in the next 15-20 years."

Having the information about specific genes that combine to express desirable traits in crop plants is an essential starting point, but such knowledge does not necessarily lead to a modified plant that will express these genes. The R&D necessary to achieve such goals requires significant time and money. Similarly, meeting all the necessary regulatory requirements can result in many years of effort before a new GM crop reaches the market. Despite the regulatory approvals and safeguards achieved to date, many consumers and political representatives across the world are not persuaded that the dangers are minimal and that adequate safeguards are in place. Hence, GM crops face significant hurdles in the years ahead.

PRECISION AGRICULTURE

Precision agriculture holds promise for increasing crop yields by reducing the use of inputs such as seed, fertilizer, and water; minimizing the negative environmental impacts of farming, and improving the quality of crops. The development of cost-effective, versatile, and highly automated forms of precision agriculture suitable for a wide range of farm types and sizes could help provide worldwide food security even in the face of resource scarcities and environmental restrictions. Trends in precision agriculture point to increasing automation of farm vehicles and implements. Within the next five to 10 years, autonomous tractors probably will begin to take on a full range of roles in large-scale farming, which will begin to resemble automated manufacturing facilities. In 10-to-15 years, technological developments and the scale of manufacturing could drive down the size of today's autonomous farming vehicles and implements. The development of smaller farm vehicles would enable farmers to use them on small sections of a field and small land holdings, leading to higher-yield, higher-intensity cultivation. The key question is whether such systems will ever be affordable for use on small plots in developing countries where the greatest productivity gains are called for.

WATER MANAGEMENT

Water management will be critical to achieving global food security because agriculture today requires irrigation for 40 percent of its production and consumes approximately 70 percent of global freshwater supplies. Currently, agricultural irrigation wastes about 60 percent of the water withdrawn from freshwater sources.

Efficient water management will be required to sustain a necessary increase in agricultural productivity. Even though desalination technologies might be economically feasible for household and industrial water, such technologies are unlikely to produce irrigation water from saline waters at a low enough cost to be feasible for agricultural use. As water scarcity increases, adopting technologies that increase water-use efficiency will be the only option farmers will have for confronting global water scarcity. The array of such technologies includes precision agriculture and GM drought-tolerant and salt-tolerant crops as well as micro-irrigation systems and hydroponic greenhouse technologies.

"Micro-irrigation technology . . . is likely to be the key technology for improving agricultural water management because it delivers a highly water-efficient solution."

Micro-irrigation technology, which has advanced considerably over the last three decades, is likely to be the key technology for improving agricultural water management because it delivers a highly water-efficient solution. Although currently applied mainly to high-value vegetable crops, micro-irrigation is suitable for all types of crops. Using today's leading micro-irrigation technologies, the percentage of water delivered to a field is some 90 percent to 95 percent compared to 35-60 percent for furrow irrigation or 60-80 precent for sprinkler systems. Such efficiency comes at a cost, however (some $2,500-$5,000 per hectare over a 10-to-15-year lifetime).

Although rain-fed agriculture is responsible for 58 precent of global cereal grain production, relatively little effort has focused on applying technology to enhance its productivity. Rain-fed areas of the world are largely regions with poverty, malnutrition, water scarcity, severe land degradation, and poor physical and financial infrastructures. Well-established inexpensive practices—such as zero-till and mulching, which transfer more water to plants rather than losing it to evaporation—are not in widespread use. New technologies that contribute to improving the yield of rain-fed agriculture while reducing the need for withdrawal from surface water sources will become increasingly important. Agricultural leaders are considering harvesting water through managed underground storage.

An increased demand for water is likely to stimulate governments to adjust their water-pricing policies to encourage water efficiency: Farmers typically pay up to a tenth the price that industry and households pay for water; thus farmers have little incentive to save water. In spite of the high costs, increasing use of precision farming in irrigated land and, in time, higher yields from GM drought-tolerant crops in rain-fed land may contribute to increasing the overall efficiency of water use in agriculture.

BIO-BASED ENERGY

If bio-based energy becomes cost competitive, it could enable advanced biofuels and other products that derive from nonfood sources to at least partially replace current food-crop-derived biofuels and petroleum feedstocks in the next 15-20 years. A transition to bio-based energy produced from nonfood biomass would radically alter world energy markets and be essential to improving food security. The nearest-term advanced biofuel is cellulosic ethanol derived from various types of biomass from agricultural and forest residues, dedicated energy crops such as perennial grasses and trees, and municipal solid waste. Other biofuels that could enter the market include drop-in biofuels, which are easily integrated with existing transportation-fuel infrastructures. Biobutanol produced by fermentation and renewable hydrocarbons produced by algae and genetically engineered organisms are examples of such drop-in biofuels.

"A transition to bio-based energy produced from nonfood biomass would radically alter world energy markets and be essential to improving food security."

To avoid conflicting with food crop production, researchers are developing technologies that use nonfood biomass feedstocks. Although production costs are higher than ethanol production from corn, some large-scale cellulosic ethanol plants are on track to begin operations in the next few years. Biodiesel, which is currently derived from food plant oils, used cooking oils, and animal fats, has seen a rapid growth worldwide, especially in Europe. Research into algae-based technologies suggests that such technologies offer attractive benefits including high productivity; the productive use of nonarable land; the use of diverse water sources (fresh, saline, and wastewater); and the recycling of carbon dioxide and other wastes.

Achieving cost competitiveness for bio-based energy technologies is the primary hurdle for commercial success. Linked to that hurdle is the highly uncertain future pricing of fossil fuel sources of energy and wider use of battery transportation technology. In addition, consistent government financial support will be necessary for the development of bio-based energy technologies, which introduces another uncertainty for the long-term viability of the technologies. For example, the United States and the European Union have aggressive biofuel mandates that include sustainability mandates for reducing greenhouse gas emissions. Although some advanced biofuel technologies could meet these standards, costs are high and the technologies are not proven on a commercial scale.

SOLAR ENERGY

Solar energy, which has substantial growth potential, could disrupt the global energy environment if it achieves a competitive cost with electricity produced from other sources of energy. Because of government subsidies and rapidly declining costs, photovoltaic technology is now widely used for electrical power generation. China is already the leading manufacturer of photovoltaic panels.

Solar thermal technology can also generate electrical power by using mirrors to concentrate sunlight, which is converted to heat in a solar collector. The heat is transferred to a heat storage medium such as molten salt, which can be used for steam generation to produce electricity. Because heat can be stored less expensively than electricity, solar thermal technology can generate electricity when the sun is not shining.

However, whether solar-photovoltaic or solar-thermal electricity-generating plants will be cost competitive with other electricity-generating fuel sources—coal, natural gas, nuclear, or wind—is unclear. Some forecasts indicate that the projected costs of electricity production from natural gas and coal will remain lower than electricity production from solar power in the next 15-20 years. Other forecasts indicate that photovoltaic electricity production will be competitive with conventional electricity production without subsidization in the next five to 10 years. Meanwhile, during the next several decades, new, highly efficient natural gas electricity-generating plants are expected to come on line and increased natural gas supplies as a result of fracking technology will maintain low natural gas prices.

Despite its position as the most abundant renewable energy resource and its theoretical potential in many regions to exceed current total energy supply as well as its benign environmental consequences, solar energy faces some formidable hurdles to reach its full potential. If government policies to provide financial and regulatory incentives for solar energy disappeared as a result of strained government budgets, solar energy might not reach a cost-competitive position in the next two decades to be a serious competitor to electricity produced from coal and natural gas. Another hurdle facing solar energy is that it is an intermittent source, generating power only when the sun is shining. Without some efficient energy storage, such as large batteries or molten salt, solar energy will not be able to fully replace other energy-generating systems. Rather, it could only operate as a hybrid system relying on other energy sources, such as natural gas, to generate electricity when the sun is not shining. Additionally, widespread use of solar energy for distributed generation of electricity will require large grid-infrastructure investments to handle the multi-directional flow of electricity in the distribution network.

HEALTH TECHNOLOGIES

Disease management technologies in development promise significant healthy longevity gains throughout the world while human augmentation technologies will likely transform everyday life, particularly for the elderly and mobility-impaired populations.

The greatest gains in healthy longevity are likely to occur in those developing countries that will experience a huge growth in the size of their middle class populations. Although the current health-care systems of such countries may be poor, developing countries are expected to make substantial progress in the longevity potential of their populations by 2030. Indeed, many leading centers of innovation in disease management are likely to be in the East.

DISEASE MANAGEMENT

Disease management is the effective control and treatment of communicable and noncommunicable illnesses. Today, physicians struggle to differentiate between many illnesses with similar symptoms. Obtaining results from detection tests can take several days, leading to delays in diagnosis, which can be life threatening. Consequently, diagnostic and pathogen-detection devices will be key enabling technologies for disease management; the future accuracy of molecular diagnostics has the power to transform medicine. The targets of molecular diagnostics include genetic information on disease presence or predisposition, and the ability to monitor the physical manifestation of a disease. One enabling technology, DNA sequencing, is advancing rapidly with some techniques currently capable of reading a human genome for about $1,000.

Molecular diagnostic devices will revolutionize medicine by providing a rapid means of testing for both genetic and pathogenic diseases during surgeries. Readily available genetic testing will hasten disease diagnosis and help physicians decide on the optimal treatment for each patient. Such personalized medicine will reduce the health-care costs associated with physicians' prescribing ineffective drugs. In addition, the declining cost of such testing will facilitate the cataloguing of many more individuals' genetic profiles, which will lead to a greater understanding of the genetic basis of many diseases. Theranostics, the combination of a diagnostic and a therapeutic

approach in one treatment, may become an important discipline for disease management, reducing hospital costs by accelerating patients' recovery times and complications caused by invasive surgery. Advances in synthetic biology will likely result in production facilities making novel treatments and diagnostics agents. Advances in regenerative medicine almost certainly will parallel these developments in diagnostic and treatment protocols. For example, replacement organs, such as kidneys and livers, could be developed by 2030.

The new disease management technologies will increase the longevity and quality of life for the world's aging population, tipping the demographic profile of many countries toward an older (but healthy) population. However, improvements in disease management technologies could be out of reach of poor people in countries that do not have health coverage for all.

Cost is the major barrier preventing molecular diagnostic technologies from becoming routinely available in physician's surgeries, although costs for genetic sequencing are rapidly decreasing. The cost per individual diagnostic test is more important than the cost of the diagnostic equipment itself. A move away from expensive biological reagents to silicon-based molecular diagnostics procedures should reduce the costs of genetic tests further. The drawback of today's genetic profiling is that the number of known disease-related genes is insufficient to provide mass screening. Synergistic technologies such as computer processing power and big data storage and analysis will be important for managing the huge amounts of data gathered by genome sequencing. However, with computing technology still advancing at a high rate computer power should not be a rate-limiting factor. Acquiring governments' approval for diagnostic tests will delay their implementation.

HUMAN AUGMENTATION

Spanning a wide gamut of technologies, ranging from implants and prosthetics to powered exoskeletons, human augmentation enhances innate human abilities, or replaces missing or defective functions such as damaged limbs. Prosthetic limbs have now reached the stage where they offer equivalent or slightly improved functionality to human limbs. Brain-machine interfaces in the form of brain-implants are demonstrating that directly bridging the gap between brain and machine is possible. Military organizations are experimenting with a wide range of augmentation technologies, including exoskeletons that allow personnel to carry increased loads and psychostimulants that allow personnel to operate for longer periods.

Human augmentation could allow civilian and military people to work more effectively, and in environments that were previously inaccessible. Elderly people may benefit from powered exoskeletons that assist wearers with simple walking and lifting activities, improving the health and quality of life for aging populations. Successful prosthetics probably will be directly integrated with the user's body. Brain-machine interfaces could provide "superhuman" abilities, enhancing strength and speed, as well as providing functions not previously available.

"The high cost of human augmentation means that it probably will be available in 15-20 years only to those who are able to pay. Such a situation may lead to a two-tiered society . . . "

As replacement limb technology advances, people may choose to enhance their physical selves as they do with cosmetic surgery today. Future retinal eye implants could enable night vision, and neuro-enhancements could provide superior memory recall or speed of thought. Neuro-pharmaceuticals will allow people to maintain concentration for longer periods of time or enhance their learning abilities. Augmented reality systems can provide enhanced experiences of real-world situations. Combined with advances in robotics, avatars could provide feedback in the form of sensors providing touch and smell as well as aural and visual information to the operator.

Owing to the high cost of human augmentation, it probably will be available in 15-20 years only to those who are able to pay for it. Such a situation may lead to a two-tiered society of an enhanced and non-enhanced persons and may require regulation. In addition, the technology must be sufficiently robust to prevent hacking and interference of human augmentation. Advances in synergistic and enabling technologies are necessary for improved practicality of human augmentation technologies. For example, improvements in battery life will dramatically improve the practicality of exoskeleton use. Progress in understanding human memory and brain functions will be critical to future brain-machine interfaces, while advances in flexible biocompatible electronics will enable better integration with the recipient of augmentations and recreate or enhance sensory experiences. Moral and ethical challenges to human augmentation are inevitable.

GAME-CHANGER 6
THE ROLE OF THE UNITED STATES

How the US evolves over the next 15-20 years—a big uncertainty—will be among the most important variables in the future shape of the international order. The United States' relative economic decline vis-a-vis the rising states is inevitable and already occurring, but its future role in the international system is much harder to assess. The extent of US power in the system is important—in the short run because of the need for systemic public goods, especially security,, and in the longer run out to 2030 because of the growing uncertainties associated with rapid geopolitical change. Even in 2030, the transition to a multipolar world will not be complete; the world's ultimate shape is far from being predetermined.

An economically restored US would be a "plus" in terms of the capability of the international system to deal with major global challenges during this long transitional period. However, a strong US would not be able by itself to guarantee that the growing global challenges—particularly in this world of rapid power diffusion—were met. A weak and defensive US, on the other hand, would make it much harder for the international system to grapple with major global challenges.

STEADY US ROLE

The United States' dominant role in international politics has derived from its preponderance across the board in most dimensions of power, both "hard" and "soft." The United States' weight in the global economy has steadily lessened since the 1960s, but it has been dropping more rapidly since the early 2000s with the rise of China's place in the world economy. Nevertheless, the US remains among the world's most open, innovative, and flexible countries. Despite being home to less than five percent of the world's population, the US accounted for 28 percent of global patent applications in 2008 and is home to nearly 40 percent of the world's best universities. US

demographic trends are favorable compared to other advanced and some developing countries. US strength also derives from high immigrant inflows and the United States' unusual ability to integrate migrants.

US industry will also benefit from increased domestic natural gas production, which will lower energy costs for many manufacturing industries. Over time, the increased domestic energy production could reduce the US trade deficit because the US would be able to reduce energy imports and may be able to export natural gas and oil. Increased domestic energy production could boost employment at home.

"The multifaceted nature of US power suggests that even as its economic weight is overtaken by China—perhaps as early as the 2020s based on several forecasts—the US most likely will remain "first among equals" alongside the other great powers in 2030 . . . "

The multifaceted nature of US power suggests that even as its economic weight is overtaken by China—perhaps as early as the 2020s based on several forecasts—the US most likely will remain the "first among equals" alongside the other great powers in 2030 because of its preeminence across a range of power dimensions and legacies of its leadership. Nevertheless, with the rapid rise of multiple other powers, the "unipolar moment" is over and Pax Americana—the era of unrivalled American ascendancy in international politics that began in 1945—is fast winding down. The graphic on page 103 shows a snapshot of the relative power and factors underlying leading countries in 2030.

A DIFFERENT SETUP GOING FORWARD

The US faces stiff economic challenges—not as clearly foreseen before the 2008 financial crisis—which will require broad-based structural reform if it is to avoid a rapid decline in its economic position. Health care is expensive and inefficient: public and private health spending is 50 percent higher per capita than that of the next highest OECD country. As the population ages, these costs are expected to rise rapidly. Secondary education is weak, with 15 year-old American students ranking only 31st of 65 countries in mathematics and 22nd in science in a survey that includes many developing countries. The US educational advantage relative to the rest of the world has been cut in half in the past 30 years. Without large-scale improvements in primary and secondary education, future US workers—which have benefited from the world's highest wages—will increasingly bring only mediocre skills to the workplace.

"Without large-scale improvements in primary and secondary education, future US workers—which have benefited from the world's highest wages—will increasingly bring only mediocre skills to the workplace."

Income distribution in the US is considerably more unequal than in other advanced countries and is becoming more so. Although incomes of the top 1 percent of Americans have soared, median household incomes have declined since 1999. Social mobility is lower and relative poverty rates are higher in the US than in most other advanced countries. Despite its high productivity and competitiveness, the US cumulative current account deficit during the last 30 years was $8.5 trillion, a reflection of extremely low household savings rates and government deficits.

The context in which US global power has operated has changed dramatically: it is just not a matter of the United States' relative economic decline, but also of the West— Washington's historic partners. Most other Western states have also suffered a stiff downturn, while developing states are accounting for a larger share of the global economy. The post-World War II era was characterized by the G-7 countries—which were allies and partners—leading both economically and politically. US projection of power was dependent on and amplified by its strong alliances with Western partners, which were forged during an extensive

struggle with fascism and then communism. For example, Europe, through NATO, has historically provided Washington with many of its key coalition partners. Even before 2008, the pressures on European security capabilities were apparent and Europe had begun a substantial defense retrenchment.

Looking ahead, regardless of the various realistic economic growth scenarios one can construct, although strong transatlantic ties will remain an important US asset, the G-7 overall will account for a decreasing share of total global military spending. In a multispeed economic world in which the West continues to experience severe fiscal constraints— which is the most likely development for the foreseeable future—the trend toward an increasingly disproportionate share of military spending by the non-G-7 will grow. Although the US will remain the leading military power in 2030, the gap with others will diminish and its ability to depend on its historic alliance partnerships will diminish even further.

The US ability to maintain near-current levels of defense spending is open to serious question. The trend for national defense spending as a share of the US economy has been downward for several decades. The US devoted on average 7 percent share of GDP to national defense during the Cold War, which dropped to below 5 percent over the past decade, including expenditures on the wars in Iraq and Afghanistan. However, spending for major entitlement programs— particularly Social Security, Medicare, and Medicaid— has grown rapidly over the past several decades. As a result, it is difficult to reverse the historic trend or increase the share in the future in the absence of a major emergency. With an aging population and the prospect of higher interest rates in the future, the rising entitlement costs will consume an increasing proportion of the Federal budget without major reform of the programs or substantially increased tax revenues.[a]

---

[a] See Cindy Williams, "The Future Affordability of US National Security," unpublished paper, 28 October 2011. According to this study, putting federal budgets on a sustainable path will require shifting about 6 percent of GDP into revenues or out of spending relative to their likely current course, according to the Congressional Budget Office. One study believes that an affordable long-term level for national defense would be between 1.6 and 2.6 percent of GDP, well below current levels.

US POWER: LINCHPIN OF THE INTERNATIONAL SYSTEM

Element of Power	Present Status	Trendline	Factors
Economic	The US share of world GDP was largely steady until 2005. It is currently around 24 percent (market rate) of world GDP, which makes the US still the single country with the largest share.	But the US share of world GDP will continue to drop, and the US will be the world's second-largest economic power in PPP terms.	China and India are gaining ground at an unprecedented rate (the US rise in the 19th century was slower as measured by gains in world GDP).
Military	The US ability to maintain near-current levels of defense spending is open to serious question. The trend for national defense spending as a share of the US economy has been downward for several decades.	Spending for major entitlement programs makes it difficult to reverse the trend of decreasing military spending.	The G-7 overall will account for a decreasing share of total global military spending. Although the US will remain the leading military power in 2030, the gap with others will diminish and Washington's ability to depend on its historic alliance partnerships will diminish even further.
Political	The US remains preeminent, though the unipolar moment has passed.	There is no competing alternative to the Western liberal order, though many rising states want less US "hegemonic" behavior.	The potential for an overstretched US facing increased demands is greater than the risk of the US being replaced as the world's preeminent political leader.
S & T	The US remains the world's leader, but Washington has growing worries about declining educational and skill levels.	China's large, sustained investments could make it close to a peer competitor by 2030.	Technology is increasingly a networked and international enterprise. Leadership in key fields will increasingly entail working with international partners.
Soft Powers	US preponderance across hard and soft powers makes it unique among great powers.	The gap with others almost certainly will narrow, but China is unlikely to rival the US in soft power in 2030.	US ability to integrate outsiders will remain a key strength for attracting the world's best talent and ensuring S&T and economic leadership.

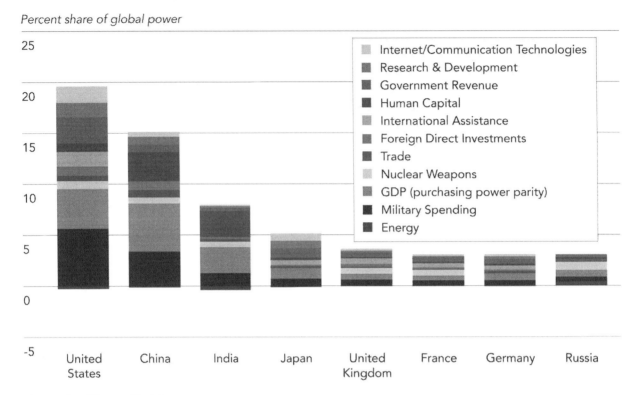

Percent share of global power

Legend:
- Internet/Communication Technologies
- Research & Development
- Government Revenue
- Human Capital
- International Assistance
- Foreign Direct Investments
- Trade
- Nuclear Weapons
- GDP (purchasing power parity)
- Military Spending
- Energy

Source: International Futures Model.

In other key domains, a similar pattern exists of a narrowing gap between the US and its competitors and between the West and the "rest." This pattern has implications for the United States' role and power in the world of 2030. The US will still be the world's S&T leader in 2030, but the gap with China, India and others will have shrunk. The US continues to have the biggest contingent of top-ranked universities while the number in Asia grows and Europe's share has diminished.

Under any scenario, the US will also have to contend with the growing diffusion of power, which would make it virtually impossible—as we stated in chapter one on the relative certainties—for any power to act hegemonically. Power has become more multifaceted—reflecting the diversity of issues— and more contextual— certain actors and power instruments are germane to particular issues. The United States' technological assets—including its leadership in piloting social networking and rapid communications—give it an advantage, but the

Internet has boosted even more the power of nonstate actors and been a key factor in the diffusion of power. In most cases, US power will need to be enhanced through relevant outside networks, friends, and affiliates that can be gathered on any particular issue. As mentioned earlier, leadership will increasingly be a function of position, enmeshment, diplomatic skill, and constructive demeanor.

MULTIPLE POTENTIAL SCENARIOS FOR THE UNITED STATES' GLOBAL ROLE

The degree to which the United States continues to dominate the international system could vary widely. Historically many such powers have played a dominant role long after their economic or even military weight has lessened in relation to others. The American economy surpassed Britain's in the late 19th century, but the US only assumed its global role during World War II. The legacy of US power—as chief architect of the post-WWII order—has a potentially long tail.

IS THERE AN ALTERNATIVE ORDER ON THE HORIZON?

The NIC sponsored several seminars with international relations experts to examine the world view of emerging powers and whether they were or would be seeking a fundamental transformation of the international order over the next couple decades. Many participants believe that today's emerging powers do not have a revisionist view of the world order along the lines offered by the Soviet Union, Imperial Japan, or Nazi Germany even though their relations with the US are ambiguous. Many emerging countries seek to use their ties with the US to advance their national interests, creating freedom for maneuver. India sees the US as a hedge against the rise of China, and Brazil recognizes Washington as a backer of its rise and guarantor of regional economic stability.

Emerging powers are likely to be particularly sensitive to future perceived slights by the US. Words like "humiliation" and "respect" cropped up repeatedly in the presentations and conversations, especially with experts from those regions. As emerging powers seek greater influence and recognition in the international order they are likely to clash diplomatically with the US. Elite and publics in emerging countries have increasingly objected to "hegemonic" behavior or extensive interventions abroad by the US. One of the attractions of a multipolar world for many of them is a lessened US dominance. Maintaining and protecting one's sovereignty would continue to be a preoccupation, particularly so long as they feel their position in the international order is not secured.

For most emerging powers, it was clear from the discussions that participants saw significant barriers to emerging powers building the political, military, and diplomatic capacity necessary to project power and influence internationally. In many ways, the intellectual capacity is even more difficult to acquire than military assets. As countries enjoy a rapid increase in their power they will need to think about the world in new ways and overcome severe domestic constraints that can impede this transition.

Participants saw China in a separate category: the US and China will be in competition with one another but they will also be required to cooperate to solve common threats and challenges and to protect mutual interests. This contrasts sharply with the Cold War which was characterized by mutual independence and ideological rivalry. For China, the principal question is whether it can continue to operate within the existing international order or if it will eventually pursue a revisionist course. There was disagreement about which was the most likely outcome. However, our interlocutors agreed that if China does seek to overturn the international order it is likely to be the result of events inside and outside China rather than the consequence of a grand design.

In an optimistic scenario, the US would address its structural weaknesses, including falling educational standards, skyrocketing health-care costs, and widening fiscal deficits. At the same time, outside the US, the euro zone would remain intact, eliminating one of the major threats to US recovery in the short-to-medium term. Continued prosperity in emerging market countries, where approximately one billion people will be added to the world middle class by 2030, could play to US economic strengths. These newly empowered consumers will demand education, entertainment, and products and services driven by information technology—all goods the US excels at producing. Moreover, as a global technological leader, the US could be motored by innovations in medicine, biotechnology, communications, transportation, or energy. For example, developments that improve the efficiency or extraction of shale natural gas and oil—of which the US possesses large reserves—will provide disproportionate benefits to the United States.

Under this optimistic scenario, we would expect the US economy to grow steadily at about 2.7 percent a year, up from 2.5 percent during the last 20 years. US growth reflects both solid labor force growth and technological advance. Average living standards would rise—almost 40 percent in this scenario—potentially engendering greater social mobility. Although the relative size of the US economy would still decline— from about a third of G20 GDP in 2010 to about a quarter in 2030 in real US dollars—the US economy would remain the world's largest at market exchange rates. In PPP terms, however, the US economy would still be surpassed by China before 2030. Trade would also still shift to the East: the US share of world trade would dip from around 12 to 10 percent, while East Asia's share would probably double from 10 to 20 percent. Though its growth would slow sharply by 2030, China would still become the central player in world trade and the largest trading partner of most countries.

" . . . a reinvigorated US would not necessarily be a panacea. Terrorism, proliferation, regional conflicts, and other ongoing threats to the international order will be affected by the presence or absence of strong US leadership but are also driven by their own dynamics."

A starkly different picture would emerge—both for the US and the international system—should the US economy not rebound and growth in the US slow to an average of 1.5 percent a year through 2030. Weaker international trade and financial arrangements, as well as spillovers from US domestic crises, would slow growth in other countries by about 0.5 percent a year. Slower growth would hold down US living standards. If seen as a country in absolute decline, the perception itself would make it harder for the US to lead.

BIG STAKES FOR THE INTERNATIONAL SYSTEM

The optimistic scenario of a reinvigorated US economy would increase the prospects that the growing global and regional challenges would be addressed. A stronger US economy dependent on trade in services and cutting-edge technologies would be a boost for the world economy, laying the basis for stronger multilateral cooperation. Washington would have a stronger interest in world trade, potentially leading a process of World Trade Organization reform that streamlines new negotiations and strengthens the rules governing the international trading system. The US would be in a better position to boost support for a more democratic Middle East and prevent the slide of failing states. The US could act as balancer ensuring regional stability, for example, in Asia where the rise of multiple powers—particularly India and China—could spark increased rivalries. However, a reinvigorated US would not necessarily be a panacea. Terrorism, proliferation, regional conflicts, and other ongoing threats to the international order will be affected by the presence or absence of strong US leadership but are also driven by their own dynamics.

The US impact is much more clear-cut in the negative case in which the US fails to rebound and is in sharp economic decline. In that scenario, a large and dangerous global power vacuum would be created and in a relatively short space of time. With a weak US, the potential would increase for the European economy to unravel. The European Union might remain, but as an empty shell around a fragmented continent. Progress on trade reform as well as financial and monetary system reform would probably suffer. A weaker and less secure international community would reduce its aid efforts, leaving impoverished or crisis-stricken countries to fend for themselves, multiplying the chances of grievance and peripheral conflicts. In this scenario, the US would be more likely to lose influence to regional hegemons—China and India in Asia and Russia in Eurasia. The Middle East would be riven by numerous rivalries which could erupt into open conflict, potentially sparking oil-price shocks. This would be a world reminiscent of the 1930s when Britain was losing its grip on its global leadership role.

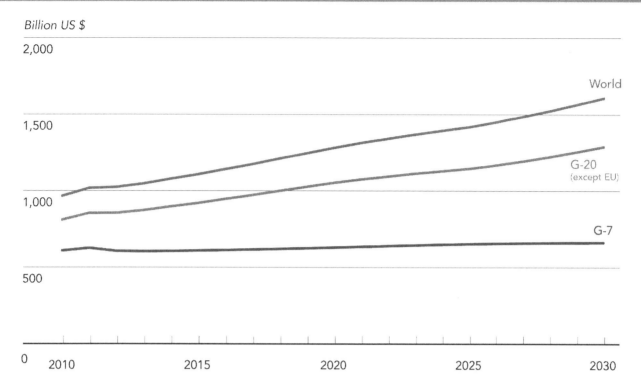

Billion US $

Source: International Futures Model.

EVENTS WILL ALSO DRIVE OUTCOMES FOR THE US ROLE

The US position in the world will be determined also by how successful it is in helping to manage international crises—typically the role of great powers and, since 1945, the international community's expectation of Washington.

Should Asia replicate Europe's 19th- and early 20th-century past and become a region divided by power struggles and rivalries, the US would be called by many—including potentially even a rising China—to be a balancer, ensuring regional stability. All countries would want and need stability to ensure their continued internal development. Potential crises that could ocur in the 2030 time frame—such as Korean unification or a tense standoff between the US and China over Taiwan—probably would lead to demands for sustained US engagement at a high level. Asia is a region with a large number of unresolved territorial disputes, including in the South China Sea where

dueling claims are likely to escalate with growing interest in exploitation of valuable seabed resources.

Other regions may require stepped up US leadership: in the Middle East and South Asia increased rivalries and the potential for both interstate and intrastate conflict are rising (see the conflict section). One can easily imagine widespread calls for strong US leadership to stave off an open Indian-Pakistani conflict or defuse a nuclear arms race in the Middle East. Humanitarian crises—particularly those involving the need for US lift and intelligence capabilities—will also help ensure continued US leadership. As we described earlier, environmental disasters are likely to be more frequent and more severe; as a result, the United States' military assets are likely to be in greater demand. Providing technological solutions for growing resource scarcities and in some cases spearheading diplomatic arrangements for better sharing of existing resources such as water are also likely to be tests of US leadership. US success or failure in

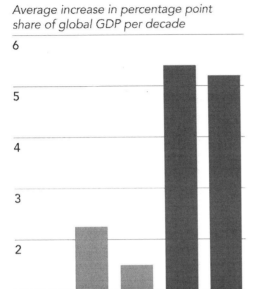

Average increase in percentage point share of global GDP per decade

UK, 1820-70	
US, 1900-50	
Japan, 1950-80	
China, 2000-20	
India, 2010-30	

Note: UK, US, and Japan data from Angus Maddison historical database, measured in 1990 International Geary-Khamis dollars. China and India data from Brookings projections, measured in 2055 PPP dollars.

Source: Brookings Institution.

managing these crises probably will directly affect the world community's perception of US power.

Historically, US dominance has been buttressed by the dollar's role as the global reserve currency. The fall of the dollar as the global reserve currency and substitution by another or a basket of currencies would be one of the sharpest indications of a loss of US global economic position, equivalent to the sterling's demise as the world's currency, contributing to the end of the British Empire in the post-World War II period. Most experts see the usurpation of the dollar as unlikely in the next 15-20 years. However, the growing global and regional use of other major currencies such as the renminbi (RMB) and euro—sharing a global status with the dollar—is probably more likely out to 2030. As Asia becomes the world's economic powerhouse and creditor, it is only a matter of time before its currencies also take on a greater global status. How

quickly or slowly that happens will have a major impact on the US global role.

"A collapse or sudden retreat of US power would most likely result in an extended period of global anarchy where there would be no stable international system and no leading power to replace the US."

FEW COMPETING VISIONS OF A NEW INTERNATIONAL ORDER—FOR THE MOMENT

The replacement of the United States by another global power and erection of a new international order seems the least likely outcome in this time period. No other power would be likely to achieve the same panoply of power in this time frame under any plausible scenario. The emerging powers are eager to take their places at the top table of key multilateral institutions such as UN, IMF, and World Bank, but they do not espouse any competing vision. Although ambivalent and even resentful of the US-led international order, they have benefited from it and are more interested in continuing their economic development and political consolidation than contesting US leadership. In addition, the emerging powers are not a bloc: they don't have any unitary alternative vision. Their perspectives—even China's—are more keyed to shaping regional structures. A collapse or sudden retreat of US power would most likely result in an extended period of global anarchy where there would be no stable international system and no leading power to replace the US. When we have discussed decreasing US power abroad, many scholars and analysts have tended to assume even greater levels of chaos and disorder would ensue than many US experts.

THE FOG OF TRANSITION

The present recalls past transition points—such as 1815, 1919, or 1945—when the path forward was not clear-cut and the world faced the possibility of different global futures. In all those cases, the transition was extended and re-balancing was partly a matter of trial and error. Domestic politics was an important factor shaping international outcomes. Going forward, US domestic politics will be critical to how the US conceives and prosecutes its international role. Many of our interlocutors stressed the need for developing a strong political consensus as a key condition for greater US economic competitiveness. A divided US would have a more difficult time of shaping a new role. The transition away from unipolarity toward new global leadership will be a multifaceted and multilayered process, played on a number of different levels and driven too by the unfolding of events, both domestically and more broadly in the rest of the world.

WORLD REBALANCED—PARALLELS WITH THE PAST?

Some of our interlocutors drew parallels between the current period and the European "long peace" after 1815 set in motion by the Congress of Vienna. Similarities include a period of rapid social, economic, technological and political change and an international system which was largely multipolar. The Europe of 1815 consisted of a diverse set of autocracies like Russia, Prussia and Austro-Hungarian Empire and liberal states such as Britain and France. In such a world, Britain occupied a special role: it managed to play an outsized role despite its lack of overwhelming power capabilities—in 1830, Russia and France were roughly the same size as Britain in terms of GNP and by 1913 the US, Russia and Germany all had larger economies. Its global financial and economic position and empire, role as offshore balancer in Europe and protector of commercial sea lanes linking its overseas dominions gave Britain the preeminent global role in the international system during the nineteenth and into the twentieth centuries.

The current multipolar system is also very diverse with an even larger number of players (think G20), and international economics and politics is much more globalized. In 1815, coming out of over 25 years of conflict, the great powers had conflicting views which they did not disguise, particularly at home. The Holy Alliance of Russia, Prussia and Austria sought to fight against democracy, revolution and secularism but ended up finding it hard to coordinate collective efforts and, in any event, their efforts proved only effective temporarily as revolutions and separatist movements continued across Europe throughout the length of the nineteenth century. A long, general peace among the great powers prevailed, mostly because no one wanted to risk imposing its will on the others for fear of the larger consequences. Equilibrium was achieved in part because of the differences. Britain's role also outlasted its demise as a first rate economic power and despite the rise of several competing states stayed preeminent in part because the others were reluctant to wrest leadership away from it until the First World War.

CHAPTER 3
ALTERNATIVE WORLDS

The graphic below compares the US share of real GDP in our four scenarios for 2030.

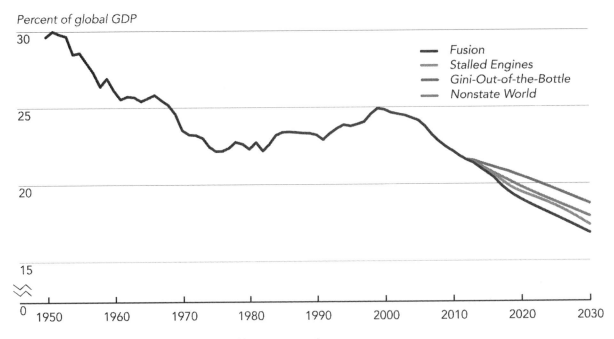

Source: McKinsey Global Growth Model; Angus Maddison; team analysis.

COMPARISON OF GLOBAL GDP COMPOSITION IN OUR 2030 SCENARIOS

The graphic below illustrates patterns in the shift in global economic clout across regions (measured in terms of their share of real global GDP) in 2010 and in our four scenarios for 2030.

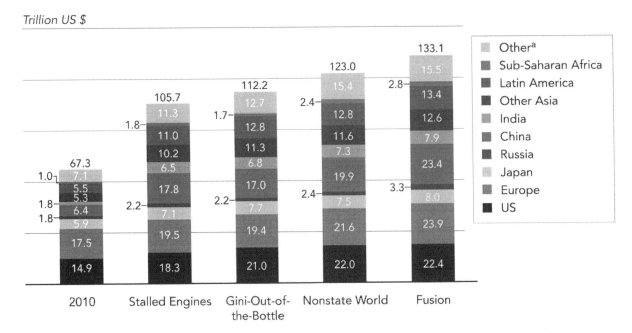

ª Other includes Eastern Europe and Central Asia, Turkey, Canada, South Asia (except India), and MENA.

Source: McKinsey Global Growth Model.

The substantial number of game-changers and complex interactions among them suggest an endless variety of scenarios. **We have sought here to delineate four archetypal futures that represent distinct pathways for future developments out to 2030. In reality, the future probably will consist of elements from all the alternative worlds.**

The graphic on the top of that page shows US share of real global GDP under the four scenarios. The graphic on the bottom of the page at left illustrates patterns in the shift in global economic clout across regions (measured in terms of regions'/countries' share of global GDP) in 2010 and in our four scenarios for 2030. The four scenarios are:

Stalled Engines–a scenario in which the US and Europe turn inward and globalization stalls.

Fusion–a world in which the US and China cooperate, leading to worldwide cooperation on global challenges.

Gini-Out-of-the-Bottle–a world in which economic inequalities dominate.

Nonstate World–a scenario in which nonstate actors take the lead in solving global challenges.

ALTERNATIVE WORLD 1
STALLED ENGINES

We chose **Stalled Engines**—a scenario in which the US and Europe turn inward and globalization stalls—as one of the bookends, illustrating the most plausible worst case. Arguably, darker scenarios are imaginable, including a complete breakdown and reversal of globalization due to a potential large-scale conflict on the order of World War I or World War II, but such an outcome does not seem probable. We believe the risks of interstate conflict will rise, but we do not expect bilateral conflict to ignite a full-scale conflagration. Moreover, unlike in the interwar period, the complete unraveling of economic interdependence or globalization would be more difficult—and therefore less likely—in this more advanced technological age with ubiquitous connections.

Stalled Engines is nevertheless a bleak future. Our modeling suggests that under this scenario total global income would be $27 trillion less than under Fusion, our most optimistic scenario. This amount is more than the combined economies of the US and euro zone today. In a Stalled Engines world, the US and Europe are no longer capable nor interested in sustaining global leadership. The US political system fails to address its fiscal challenges and consequently economic policy and performance drift. The European project unravels. Greece's exit from the euro zone triggers the rapid, unmanaged exit of the rest of the periphery. More nationalist, even nativist, parties rise to claim positions of influence in coalition governments. By the 2020s, it looks like only a limited free trade zone will remain.

Economic growth continues in major emerging markets and accounts for approximately three quarters of global growth. Nonetheless, fundamental economic and political reforms remain elusive in China and India. Corruption, social unrest, weak financial systems, and chronically poor infrastructures slow their growth rates. China's growth falls, for example, from 8 percent at the start of the period to around 3 percent by 2030.

As pressures grow everywhere for disengagement and protectionism, the global governance system is unable to cope with a widespread pandemic that triggers panic. Rich countries wall themselves off from many developing and poor countries in Asia, Africa, and the Middle East. By disrupting international travel and trade, the severe pandemic helps to stall out, but does not kill globalization.

On the sidelines of the annual Davos meeting, a number of multinational CEOs gather to discuss what they see as globalization stalling out. One of their members has asked the director of her "Strategic Vision" office to write a short paper describing the downward spiral, which is used as the basis for the discussion. The following is an extract from that paper:

WORLDCORP *Strategic Vision Group*
1800 Ladbroke Lane, Suite 615
London, England
W10 5NE

I have to confess I did not see it coming, but we have to face up to the fact that we are in a new world—one in which globalization is no longer a given. You may ask how this came about. The key was the inward turn of the United States. I think all of us thought that the discovery of shale gas meant that the US was "back" despite all the domestic squabbling. Clearly, we did not take into consideration the US legal system. Not only did our earlier inflated estimates fall victim to slower-than-anticipated technological improvements in extraction efficiency and deposits that proved to be at the lower end of initial forecasts, but we failed to factor in the costly series of lawsuits against the energy producers.

Then we were hit with a double whammy. Just when we thought Europe was digging itself out from Greece's unruly exit from the euro zone and negotiating a new political and economic pact, the French people have revolted in the latest referendum on a new EU treaty. It was a devastating defeat for the French Government and now a huge problem for everyone else. It is not clear that a new deal can be devised given the wide margin of defeat for the former treaty proposal. Increasingly, German elites are saying that Germany doesn't need the EU anymore: they want to get out now.

I'm not sure the developing world understands the seriousness of these changes. I think there was, on their part, a certain schadenfreude—rejoicing—about the West's problems. China welcomed the US decision to draw down its overseas forces, seeing it as a guarantee of US non-interference, though Chinese "liberals" are chagrined because they saw a strong US as keeping the pressure on Beijing for reforms. Beijing expects Vietnam and The Philippines to gradually back down in the South China Sea without strong US support.

China has its own share of problems. Fundamental economic and political reforms have stalled; corruption and social unrest is slowing growth rates, which perhaps explains why the government is fomenting nationalism and becoming more adventurist overseas.

Many Indian strategists have been leery of putting too much trust in the US; the recent US drawdown confirms they were right. New Delhi has few other natural partners. India worries a lot about its influence in Central Asia. A Taliban coup recently occurred in which all the other factions—which had formed the government—were brutally suppressed. India, which blames Pakistan, sought Western help but was largely rebuffed.

1

Indian distrust of China has also grown to the extent that no more BRIC summits are being held. Chinese and Indian diplomats won't sit together even in a multilateralist setting. China recently completed a 38,000-megawatt dam on the Brahmaputra close to the disputed border with India and has begun building another. China's decision to test Vietnam's determination to stand up to Beijing in the South China Sea has Indian officials on edge. In Delhi's view, China's aggression appears to be unstoppable without a greater US willingness to intervene. It appears to be only a matter of time before China's blue water navy extends its sway farther west into the Indian Ocean.

The global economy has suffered the consequences of the escalating tensions among the emerging powers. Global growth is now trending downward. Poorer countries, particularly, are suffering: during bad harvest years, more countries are creating export bans, exacerbating food shortages and price spikes.

Another turning point was when the Middle East boiled over. Sunni-Shia violence exploded in the Gulf. Iran intervened to protect Shia in Bahrain, prompting Saudi military retaliation. Iran then announced that it would start testing a nuclear device. The US debated whether to send the Sixth Fleet to the Gulf to ensure the free flow of oil, but Washington decided to take a "wait-and-see" approach. If I have to choose a moment when it was clear that the US role had changed, this was it. Even the Chinese got worried about a diminishing US role and sent their fleet to the Gulf of Oman.

There appears to be no end in sight to the Sunni-Shia tensions. Saudi Arabia and Iran—both hit by lower energy prices because of the global growth slowdown—have nevertheless increased tensions by launching a proxy war in Syria and Lebanon. Hizballah has also launched its first large-scale cyber attack against Israel and the United States.

With large amounts of arable land, unconventional energy reserves (if the lawyers ever allow them to be tapped), and adequate water resources, the US can be more self-sufficient than most other countries. The growing disorder outside the US has strengthened those in favor of disengagement. In China, however, the party is increasingly under fire for what many Chinese people view as gross mismanagement of the economy. A coordinated general strike has been ongoing in several of the major cities. India's development has also substantially slowed. No government stays in power long and there is a constant reshuffling of government posts among coalition partners.

As with most ill fortune, troubles tend to come in waves: a deadly virus—which scientists had warned about repeatedly—has erupted in Southeast Asia. Ironically, with the increased security and border controls, the US, some Europeans, and even China are better able to weather the pandemic, which is spreading quickly. Flights have been cancelled and ship transports have been stopped. There are reports of tens of millions of deaths. Twitter tried to operate even at the height of the pandemic, but a number of governments pulled the plug, saying that the use of social media was responsible for the increasing panic. The virulent strain spread quickly outside Southeast Asia to South Asia and along the trade and travel routes to the Middle East and Africa.

As a result of the pandemic, there is now a new map of the world in everybody's mind. I can remember when the world map was the British Empire with a quarter of the Earth's surface colored in pink. Then we had the map of the Free World with Washington as its capital. Now the new mental map shows a devastated Southeast Asia and portions of India, the Horn of Africa, and parts of the Gulf. Many of these areas are still not getting any international assistance.

This new mental map, created by what happened to the poor and destitute and their being shunned by the rich countries, including China, is widening the gulf between North and South and East and West. The new map will be what survivors in the developing world carry around in their minds and, consciously or not, will inform thinking for a generation on world affairs.

Even in the rich, developed countries, which were spared the worst impact from the pandemic, the death toll reached several million—the youth were particularly susceptible. I can't tell you the psychological impact on the rich survivors. The worldwide pandemic has put globalization even more in disfavor. It was the coup de grace for many, sealing the case against what was seen as the rampant globalization earlier in the 21st century.

Western multinationals have seen forced nationalization in Southeast Asia, India, and Africa. Governments there say that those businesses which ceased their operations during the pandemic lost their rights to resume their businesses afterward.

Still, I noticed that Facebook is becoming more popular and that young people are also beginning to travel and study abroad. Maybe this augurs a rebound in globalization's fortune . . .

3

HOW GAME-CHANGERS SHAPE SCENARIO:

Global Economy	All boats sink in this scenario. Slower global growth is accompanied by higher food prices.
Conflict	A new "great game" ramps up in Asia. Sunni-Shia violence erupts in the Middle East, pitting Iran against Saudi Arabia. Outside powers such as the US and Europe decline to intervene.
Regional Stability	Southeast Asia and portions of India, the Horn of Africa, and parts of the Gulf are hit hard by the pandemic, undermining stability. Even before the pandemic, the breakdown in global governance has meant an increasingly unstable Central Asia and Middle East.
Governance	Multilateralism comes to a halt following a worldwide pandemic. Rich countries panic and try to isolate poorer countries where the outbreak started and is more severe. Resentments build between East and West and North and South.
Technology	Lack of technological improvements means the shale gas revolution is delayed. By end of scenario, however, IT connections are source of renewal, preserving globalization.
US Role in the World	The US turns inward. The US public is no longer as interested in sustaining the burdens of global leadership and, following the pandemic, is more interested in building a Fortress America.

HOW MAJOR POWERS/REGIONS FARE IN SCENARIO:

Europe	Preoccupied by domestic turmoil, Europe sits with the US on the sidelines.
Russia	Russian power in the Near Abroad has grown with the US pullback from Afghanistan and Central Asia.
China	Fundamental economic and political reforms have stalled; corruption and social unrest is slowing growth rates, which perhaps explains why the government is fomenting nationalism and becoming more adventurist overseas.
India	A US withdrawal from Asia leaves India having to fend on its own against what it sees as an increasingly aggressive China.
Brazil/Middle Tier Powers	Brazil and the rest of South America are less affected by growing geopolitical tensions and the worldwide pandemic. As a major food exporter, Brazil has benefited from rising prices. It seeks to fill the vacuum created by a withdrawn US and Europe.
Poor Developing States in Africa, Asia and Latin America	Poorer states suffer enormously in this scenario from rising geopolitical tensions and food inflation. Pandemic deaths are greatest in poorer countries, and recovery will be difficult with the breakdown in global economic and technological cooperation.

ALTERNATIVE WORLD 2
FUSION

Fusion is the other bookend, portraying what we see as the most plausible best case. This is a world in which the specter of a spreading conflict in South Asia triggers efforts by the US and China to intervene and impose a cease-fire. China and the US find other issues to collaborate on, leading to a sea change in their bilateral relations, as well as to broader worldwide cooperation on global challenges. This scenario would only be possible through strong political leadership that overrules cautious domestic constituencies and forges stronger international partnerships. As a result, trust between societies and civilizations would increase.

In a Fusion world, economic growth resumes as the initial collaboration on security is widened to include intellectual property and innovation to deal with resource issues and climate change. China, bolstered by the increasing role it is playing in the international system, begins a process of political reform. With the growing collaboration among major powers, global multilateral institutions are reformed and made more inclusive. In other words, political and economic reforms move forward hand-in-hand.

In this scenario, all boats substantially rise. Emerging economies continue to grow faster than advanced economies, but GDP growth in advanced economies also accelerates. The global economy nearly doubles by 2030 to $132 trillion that year. The American Dream returns, with per capita incomes rising $10,000 in ten years. Chinese per capita incomes also rapidly increase, ensuring that China avoids the middle-income trap. In Europe, the euro zone crisis proves to be the catalyst for deep political and economic restructuring.

In addition to political leadership in states, the role of nonstate actors is also key. Technological innovation—rooted in expanded exchanges and joint efforts at the university- and research-lab level—is critical to the world staying ahead of the rising resource constraints that would result from the rapid boost in prosperity.

In 2030, the East-West Center—founded in 1960 by the US Congress to promote better relations and understanding among the people and nations of the United States, Asia, and the Pacific through cooperative study, research, and dialogue—has decided to change its name to the Center for Global Integration. The inaugural address for the rechristened institution will be given by a noted archaeologist whose works underlining the similarities among civilizations are being rediscovered, winning public acclaim for his foresight. In recent years, he was beginning to doubt whether he was right, as he recounts here.

The growing tensions between the great powers had him on the brink of recanting what seemed like an overly optimistic view of global trends. In his address (excerpted right), he explains why those doubts have now dissipated and he is returning to his earlier rosy outlook.

CENTER FOR GLOBAL INTEGRATION

To: Center for Global Integration

From: Dr. Arthur E. Kent

Subject: Inaugural Address Transcript

If you had asked me anytime during the second decade of the 21st century, I would have told you that we were headed into a world catastrophe. It felt like what we read about the runup to the First World War when there were mounting frictions between the great powers. In this case there was sparring between China and India, China and the US, and the US and Europe over Middle East policy and among the US, India, and Pakistan over Afghanistan.

Talk about the Great Game—everybody seemed to be playing it despite knowing the harm it was doing to the global economy. The West was having a bad economic decade. The needed political and structural reforms in both the US and Europe were taking time to produce a payoff. Much of Europe was dealing with the dramatic aging of its population. The United States was bogged down in long-running partisan debates.

The surprise was China. Everyone assumed that it would continue to advance. No one anticipated the leadership's decisionmaking paralysis and how the internal wrangling was taking a toll on China's economic growth. As Metternich was wont to say about France at the Congress of Vienna, if China sneezes everyone else catches a cold. China did more than make everyone get an economic cold. China's leaders—despite or maybe because of the downturn—ramped up military spending, causing everyone's nerves to get on edge.

In this environment of slowing global growth and increasing distrust, Indo-Pakistani tensions also flared: in a year of drought, Pakistan accused India of holding back much-needed relief with its refusal to open its dams along the Indus. Delhi viewed the increased militant infiltration in Kashmir as a Pakistani provocation. It also detected Islamabad's hand in a plot by extremists to blow up the Mumbai stock exchange. India mobilized its army.

1

The major powers were scrambling. Beijing sent a secret envoy to Washington with a cease-fire plan. Together the US and China brought the plan to the UN Security Council. China promised to inject massive amounts of humanitarian and development aid if Pakistan ceased further retaliation. The US and Europe threatened massive sanctions if India did not withdraw. The US and China are cosponsoring peace talks in Geneva to settle issues such as Kashmir and Pakistani support for militant groups.

No one would have predicted such a positive outcome. A lot depended on the personal ties between US and Chinese leaders. Both leaderships disregarded the objections raised by mid-level bureaucrats to cooperating with the other and have been awarded Nobel Peace Prizes for their joint initiative. The leaders saw the danger of a major war for everyone's future and acted. They also wanted to do more: hence their decision to ignite a global technological revolution.

Developing technological solutions to major challenges had an electrifying effect, particularly for younger generations. Whereas the 2010s were all "doom and gloom," the 2020s turned suddenly into a golden age for technology. Mechanisms for global sharing of innovation were established by China and the United States. Global education exchanges flourished like never before. Turkey, Russia, and Israel, for example, became creative hotbeds for cross-cultural fertilization. Knowledge industries spread into Africa and Latin America.

In this collaborative environment, a global consensus for action on clean energy and food security emerged. US labs led in producing new materials to support improved energy storage. Scientists based in India worked on more decentralized energy systems serving rural areas. Brazil became the center for work on a new green revolution.

The Gulf states have seen the writing on the wall and are rapidly diversifying their economies. Their efforts to develop strong universities—which began with US and Western help—have paid off for the region. The Gulf states now have a highly trained and entrepreneurial elite. A sort of contagion took hold—somewhat along the lines of what happened in Asia in the 1970s and 1980s—and the Middle East is experiencing rapid economic development.

Years from now I think that historians will see changing immigration and mobility as the foundation for the growing political and technological cooperation. For good or for ill, a cosmopolitan elite with ties to multiple countries has formed: these elites are comfortable working and living in multiple places. Even the less skilled are more mobile, filling in gaps in many aging societies. The increasing spread of biometrics has meant that government authorities can now easily track flows of people. The number

2

of "illegals" in America or Europe has dropped. As a result, governments are more confident about allowing expanded flows of workers.

There is less talk of declinism—the United States' or Europe's. World attention is now more focused on how to protect the biosphere given the rampant growth unleashed by greater international cooperation. Plant and insect species are dying off at an alarming rate due to the rampant urbanization and agricultural revolutions. The size of the middle class has exploded across the globe. Even Western middle classes are getting richer. It is a never-ending cycle. New technologies are replacing or making available resources go farther, but the growing number of nouveau riche are causing cities to swell and rural areas to depopulate. Other environmental concerns have also become troubling. Several recent typhoons have been unusually powerful, causing an unprecedented number of deaths and greater physical destruction than ever before. Arctic ice melted at a far more rapid rate than anticipated, and rampant exploitation of resources in the Arctic has begun. Methane gas levels are rising rapidly, exacerbating climate change scientists' fears.

South Asia is still a concern. Cooperation elsewhere and pressure from other powers such as China and the US have persuaded the Indians and Pakistanis to increase their strategic dialogue and to begin to open trade flows. India's rapid economic expansion fuels distrust, suspicion, and envy among Pakistanis. Pakistan has not ceased its nuclear modernization program, and Afghanistan is a still a battleground for competing interests.

A page has been turned in human history—no more competition over resources . . .

3

HOW GAME-CHANGERS SHAPE SCENARIO:

Global Economy	All boats substantially rise. Emerging economies continue to grow faster than advanced ones, but GDP growth in advanced economies also accelerates. The global economy nearly doubles by 2030 to $132 trillion that year. Chinese per capita incomes rapidly increase, ensuring that China avoids the middle-income trap.
Conflict	The specter of a spreading conflict in South Asia triggers intervention by the US and China, leading to a cease-fire and settlement. Such success breeds broader cooperation on global and regional challenges, lowering risks of conflict.
Regional Stability	Tensions remain in South Asia, the Middle East, and elsewhere, but increased multilateral cooperation on poverty and climate change lessens the risks of instability. Europe rebounds. A liberal China increases possibilities for regional security in Asia.
Governance	Cooperation, initially based on the US and China coming together, quickly spreads. Greater democratization takes hold first with a more liberal regime in China. Reform of the multilateral institutions is a final stage, following deepening cooperation among powers.
Technology	The rapid expansion of scientific knowledge is a key factor in sustaining a more cooperative world. Technological innovation is also critical to the world staying ahead of the rising resource constraints that would result from the rapid boost in prosperity posited under this scenario.
US Role in the World	The American Dream returns, with per capita incomes rising $10,000 in ten years. The United States' technological surge and efforts to end conflicts are the basis of US leadership. Talk of US declinism has abated in this new environment where cooperation has replaced competition among the great powers.

FUSION

HOW MAJOR POWERS/REGIONS FARE IN SCENARIO:	
Europe	In Europe, the euro zone crisis proves to be the catalyst for deep political and economic restructuring.
Russia	As technology becomes the source of international legitimacy and status, Russia starts rebuilding its S&T sector. Russia becomes a creative hotbed for cross-cultural fertilization.
China	China emerges stronger with its soft power enhanced and begins to move toward democracy. It assumes increased global and regional roles.
India	India's high-tech industries benefit greatly from the new cooperative environment. While Sino-Indian ties improve, India still struggles to overcome historic tensions with Pakistan. The advances in energy and water help to ensure continued economic development.
Brazil/Middle-Tier Powers	Brazilian scientists are on the forefront of the new green revolution for Africa. With more cooperation among the great powers, middle-tier powers find that they play less of a global role than when US and China competed for their support.
Poor Developing States	Poor states benefit greatly from the technological advances in food and energy. Some states continue to teeter on the edge of failure, but many more are doing better in the cooperative atmosphere.

GINI OUT-OF-THE-BOTTLE

In ***Gini Out-of-the-Bottle,***[a] inequalities within countries and between rich and poor countries dominate. The world becomes wealthier—as global GDP grows—but less happy as the differences between the haves and have-nots become starker and increasingly immutable. The world is increasingly defined by two self-reinforcing cycles—one virtuous leading to greater prosperity, the other vicious, leading to poverty and instability. Political and social tensions increase. Among countries, there are clear-cut winners and losers. Countries in the euro zone core that are globally competitive do well, while others on the periphery are forced out. The EU splinters and eventually falters. The US remains the preeminent power, achieving an economic turnaround fueled by its new energy revolution, technological innovation, prudent fiscal policies, and the relative weakness of many potential competitors. Without completely disengaging, however, the United States no longer tries to play "global policeman" on every security threat.

Parts of Africa suffer the most. The secessions of Eritrea from Ethiopia and South Sudan from Sudan are seen in retrospect as precursors of this era in which the boundaries across the Sahel are redrawn. States fragment along sectarian, tribal, and ethnic lines. The shale oil and gas revolution that benefits the US proves disastrous for those African countries dependent upon oil exports. The failed states in Africa and elsewhere serve as safehavens for political and religious extremists, insurgents, and terrorists.

The transformed global energy market and Saudi Arabia's failure to diversify its economy hit Riyadh particularly hard. Saudi Arabia's economy barely grows during this period while its population continues to increase. Saudi per capita income declines from almost $20,000 today to just over $16,000 by 2030. In the face of this economic challenge, the Kingdom no longer possesses the resources to play a major regional role.

Elsewhere, cities in China's coastal zone continue to thrive, but inequalities increase. Social discontent spikes as middle-class expectations are not met except for the very "well-connected." Fissures appear within China's leadership as members struggle for wealth, which in turn breeds self-doubt, undermining the legitimacy of the ruling institutions. Having an increasingly difficult time governing, the party reverts to stirring nationalistic fervor.

In this world, the lack of societal cohesion domestically is mirrored at the international level. With Europe weakened and the US more restrained, international assistance to the most vulnerable populations declines. Major powers remain at odds; the potential for conflict rises. An increasing number of states fail, fueled in part by the lack of much international cooperation on assistance and development. Economic growth continues at a moderate pace, but the world is less secure owing to political and social fissures at all levels.

In 2028, the Editor of the New Marxist Review *launched a competition for the best short essay on the meaning of Marx and Communism 210 years after Marx's birth in 1818. To her surprise, the journal was flooded with thousands of submissions. She was having a hard time sifting through the piles and selecting a winner, but she found one that pulled together many of the recurring themes. The essay made the case that Marx isn't dead but is instead thriving and doing better in the 21st century than anybody could have imagined just 15 or 20 years ago. The following are excerpts from that essay.*

---

[a] The "Gini" in this scenario title refers to the *Gini Coefficient*, which is a recognized statistical measurement of inequality of income.

Marx Updated for the 21st Century

The breakup of the EU a couple years ago was a classic case of Marxist inevitability. In a sense, what we saw was a transposition of the class struggle onto a larger regional landscape with northern Europeans in the role of exploitative bourgeoisie and the Mediterranean South the defenseless proletariat. These tensions—as Marx (and Lenin, by the way) tell us—cannot be resolved except through conflict and breakup. At first it looked like the process of reorganizing the EU into tiers could be orderly with the less well-off taking a backseat without much fuss.

Unfortunately, Brussels did not address growing resentments among the have-nots. Practically overnight, we saw this process turn into chaos. EU Commission offices were attacked and burned down, not just by rioters in many southern European cities, but also in major cities in the richer north. For a while it looked like we would see a reenactment of the 1848 revolutions: unemployed youth in even the better off northern European countries taking to the streets in sympathy.

The EU's websites were hacked into; its internal system was inoperable for months due to sabotage. The class struggle is widening into a new dimension that did not occur to Marx. A generational war appears to be afoot. The recently organized youth parties in England and France are calling for cutbacks in social entitlements for the elderly. They also want higher education fees to be drastically cut.

We've seen growing class divisions elsewhere, pointing to a potential global revolution. Beijing's power over the provinces has been declining. China's coastal cities continue to do relatively well because of their overseas commercial links and richer domestic markets. Government efforts to build up the new interior cities have floundered. Little investment money is flowing in. A Maoist revival is under way there and a party split seems inevitable. The Chinese should have known better. They inducted too much of the rising bourgeoisie into the party. This was bound to create conflict with the real workers. I don't see any resolution except through more class warfare and conflict.

The Marxist- and Maoist-inspired insurgencies are increasingly spreading in rural areas all over the world. India has a long history of Naxalist insurgencies, which continue to grow stronger. Interestingly, counterparts are rising up in urban areas. There you see a lot more crime; much of it is sophisticated, making it impossible for the bourgeoisie to wall themselves

1

off into gated communities. I know of some bourgeois families that have reverted back to paying for everything with cash. Every time they have banked online or used a credit card, cybercriminals—who appear to have composed a list of targets—siphon off funds from their accounts and charge enormous sums to their credit cards. Banks are finding maintaining security to be increasingly costly.

In the Middle East and parts of Africa, unfortunately from a Marxist point of view, the terrorists and insurgents are still falling back on religion or ethnicity. The Saudi authorities are reeling from increased homegrown terrorists attacking the wealthy, citing their irreligious behavior. Every day in Saudi Arabia or one of the Gulf countries another luxury mall is bombed by self-styled jihadists.

Nigeria is virtually split with the Christian communities under siege in the North. The transposition of the class conflict along sectarian, tribal, and ethnic lines in Africa means the old "colonialist" map has been virtually torn up. By my count, there are ten new countries on the African continent alone. In the Middle East, we now have a Kurdistan, carved out from several countries. Winston Churchill and Gertrude Bell—architects of a united Iraq after World War I—would be spinning in their graves. Of course, the West and China have yet to recognize many of these partitions. They are like ostriches with their heads in the sand. There's too much veneration for those so-called "venerable statesmen" who drew up the old imperialist maps in the 19th and 20th centuries.

I'm not sure that the US is yet ripe for revolution. It's done too well from shale gas. The working class there got lulled by the increased manufacturing possibilities as businesses moved back from Asia when US domestic energy prices dropped. But it could be just a matter of time. Entitlement reform in the 2010s didn't happen because US growth picked up. US debt has continued to climb: it is only a matter of time before entitlements will be back on the political agenda. The onset of a global downturn with all the turmoil in Europe and elsewhere is beginning to stir up class tensions. The US thinks it is immune, but we'll see. Unfortunately, opposition activists in America no longer read Marx.

One thing Marx would have reveled in is the power that the proletariat now has. These revolutionary groups have many more destructive means at their disposal, from drones and cyberweapons to bioweapons. I worry that the tensions could get out of hand and the counterrevolutionaries will strike before the downtrodden have built up their strength and perfected tactics. In a sense, with the wider access to lethal weapons, there is less inequality than Marx imagined.

However, the bourgeoisie are beginning to understand. The wealthy cities and towns will no doubt build up their security forces to deal with the constant disruptions and riots. The US,

2

some Europeans, Chinese Communist Party leaders, Russian oligarchs, and others are talking about a global initiative against cybercrime. It's paradoxical. Years ago, the US and Europeans were glib about the need to keep the Internet uncensored and available to all. The Chinese and Russians were concerned about such freedoms getting out of hand and tilting the balance too much in favor of empowered individuals. Suddenly, the scales have dropped from the Americans' eyes and class interest is back in vogue.

Oh—that Marx could see that the class struggle never did die. Globalization has just spawned more of it . . .

HOW GAME-CHANGERS SHAPE SCENARIO:

Global Economy	The global economy grows at rate of 2.7%, much better than in Stalled Engines but less well than in Fusion or Nonstate World. The US achieves an economic turnaround fueled by its new energy revolution and the relative weakness of many potential competitors. By contrast, growth slows in China with fears rising that the country will not escape the middle-income trap. Countries in the euro zone core that are globally competitive do well, some on the periphery are forced out. The EU splinters and eventually falters.
Conflict	Rural-urban and class tensions erupt, particularly in Africa and parts of the Middle East and Asia. The scope of conflicts grows as insurgents and terrorists employ drones, cyber attacks and bioweapons
Regional Stability	Parts of Africa fare the worst with increasing fragmentation along sectarian, tribal, and ethnic lines. Middle East borders are redrawn with an emerging Kurdistan. Political, social, and generational conflict is rampant in Europe, China, and India.
Governance	The lack of societal cohesion domestically is mirrored at the international level. With Europe weakened and the US more restrained, international assistance to the most vulnerable populations declines. More states fail and more are partitioned.
Technology	The fracking technology behind the US energy revolution hits energy producers like Saudi Arabia very hard. States increasingly worry that technology has given individuals too much power. By the end of scenario, Western powers are joining with China, Russia, and others to restrict Internet freedoms.
US Role in the World	The US becomes more restrained in fighting global fires: the few that threaten clear national interests are extinguished, but many are allowed to burn. By the end of the scenario, however, the US is beginning to ally with authoritarian states to try to restore some order because of growing nonstate threats.

HOW MAJOR POWERS/REGIONS FARE IN SCENARIO:	
Europe	Collective Europe is a shell; there is more diversity than uniformity across countries. The euro crisis turned out to be a devastating blow to aspirations for a Europe as a whole playing a dynamic role in the international arena.
Russia	Inequalities at home become a bigger issue with Russian elites allying with counterparts in US, Europe, and China to stem the rise of cybercriminals.
China	China struggles to maintain its previous high economic growth rate as divisions between urban and rural populations grow. Owing to increasing discontent at home, the regime is losing legitimacy. A Maoist revival is under way with growing divisions in the party.
India	India struggles to keep up its growth rate as the rural Naxalite insurgency spreads.
Brazil/Middle-Tier Powers	Brazil's efforts to fight inequality pay off with less domestic instability than in most other states. The rise of Kurdistan is a blow to Turkish integrity, increasing the risks of major conflict in its surrounding neighborhood.
Poor Developing States in Africa, Asia, and Latin America	Poor states suffer from the overall slower economic growth rates. Domestic conflicts worsen the outlook for food production. Humanitarian crises overwhelm the international system's ability to provide assistance.

In a **Nonstate World,** nongovernmetal organizations (NGOs), multinational businesses, academic institutions, and wealthy individuals, as well as subnational units, such as megacities, flourish and take the lead in confronting global challenges. New and emerging technologies that favor greater empowerment of individuals, small groups, and ad hoc coalitions spur the increased power of nonstate actors. A transnational elite—educated at the same global academic institutions—emerges that leads key nonstate actors (major multinational corporations, universities, and NGOs). A global public opinion consensus among many elites and middle-class citizens on the major challenges—poverty, the environment, anti-corruption, rule-of-law, and peace—form the base of their support and power. Countries do not disappear, but governments increasingly see their role as organizing and orchestrating "hybrid" coalitions of state and nonstate actors which shift depending on the challenge.

Authoritarian regimes—preoccupied with asserting the primacy and control of the central government—find it hardest to operate in this world. Smaller, more agile states where the elites are also more integrated are apt to be key players—punching way above their weight—more so than large countries, which lack social or political cohesion.

Global governance institutions that do not adapt to the more diverse and widespread distribution of power are also less likely to be successful. Multinational businesses, IT communications firms, international scientists, NGOs, and groups that are used to cooperating across borders thrive in this hyper-globalized world where expertise, influence, and agility count for more than "weight" or "position." Private capital and philanthropy matter more, for example, than official development assistance. Social media, mobile communications, and big data are key components, underlying and facilitating cooperation among nonstate actors and with governments.

In this world, the scale, scope, and speed of urbanization—and which actors can succeed in managing these challenges—are critical, particularly in the developing world. National governments that stand in the way of these clusters will fall behind.

This is a "patchwork" and uneven world. Some global problems get solved because networks manage to coalesce, and cooperation exists across state and nonstate divides. In other cases, nonstate actors may try to deal with a challenge, but they are stymied because of opposition from major powers. Security threats pose an increasing challenge: access to lethal and disruptive technologies expands, enabling individuals and small groups to perpetrate violence and disruption on a large scale. Terrorists and criminal networks take advantage of the confusion over shifting authorities among a multiplicity of governance actors to acquire and use lethal technologies. Economically, global growth does slightly better than in the Gini Out-of-the-Bottle scenario because there is greater cooperation among nonstate actors and between them and national governments on big global challenges in this world. This world is also more stable and socially cohesive than Nonstate World and Stalled Engines.

In 2030 an historian is writing a history of globalization and its impact on the state during the past 30 years. He had done a doctoral thesis on the 17th century Westphalian state system but hadn't managed to land an academic job. He was hoping that a study of a more recent period would give him a chance at a big-time management consultancy job. Following is a synopsis of his book, The Expansion of Subnational Power.

Globalization has ushered in a new phase in the history of the state. Without question, the state still exists. The continuing economic volatility in the global economy and need for government intervention shows that the state is not going away. However, it would also be wrong to say that the powers of the state have remained the same. During the past 30 years, subnational government authorities and the roles of nonstate bodies have greatly expanded. This has been especially the case in Western democracies, but the increase in subnational power has spread far and wide; the West no longer has a monopoly.

The expansion has been fueled by the formation of a transnational elite who have been educated at the same universities, work in many of the same multinational corporations or NGOs, and vacation at the same resorts. They believe in globalization, but one that relies on and benefits from personal initiative and empowerment. They don't want to rely on "big" government, which they see as oftentimes behind the curve and unable to react quickly in a fast-moving crisis.

This "can-do" and "everyone-can-make-a-difference" spirit has caught on with the rising middle classes around the world, which are increasingly self-reliant. It's fair to say that in a number of cases, the rising middle classes distrust the long-time elites who have controlled national governments in their countries. Hence, for the rising middle classes, working outside and around government has been the way to be upwardly mobile. Denied entry at the national level, many—when they seek elected office—see cities as steppingstones to political power.

This new global elite and middle class also increasingly agree on which issues are the major global challenges. For example, they want to stamp out cronyism and corruption because these factors have been at the root of what has sustained the old system or what they term the ancien regime. The corruption of the old elites has impeded upward mobility in many countries. The new elites believe strongly in rule-of-law as a way of enforcing fairness and opportunity for all. A safe and healthy environment is also important to ensuring quality of life. Many are crusaders for human justice and the rights of women.

Technology has been the biggest driver behind the scenes. With the IT revolution, all the nonstate bodies, from businesses to charities to universities and think tanks, have gone global. Many are no longer recognizable as American, South African, or Chinese. This has been disconcerting to central governments—particularly the remaining authoritarian ones—which do not know whether to treat them as friend or foe.

1

The technological revolution has, in fact, gone way beyond just connecting people in far-flung parts of the world. Owing to the wider access to more sophisticated technologies, the state does not have much of an edge these days. Weapons of Mass Destruction (WMD) are within the reach of individuals. Small militias and terrorist groups have precision weaponry that can hit targets a couple hundred miles away. This has proven deadly and highly disruptive in a couple of instances. Terrorists hacked into the electric grid and have brought several Middle Eastern cities to a standstill while authorities had to barter and finally release some political prisoners before the terror-hackers agreed to stop.

Many people fear that others will imitate such actions and that more attacks by ad hoc groups will occur. We have seen in the past decade what many experts feared for some time: the increasing overlap between criminal networks and terrorists. Terrorists are buying the services of expert hackers. In many cases, hackers don't know for whom they are working.

A near-miss bioterrorist attack occurred recently in which an amateur's experiments almost led to the release of a deadly virus. Fortunately, the outcry and panic led to stronger domestic regulations in many countries and enormous public pressure for greater international regulation. As an example of the enhanced public-private partnership, law enforcement agencies are asking the bio community to point out potential problems. In light of what could happen, the vast majority of those in the bio community are more than eager to help. However, most everyone has recognized that action at the country level is needed too. Thus, the original intent of the Westphalian system—to ensure security for all—is still relevant; since the near-miss bioterror attack, no one is talking about dispensing with the nation-state.

On the other hand, in so many other areas, the role of the central government is weakening. Consider food and water issues. Many NGOs sought central government help to institute country-wide plans, including pricing of water and reduced subsidies for subsistence farmers. There was even that huge G-20 emergency summit—after the wheat harvests failed in both the US and Russia and food riots broke out in Africa and the Middle East—which called for a new WTO round to boost production and ensure against growing export restrictions. Of course, all the G-20 leaders agreed, but when they got back home, the momentum fell apart. The momentum took a dive not just in the US and the EU, where the lobbyists sought to ensure continued subsidies, but also in places like India where subsistence farmers constitute important political constituencies for the various parties.

Five years later no progress has been made in restarting a World Trade Organization round. On the other hand, megacities have sought their own solutions. On the frontlines in dealing with food riots when they happen, many far-sighted mayors decided to start working with farmers in the countryside to improve production. They've dealt with Western agribusiness to buy or lease land to increase production capacities in surrounding rural areas. They are increasingly looking outside the countries where the urban centers are located to

2

negotiate land deals. At the same time, "vertical farming" in skyscrapers within the cities is being adopted.

This effort of each megacity looking after itself probably is not the most efficient. Many people not living in well-governed areas remain vulnerable to shortages when harvests fail; those living in the better-governed areas can fall back on local agricultural production to ride out the crisis.

In general, expanded urbanization may have been the worst—and best—thing that has happened to civilization. On the one hand, people have become more dependent on commodities like electricity and therefore more vulnerable when such commodities have been cut off; urbanization also facilitates the spread of disease. On the other hand, it has also boosted economic growth and meant that many resources—such as water and energy—are used more efficiently. This is especially true for many of the up-and-coming megacities—the ones nobody knew about 10 or 15 years ago. In China, the megacities are in the interior. Some of them are well planned, providing a lot of public transportation. In contrast, Shanghai and Beijing are losing businesses because they have become so congested. Overall, new or old, governance at the city level is increasingly where the action is.

We've also seen a new phenomenon: increasing designation of special economic and political zones within countries. It is as if the central government acknowledges its own inability to forge reforms and then subcontracts out responsibility to a second party. In these enclaves, the very laws, including taxation, are set by somebody from the outside. Many believe that outside parties have a better chance of getting the economies in these designated areas up and going, eventually setting an example for the rest of the country. Governments in countries in the Horn of Africa, Central America, and other places are seeing the advantages, openly admitting their limitations.

3

HOW GAME-CHANGERS SHAPE SCENARIO:

Global Economy	Global growth does slightly better than in the *Gini Out-of-the-Bottle* scenario because there is greater cooperation among nonstate actors and between them and national governments on major global challenges. This world is also more stable and socially cohesive.
Conflict	Security threats pose an increasing challenge as access to lethal and disruptive technologies expands. Terrorists and criminal networks take advantage of the confusion over shifting authorities and responsibilities and the multiplicity of governance actors to establish physical and virtual safe havens.
Regional Stability	Regional institutions become more hybrid as non governmental bodies become members and sit side-by-side with states. Mayors of mega-cities take a lead in ramping up regional and global cooperation. There is increasing designation of special economic and political zones within regions to spur economic development.
Governance	Countries do not disappear, but governments increasingly see their role as organizing and orchestrating "hybrid" coalitions of state and nonstate actors that shift depending on the challenge. Multinational businesses, IT communications firms, international scientists, NGOs and groups that are used to cooperating across borders thrive in this hyper-globalized world where expertise, influence, and agility count for more than "weight" or "position."
Technology	Social media, mobile communications, and big data are key components, underlying and facilitating cooperation among nonstate actors and governments.
US Role in the World	The US has an advantage because many nonstate actors—multinationals, NGOs, think tanks, and universities—originated there, but they increasingly see themselves as having a global identity. The US Government maximizes its influence when it organizes a hybrid coalition of state and nonstate actors to deal with global challenges.

HOW MAJOR POWERS/REGIONS FARE IN SCENARIO:

Europe	Europe thrives as it uses its soft powers—NGOs, universities, and global finance and business—to boost its standing. The emphasis on coalition and inclusivity in this world plays to the Europeans' strength of coalition-building to solve challenges.
Russia	Moscow is increasingly concerned about security threats posed by the growth of terrorist and criminal organizations. Russia finds it difficult to work with the proliferation of global nonstate actors in the international arena.
China	China as an authoritarian regime is preoccupied with asserting the primacy and control of the central government and finds it difficult to operate in this world.
India	India has the potential to flourish with its elites imbedded in global business and academic networks. If it manages its urban challenges, it also can serve as a trailblazer to others in the developing world, grappling with rapid urbanization.
Brazil/Middle-Tier Powers	Middle-tier powers play an outsized role where size and weight are less important than engagement in networks. The degree to which they have a highly developed nonstate sector will be an important determinant of success in this world.
Poor Developing States in Africa, Asia, and Latin America	The degree to which developing states manage urbanization will determine whether they thrive or fail in this world. National governments that stand in the way of emerging urban clusters are likely to fall behind those who use urbanization to bolster economic and political prospects.

ACKNOWLEDGEMENTS

The list of those who helped us to compile **Global Trends 2030** is long and extensive. With each new edition, we have benefited from a broader and more diverse array of contributors from around the world, including individual scholars and experts, universities, think tanks, science labs, businesses, and government institutions. Given the impossibility of mentioning everyone who has participated in the multitude of conferences, workshops, individual meetings, and other activities associated with producing this report, we would like to mention a number of organizations and individuals whose contributions were particularly notable:

The Atlantic Council of the United States (ACUS) was foremost in organizing a set of workshops on key themes and also conferences in Silicon Valley and multiple countries overseas. Mr. Fred Kempe, ACUS President and CEO; Mr. Barry Pavel, Director of ACUS' Brent Scrowcroft Center for International Security; Dr. Banning Garrett; and Mr. Carles Castello-Catchot opened doors to a diverse set of expert groups we would not have had the opportunity to engage with otherwise. Ms. Ellen Laipson, President of the Stimson Center, hosted the initial workshop on the track record of previous Global Trends works, which helped us to avoid some past pitfalls. Mr. David Michel's work at Stimson on maritime and environmental trends also was of critical value.

The International Futures model of the Frederick S. Pardee Center at the University of Denver, with support from Professor Barry Hughes and Dr. Jonathan Moyer, provided an overall framework that enabled us to explore possible futures across a wide range of domains, from geopolitics to health and education. McKinsey & Company was instrumental in helping us think through the scenarios and model the possible economic trajectories of our alternative futures with the help of its proprietary Global Growth Model.

Princeton Professor John Ikenberry has led quarterly meetings of international relations scholars with the NIC for the past decade, providing numerous opportunities to explore many of the ideas about the changing international system featured in Global Trends 2030 and its predecessor volumes. Dr. Gregory Treverton, RAND Corporation, organized a pivotal workshop on the changing nature of power for this study. Drs. William Ralston and Nick Evans of Strategic Business Insights, Inc. provided critical thinking and expertise on disruptive technologies. Dr. Bernice Lee and her team at the Royal Institute of International Affairs (Chatham House) provided extensive research on resource scarcities. Dr. Steve Szabo hosted several meetings on resource issues at German Marshall Fund's Transatlantic Academy. Dr. Xenia Dormandy of Chatham House shared with us her research on nonstate actors. Mr. David Low and his team at Oxford Analytica organized a workshop on the future of terrorism, which provided the basis for the treatment of terrorism in the text. Mr. Jonathan Paris, a London-based analyst, member of Chatham House, and Nonresident Senior Fellow with the Atlantic Council, provided help with Middle East futures and organized several overseas meetings for us.

The Department of Energy laboratories were very generous with their help: Drs. Alvin Sanders and Richard Snead at Oak Ridge organized a workshop on natural disasters and, at Sandia, Drs. Howard Passell, Russ Skocypec, Tommy Woodall and others undertook extensive work on resource sustainability and its impact on state fragility. A number of experts and scholars provided critical inputs and reviews of the draft: Dr. Daniel Twining, German Marshall Fund; Professors William Inboden and Jeremi Suri, University of Texas; Mr. Philip Stephens, Financial Times; Professor Christopher Layne, Texas A & M; Dr. Richard Cincotta, Stimson Center; Professors Tom Fingar, Paul Saffo and Ian Morris, Stanford University; Professors John Kelmelis and Darryl Farber,

Penn State University; Drs. David Gordon and Ash Jain, Eurasia Group; Dr. Giovanni Grevi, FRIDE (Fundacion par alas Relaciones Internacionale); Ms. Rosemarie Forsythe, Exxon Mobil Corporation; Professor Jack Goldstone, George Mason University; Dr. Dan Steinbock, Research Director of International Business, India, China & America Institute; Deputy Director Olivier Erschens, Centre d'Etudes Strategiques Aerospatiales; Professor Sumit Ganguly, Indiana University; Professor Emile Nakhleh, University of New Mexico; Dr. James Shinn, Princeton University; Ms. Catarina Tully, Director, FromOverHere, Ltd; Drs. Fiona Hill and Justin Vaisse, Brookings Institution; Dr. David Shorr; The Stanley Foundation; Mr. Kari Mottola; Special Adviser at the Finnish Ministry of Foreign Affairs; Mr. Arturo Lopez-Levy, University of Denver; Dr. Mark Fitzpatrick, International Institute for Strategic Studies; Dr. Malcolm Cook, Flinders University; Dr. Patrick Cronin, Center for New American Security (CNAS); Dr. Cho Khong, Shell Corporation; Dr. Alexander Van de Putte; Mr. Herve de Carmoy; and Mr. Alexandre Adler, Le Figaro.

A number of academic institutions hosted events at which we received input and reactions which proved critical to the final draft. These institutions include the LBJ School of Public Affairs at the University of Texas; the International Security Program at the University of Notre Dame; Stanford University; University of New Mexico; Indiana University School of Public and Environmental Affairs and Center for the Study of the Middle East; the Frank Batten School of Leadership and Public Policy at the University of Virginia; Princeton University; the Naval Postgraduate School; and Penn State University.

The Bush School at Texas A & M hosted a two-day gaming exercise to test theories of future US power and impact on the international system. The Inter-American Dialogue hosted a meeting at Georgetown University to discuss the impact of global trends on Latin America. Mr. Sergio Bitar has been especially active in thinking about those impacts. The Tobin Project in Cambridge, Massachusetts—which seeks to close the gap between scholars and government practitioners—brought together academics from around the country to critique the draft. Other US institutions and organizations which hosted us for a review of the draft include the Santa Fe Institute, NASA; the Brookings Institution, CNAS, the RAND Corporation, the Eurasia Group, CENTRA Technologies, Facebook, Twitter, Google, CISCO, Bloom, Numenta, and the Aspen Security Forum.

Our overseas interlocutors were immensely helpful. Our effort and the EU's recent global trends publication under the direction of Dr. Alvaro de Vasconcelos, former Director of the EU's Institute for Security Studies, have been conducted almost in tandem. We have held several joint meetings on the same topics and have learned

from one another. The inter-institutional group behind the EU global trends effort includes Mr. James Elles, Member of the European Parliament; Mr. Jean-Claude Thebault, Director-General, Bureau of European Policy (BEPA), EU Commission; Dr. Joao Marques de Almeida, BEPA; Messrs. Leo Schulte Nordholt and Matthew Reece, both with the General Secretariat of the EU Council—all of whom provided key insights on the future of Europe and the world. Swedish Foreign Minister Carl Bildt hosted a dynamic lunchtime discussion at the outset of our effort; other Swedish practitioners and thinkers— Dr. Lars Hedstrom, Director of the National Defence College; Professor Bengt Sundelius, Civil Contingencies Agency; Dr. Anna Jardfelt, Director of Swedish Institute of International Affairs; and Dr. Bates Gill, former Director of the Stockholm International Peace Research Institute— have stimulated our thinking and hosted meetings. In the UK, Wilton Park hosted a joint Foreign and Commonwealth Office-NIC conference on Middle East futures; Dr. Robin Niblett, Director of Chatham House, who holds regular exchanges with the NIC, also organized several workshops for us. In France, Dr. Bruno Tertrais, Research Director at the Fondation pour la Recherche Strategique in Paris, hosted a roundtable discussion that was instrumental in shaping our thinking on Europe. We also benefited from an exchange with Drs. Nicolas Regaud and Guillaume de Rouge in the MoD's Directorate for Strategic Affairs on their publication, Horizons Strategiques. In the Netherlands, Dr. Jair van der Lijn at the Clingendael think tank arranged a lively discussion on the draft. In Canada, Dr. Peter Padbury of the Horizons office, along with experts at other government agencies, shared their work and hosted a meeting on the draft and futures methodology. In the United Arab Emirates (UAE), Dr. Anwar Gargash, Foreign Affairs Minister of State, hosted a discussion for us on the UAE's perspectives on global trends.

In China, we were hosted by China Institutes of Contemporary International Relations, the China Institute of International Studies, the China Center for Contemporary World Studies, the Shanghai Institute of International Studies, and the China Foundation for International Strategic Studies; several of these organizations are far advanced on their own studies of global trends. In Singapore, Dr. Ping Soon Kok, Senior Director of the National Security Coordination Centre in the Prime Minister's Office, arranged a week-long series of exchanges, reflecting the depth of experts' thinking on the future. In India, the Observer Research Foundation Centre for Policy Research, Gateway House, Center for Peace and Conflict Studies, and Institute for Defence Studies hosted us for meetings. In Russia, Dr. Alexander Dynkin, Director of the Institute of World Economy and International Relations (IMEMO), hosted a meeting in which we compared results of IMEMO's own published study, *Global Outlook 2030*, with our *Global Trends 2030* draft.

We visited several African countries to gain reactions to the draft. In South Africa, in addition to meetings with government officials, we held meetings with the South Africa Institute of International Affairs and Institute of Security Studies. In Nigeria, we met with government officials and were hosted by the Ken Nnamani Centre, the Centre for Democracy and Development, the Institute for Peace and Conflict Resolution, and the Centre for the Study of Economies of African (CSEA). In Kenya, we briefed the President's National Security Advisory Committee and met with the Kenya Institute for Public Policy Research and Analysis and UN Habitat offices. In Ethiopia, Dr. Martin Kimai, Director of Conflict Early Warning and Response Mechanism, organized a discussion on the draft. The Global Futures Forum hosted a meeting in Botswana, which we attended, that gathered together technology practitioners from around the continent. In Brazil, we met with the Institute Fernando Cardoso, Instituto de Pesquisa de Relacoes Internacionaios, IBM Research Brazil, and Fapsep Foundation.

The GT 2030 blog, an innovation for this edition, generated wide-ranging discussions on key themes. We relied on the help of many of our Intelligence Community Associates and other experts for the management of the weekly themed discussions, including Drs. Daniel Twining, Ash Jain, William Burke-White, Thomas Mahnken, Peter Feaver, Jackie Newmyer Deal, Steve Weber, Andrew Erdmann, William Inboden, Richard Cincotta, Ralph Espach, Allan Dafoe, Howard Passell, and Cung Vu.

Within the US Government, special thanks goes to Dr. Susan Nelson, Ms. Christina Condrey, Ms. Rachel Warner, Ms. Judith Van Zalen, and Mr. Nate Price in the State Department's Bureau of Intelligence and Research. They spent countless hours making the arrangements for many of the meetings with outside organizations and experts.

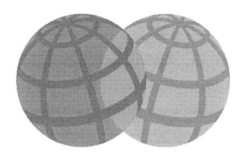

This assessment was prepared under the auspices of the Counselor, National Intelligence Council.

Questions about this paper or requests for copies can be directed to the Counselor, Dr. Mathew Burrows on 703-482-0741.

This publication can be found on www.dni.gov/nic/globaltrends

17299216R00095

Made in the USA
Middletown, DE
17 January 2015